The Washington One-Day Trip Book

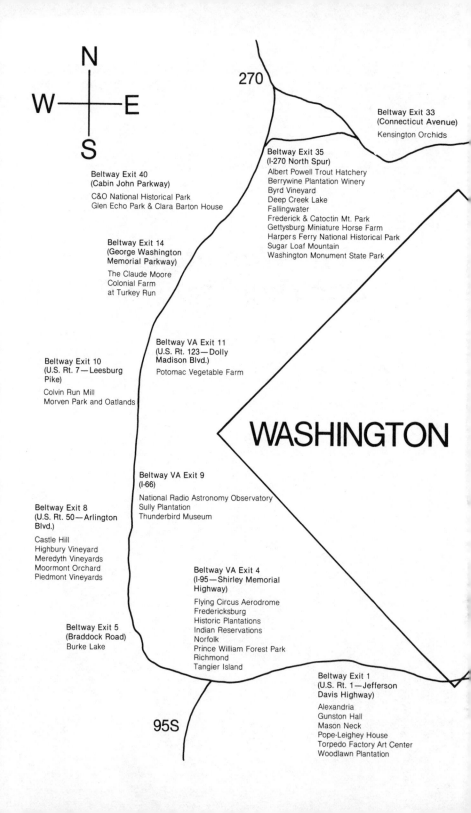

N
W · E
S

270

Beltway Exit 33
(Connecticut Avenue)
Kensington Orchids

Beltway Exit 35
(I-270 North Spur)
Albert Powell Trout Hatchery
Berrywine Plantation Winery
Byrd Vineyard
Deep Creek Lake
Fallingwater
Frederick & Catoctin Mt. Park
Gettysburg Miniature Horse Farm
Harpers Ferry National Historical Park
Sugar Loaf Mountain
Washington Monument State Park

Beltway Exit 40
(Cabin John Parkway)
C&O National Historical Park
Glen Echo Park & Clara Barton House

Beltway Exit 14
(George Washington
Memorial Parkway)
The Claude Moore
Colonial Farm
at Turkey Run

Beltway VA Exit 11
(U.S. Rt. 123—Dolly
Madison Blvd.)
Potomac Vegetable Farm

Beltway Exit 10
(U.S. Rt. 7—Leesburg
Pike)
Colvin Run Mill
Morven Park and Oatlands

WASHINGTON

Beltway VA Exit 9
(I-66)
National Radio Astronomy Observatory
Sully Plantation
Thunderbird Museum

Beltway Exit 8
(U.S. Rt. 50—Arlington
Blvd.)
Castle Hill
Highbury Vineyard
Meredyth Vineyards
Moormont Orchard
Piedmont Vineyards

Beltway VA Exit 4
(I-95—Shirley Memorial
Highway)
Flying Circus Aerodrome
Fredericksburg
Historic Plantations
Indian Reservations
Norfolk
Prince William Forest Park
Richmond
Tangier Island

Beltway Exit 5
(Braddock Road)
Burke Lake

Beltway Exit 1
(U.S. Rt. 1—Jefferson
Davis Highway)
Alexandria
Gunston Hall
Mason Neck
Pope-Leighey House
Torpedo Factory Art Center
Woodlawn Plantation

95S

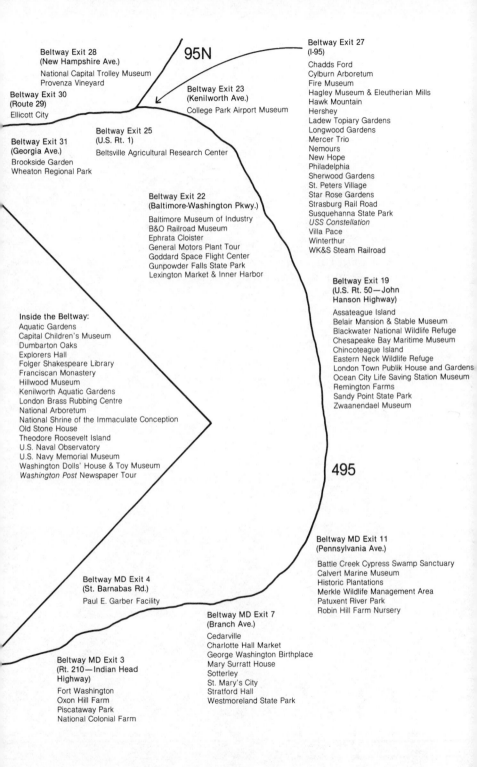

95N

Beltway Exit 28
(New Hampshire Ave.)
National Capital Trolley Museum
Provenza Vineyard

Beltway Exit 30
(Route 29)
Ellicott City

Beltway Exit 23
(Kenilworth Ave.)
College Park Airport Museum

Beltway Exit 27
(I-95)
Chadds Ford
Cylburn Arboretum
Fire Museum
Hagley Museum & Eleutherian Mills
Hawk Mountain
Hershey
Ladew Topiary Gardens
Longwood Gardens
Mercer Trio
Nemours
New Hope
Philadelphia
Sherwood Gardens
St. Peters Village
Star Rose Gardens
Strasburg Rail Road
Susquehanna State Park
USS Constellation
Villa Pace
Winterthur
WK&S Steam Railroad

Beltway Exit 25
(U.S. Rt. 1)
Beltsville Agricultural Research Center

Beltway Exit 31
(Georgia Ave.)
Brookside Garden
Wheaton Regional Park

Beltway Exit 22
(Baltimore-Washington Pkwy.)
Baltimore Museum of Industry
B&O Railroad Museum
Ephrata Cloister
General Motors Plant Tour
Goddard Space Flight Center
Gunpowder Falls State Park
Lexington Market & Inner Harbor

Beltway Exit 19
(U.S. Rt. 50—John
Hanson Highway)
Assateague Island
Belair Mansion & Stable Museum
Blackwater National Wildlife Refuge
Chesapeake Bay Maritime Museum
Chincoteague Island
Eastern Neck Wildlife Refuge
London Town Publik House and Gardens
Ocean City Life Saving Station Museum
Remington Farms
Sandy Point State Park
Zwaanendael Museum

Inside the Beltway:
Aquatic Gardens
Capital Children's Museum
Dumbarton Oaks
Explorers Hall
Folger Shakespeare Library
Franciscan Monastery
Hillwood Museum
Kenilworth Aquatic Gardens
London Brass Rubbing Centre
National Arboretum
National Shrine of the Immaculate Conception
Old Stone House
Theodore Roosevelt Island
U.S. Naval Observatory
U.S. Navy Memorial Museum
Washington Dolls' House & Toy Museum
Washington Post Newspaper Tour

495

Beltway MD Exit 11
(Pennsylvania Ave.)
Battle Creek Cypress Swamp Sanctuary
Calvert Marine Museum
Historic Plantations
Merkle Wildlife Management Area
Patuxent River Park
Robin Hill Farm Nursery

Beltway MD Exit 4
(St. Barnabas Rd.)
Paul E. Garber Facility

Beltway MD Exit 7
(Branch Ave.)
Cedarville
Charlotte Hall Market
George Washington Birthplace
Mary Surratt House
Sotterley
St. Mary's City
Stratford Hall
Westmoreland State Park

Beltway MD Exit 3
(Rt. 210—Indian Head
Highway)
Fort Washington
Oxon Hill Farm
Piscataway Park
National Colonial Farm

For my father, Harry Ockershausen, with loving gratitude for the memories of our many Sunday afternoon adventures.

The Washington One-Day Trip Book

101 Offbeat Excursions
In and Around the Nation's Capital

Jane Ockershausen Smith

EPM Publications
McLean, Virginia

Library of Congress Cataloging in Publication Data

Smith, Jane Ockershausen
  The Washington one-day trip book.

  Previously published as: The one-day trip book. c1978.
  Includes index.
  1. Washington Region—Description and travel—Guidebooks.
I. Title. II. Title: The Washington 1-day trip book.
F192.3.S57 1984
917.53'044   83-25417   ISBN 0-914440-70-5

Notice: Telephone numbers and admission fees change so frequently
that they have not been included in most listings. For those sites where
appointments are necessary or special events are scheduled, phone
numbers are cited. Days and hours of operation are given, but it is
always best to call ahead and check. Consult telephone directories for
numbers.

Cover and book design by Howard Clare

CONTENTS

SUMMER

How to use This Book

Families that wait all year for their two-week vacation during the summer months are unnecessarily missing a lot of fun. Short excursions spaced weekly or monthly throughout the year can give a lift to the gray days of winter and provide economical mini-vacations. Even though a few of the places in this book may seem too far away for a one-day trip, people with energy, determination and little money will find them feasible and an exciting challenge. There are numerous offbeat and diverse destinations within a day's drive from the Washington area that are ignored in official guidebooks. This book will give you an idea of what to expect at each spot so you can select the places that most appeal to your family.

Equally as important as knowing what to expect is knowing when to visit various places. The right time of year can transform an otherwise merely pleasant hillside into a truly breathtaking vision. People with a horticultural bent can follow the calendar year round and see a multitude of flowers at their peak of perfection. For spring in December, try the Christmas display at Longwood Gardens or enjoy the start of spring itself by viewing the lakeside display of yellow and white daffodils at Pennsylvania's Longwood Gardens and the banks of blossoming azaleas at Norfolk's Botanical Garden, Delaware's Winterthur, Maryland's London Town or Washington's National Arboretum. Wild flower paths at Morven Park in Virginia, Bowman's Hill in Pennsylvania and Cylburn Arboretum in Baltimore are at their best in springtime also. In June the acres of roses at Pennsylvania's Star Rose Gardens offer a stunning view. In late July the water lilies and lotuses are in full flower at the Aquatic Garden in Washington. The enormous lotus blossoms, dwarfing all other flowers, are well worth a special visit.

Garden trips are not the only ones that require proper planning for maximum enjoyment. Surprisingly, the same careful attention to timing can pay dividends on some of the more popular attractions such as Hersheypark and Carter's Grove Plantation, which lose a great deal of their charm if visited on a crowded weekend. This book offers guidelines and suggestions for planning your trips wisely.

Excursions are included that will appeal to a wide spectrum of special interests; a topical index offers a cross reference for your convenience. For instance, once the hiker has discovered the seemingly endless trails at Prince William Forest Park in Virginia, or Cedarville State Park in Maryland, he will want to return again and again, or he may want to try the more challenging hike up Pennsylvania's Hawk Mountain or Maryland's Sugar Loaf Mountain. Naturalists will find much to interest them such as the elusive eagles at Mason Neck in Virginia, the circling birds of prey at Hawk Mountain, the thousands of migrating geese at Maryland's Blackwater, Eastern Neck and Merkle Wildlife Refuges and the developing fish at the Albert Powell Trout Hatchery in Maryland. Here again timing is an important element in planning your trip because wildlife, like flowers, follow a natural schedule to which the visitor must become attuned.

History buffs can plan a nice combination package, either for one long trip or for several excursions, that will illustrate colonial life at the various economic levels. Starting at the lowest rung you can see dirt farmers at work on Virginia's Claude Moore Colonial Farm at Turkey Run. Go from there to the small freeholder's homestead at Maryland's National Colonial Farm. A higher step on the economic ladder is represented by the small Maryland river plantation, Sotterley, and the Virginia plantation, Sully. City life can be explored in Old Town Alexandria, river boat commerce at the Colvin Run Mill and colonial ferry service at the Publik House at London Town. These places show what life was like and provide an interesting educational experience for all, as well as some fascinating architectural sidelights.

Those interested in the arts can vary their trips between work which is being created and that which has been tested by time. Virginia's Torpedo Factory Art Center is a multimedia lesson in art with more than 200 artists demonstrating and displaying their crafts. Another living studio is the Glen Echo Workshops where crafts are not only taught but also sold. Crafts are an integral part of a visit to Pennsylvania's New Hope, St. Peters Village, Chadds Ford or Peddler's Village. The art of the past can be seen at Richmond's Virginia Museum, the Philadelphia Museum of Art and Rodin Museum and the Brandywine River Museum at Chadds Ford.

Many excursions offer an opportunity to visit more than one spot during your trip. To make it easier to plan a full day for families with diversified interests, there is a map at the front of the book which groups the excursions geographically. A quick glance will alert you to other places included in the book that are in the vicinity of your planned outing. For example, if you are heading for Chadds Ford you might also consider stopping at Winterthur, the Eleutherian Mills, Gunpowder State Park, Nemours, Longwood Gardens, Hagley Museum, Brandywine Battlefield, Nature Trail and Museum or Star Rose Gardens.

Mothers will discover when perusing this book that many of these excursions are hidden right in their own neighborhoods or within a very short driving distance. Brief trips provide a welcome respite from the norm. A mother can take preschoolers to many entertaining places without involving the whole family. She might want to bring older daughters to the Washington Dolls' House and Toy Museum or to Alexandria's Lee-Fendall House. Among other trips that lend themselves to solo efforts on Mom's part are Oxon Hill Farm, Kenilworth Aquatic Gardens, the National Arboretum, Claude Moore Colonial Farm and Brookside Gardens at Wheaton Regional Park. These trips are quite economical because in many cases the destinations are only a few minutes from a

Beltway exit. Taking a picnic lunch adds a special treat for the children and eliminates the need for finding a restaurant in the area and spending a lot of money for food.

One obstacle to family excursions for many is the difficulty in persuading Dad to spend his leisure time behind the wheel exploring the countryside. If this is the case, a judicious selection of initial excursions may win him over because there are many which should particularly appeal to him and at the same time keep the driving to a minimum. Try starting in Maryland with a tour of the Provenza Vineyard in late summer or the Goddard Space Flight Center on a winter day. For an indoor trip, consider Washington's U.S. Naval Observatory or the Baltimore and Ohio Railroad Museum. These are trips, as are so many of them in this book, that are fun for all; adults can appreciate them just as much as children and sometimes even more.

It is helpful to know that small groups such as the family or even individuals can tour various attractions without having to be part of a larger organization. We may pass a spot like Goddard Space Flight Center or the U.S. Naval Observatory for many years and each time make a mental note to stop. The information here will help you realize how welcome you are at these installations and how easy it is to avail yourself of their facilities. The next time you have out-of-town guests, instead of revisiting the familiar landmarks, try a diversion from the official guidebooks and choose some of these offbeat places.

The topical cross reference in the back of the book contains two unique sections. One includes those places that are accessible to or particularly planned for the handicapped visitor. These include the Fragrance Gardens at Maryland's Brookside Garden, Pennsylvania's Longwood Garden and Virginia's Botanical Garden. Also, rugged natural parks such as the Patuxent River Park in Maryland have special trails.

The second section is a guide to those spots accessible by boat. Boating has become increasingly popular in this area and many families have discovered the desirability of breaking up their days on the water with some excursions on terra firma. Stops at London Town, Tangier or St. Michael's to see the Chesapeake Bay Maritime Museum are only some of the ports suggested.

A new section created especially for this revised edition provides information about 101 annual events. If you check this list at the end of each chapter before planning your excursions, you will be able to schedule your arrival at many sites for those occasions when something special is happening. Excursions in the book that do plan annual events include Morven Park, the Trolley Museum, London Town, Fredericksburg, Mary Surratt House, Colvin Run Mill, Brookside Gardens, Cedarville and Gunston Hall, to name just a few.

The excursions in this book are unusual, enjoyable and informative. Remember, short trips are economical trips. Start by selecting excursions that seem both feasible and of particular appeal to you and your family and then be adventurous and try others. The trips are grouped seasonally although a great many places can be visited any time of the year. Quite a few spots do have an optimum time and others are just open during certain months, so it's always a good idea to read all the information about the excursion before starting. One-day trips can provide enrichment for the whole family and form bonds of experiences enjoyed together that children will long remember.

WINTER

ALEXANDRIA AND TORPEDO FACTORY ART CENTER
An Explosion of Art and History Full Steam Ahead

Many of us in this area are geographical victims, blinded by our proximity to interesting and historical sites which to us are no more than names on the passing road signs. We are well rewarded when we make the effort to explore these places. A day spent getting acquainted with Alexandria, Virginia, offers art, architecture, history, antiques and crafts from around the world. Alexandria, with its roots in America's past, its cobblestone streets, lovely old houses and riverside studios, offers a veritable smorgasbord of options for a one-day visit.

A good place to begin is the Ramsey House Visitor's Center at 221 King Street. This is the oldest house in Alexandria, having been moved down river in 1749 by William Ramsey from its previous location to the newly established city. William Ramsey, a successful merchant, was anxious to get the jump on his competitors. A stop at Ramsey House will let you get a head start on the less well-prepared explorers because there you will find numerous pamphlets, maps, parking information and a free film that will acquaint you with Alexandria's many charms. The center is open 9:00 a.m. to 5:00 p.m. daily except Thanksgiving, Christmas and New Year's Day.

Farther down King Street in a renovated warehouse on the Alexandria waterfront you will find the Torpedo Factory

Art Center. It is a treasure trove of art studios located in a building with a colorful history.

The factory was used during both World Wars to manufacture torpedoes. Later captured war records were stored there. Upon completion of the 1983 renovations a 3,000-pound Mark 14 torpedo case built at this factory in 1944 was given to the art center as a memento of the building's past.

Today 200 juried professional artists have studios here and some 43,000 people a month visit this art center. You'll see painters, sculptors, potters, fiber artists, printers, stained glass workers, jewelers and musical instrument makers. The new studios have large windows and open doors. You can watch the artists at work, see a representative sampling of their crafts and purchase artwork.

Within the Torpedo Factory Art Center are four galleries run by non-profit organizations of artists and craftsmen: The Art League offers day and evening classes and holds juried art shows; The Potomac Craftsmen is a fiber artist organization; The Scope Gallery includes pottery and ceramics; and the Enamelist Gallery is for fire enameling.

The center is also home to the Alexandria Urban Archaeology Program, which has a museum and research lab on the second floor. This is a unique program; Alexandria is one of the few cities in the United States to have an archaeological program for conserving sites within an urban environment. The purpose of this program is to help the interested public interact with trained archaeologists in uncovering, preserving and understanding artifacts from Alexandria's past. The museum has a working lab so that staff and volunteers can reconstruct and catalog artifacts. Permanent exhibits include ceramic and glassware from Old Town sites.

The Torpedo Factory Art Center is open daily from 10:00 a.m. to 5:00 p.m. If your budget will not allow you to sample the many in-town restaurants you may want to pack a picnic lunch and take a midday break at the waterfront park right next to the center on North Union Street.

If you have only a day, it would be impractical to attempt to take in all of Alexandria's historical sites. You'll have to be selective and save some for another visit. One historical must is Christ Church at 118 N. Washington Street, where Washington once had a pew and many subsequent presidents have worshiped. Visitors are welcome from 9:00 a.m. to 5:00 p.m. daily except Sunday when the hours are 2:00 until 5:00 p.m.

A quite different site is Fort Ward Museum, which was one of the 68 forts built to protect Washington during the Civil War. Fort Ward is the only one of the ring of forts, collectively called the Defenses of Washington, that remains. The museum buildings, officer's hut and rifle trenches have all been restored or reconstructed. The Fort Ward Museum is open at no charge 9:00 a.m. to 5:00 p.m. daily and noon to 5:00 p.m. on Sunday.

Alexandria also has two homes closely associated with the Lee family. The Lee-Fendall House at 429 N. Washington Street is interesting because it was there that "Light Horse Harry" Lee wrote the moving farewell address from the citizens of Alexandria to George Washington when he headed for his inauguration in New York.

Across the street at 607 Oronoco Street is the Boyhood Home of Robert E. Lee, where young Robert lived for more than ten years. Both houses are open on weekdays from 10:00 a.m. to 4:00 p.m. and on Sundays from noon to 4:00 p.m. The Lee-Fendall House is closed on Mondays and the Boyhood Home of Robert E. Lee is closed from mid-December to the end of January. Admission is charged at both.

Also to be explored is the Carlyle House, built so early in Alexandria's development that the town building ordinances had yet to be written. It is therefore the only house in the city that was not built in line with the street. The house has a fascinating history as you will discover on your tour. Hours are Tuesday through Saturday from 10:00 a.m. to 5:00 p.m. and Sunday from noon to 5:00 p.m. If you want to end your day as so many colonial leaders once did, why not stop for a light repast at Gadsby's Tavern at 134 North Royal Street?

Directions: Take Beltway Virginia Exit 1, U.S. 1, north into Alexandria. Turn right on Franklin Street, then make a left on Washington Street. Next make a right on King Street. The Ramsey House Visitor's Center is located at the intersection of King and Fairfax Streets. For the Torpedo Factory Art Center continue down King Street toward the river to Union Street and turn left. For Fort Ward Museum go up King Street to Kenwood Avenue and make a right. Then take a left on West Braddock. Continue on West Braddock for approximately one mile and Fort Ward will be on the right.

BALTIMORE MUSEUM OF INDUSTRY
Industrial Strength Foray

It is always exciting to watch a museum get off the ground, and the Baltimore Museum of Industry is still considered a comparative newcomer, having opened on November 22, 1981. The museum's well-chosen motto is, "A working museum for a working city." Its location in the old 1865 Platt Packing Company, an oyster cannery, puts the museum in the middle of the still active south Baltimore-Locust Point Industrial District, midway between the Inner Harbor and Fort McHenry.

The bustle of this busy area around the museum is echoed within, where three demonstration areas draw visitors into the work being done. The focus is on the people who worked in Baltimore's major industries, past and present. Here you can see the jobs they did and the tools and equipment they used.

One of the principal areas of interest is the turn-of-the-century belt-driven machine shop. The floor-to-ceiling belts turn flywheels and planing machines. Volunteers operate the old machinery, using it to make nuts and bolts for the museum's own collection of antique equipment. One old piece is a Simplex clock whose ribbon told the payroll master how many hours each employee worked.

The next re-created "work setting" is the old-time print shop. Here there are presses that date back to 1820. In fact, you will be shown the evolution of the printing machines from the cumbersome early models like the 1870 Baltimore Jobber printing press to the more "modern" 1952 version of the linotype. Visitors can help "pull the devil's tail" on a vintage press. One try at the hard-to-move lever and you'll see why printers often had over-developed left arms.

In the composite case you'll see drawers filled with hand-set type. You'll also understand why a printer had to "mind his P's and Q's." The printer's ability to select the correct type was rather like a touch typist's technique and a good printer had to be as fast as a good typist.

Everybody gets a chance to join in and work the Poco press (circa 1900) where a single copy was printed before it was sent to be copied in any large quantity. You'll produce a copy that reads, "I printed this."

Visitors also get a chance to participate in the last work area, the garment shop. You'll see a 1914 long distance moving car like those used in Baltimore to deliver pre-cut bundles of material to the homes where the sewing was done in the days when the garment industry was a cottage trade. Just a minute on the 1887 Wheller and Wilson sewing machine will demonstrate how hard it was to work all day on this treadle machine.

Shortly after the cottage trade developed Baltimore had a number of lofts where specialized machines performed various functions. At the museum you can see a belt-looper, a hand-operated button stitcher and both a small and a large basting machine. There are also irons used in the garment business that are so heavy many visitors are unable to lift them from the table.

In addition to these work areas there are visual reminders of other early Baltimore businesses, as well as artifacts and equipment from such diverse industries as canning and shipping and even an 1895 drug store that once stood on the corner of Eastern Avenue and Conkling Street in Baltimore.

Before you leave be sure to see the S.S. Baltimore, one of the last steam engine tugboats on the East Coast. This tugboat was recovered from a watery grave in the Sassafras River and is being restored. It is currently anchored outside the museum.

The Baltimore Museum of Industry at 1415 Key Highway is open Saturday from 10:00 a.m. to 5:00 p.m. and Sunday from 12:00 to 5:00 p.m. Admission is charged.

If at all possible, since you're so nearby, try to at least make a brief stop at Fort McHenry National Monument and Historic Shrine. The fort figured prominently in the War of 1812. It was the flag flying over this fort that inspired Francis Scott Key to write our national anthem, The Star Spangled Banner. A film tells the story of this "star" fort. There are reconstructed barracks, guardhouses and a powder magazine. Hours are 9:00 a.m. to 5:00 p.m. daily. On summer evenings the fort stays open until 8:00 p.m. The fort is closed Christmas and New Year's Day. You can also picnic at this fort or just walk along the mile-long waterfront path.

Directions: Take Beltway Exit 22, the Baltimore-Washington Parkway, into Baltimore. It will become Russell Street. Continue up to Pratt Street and then make a right to the Inner Harbor. Turn right at Light Street and follow signs for Fort McHenry. For the Baltimore Museum of Industry turn left at Key Highway and continue past Bethlehem Steel to the museum at 1415 Key Highway. For Fort McHenry continue on Key Highway to Lawrence Street and then turn right on Fort Avenue which will lead you to the gate of Fort McHenry.

CAPITAL CHILDREN'S MUSEUM
A-MUSEum

One of Washington's most captivating, but all too frequently overlooked, attractions just keeps getting better. Capital Children's Museum is a museum for children of all ages that stimulates both the senses and the mind. The working philosophy of this museum is predicated on the Chinese proverb:

I hear and I forget
I see and I remember
I do and I understand

Here children "do," as this is definitely a hands-on museum. Youngsters can paint with a computer, bake a tortilla, launch a satellite, crawl through a manhole, print a poster, read an electronic newspaper, move water with an Archimedean screw, fashion a yarn necklace, experiment with lasers and much, much more.

One of the museum's major exhibits is Communications Hall. Exploration of this multi-faceted topic begins in a reproduced Ice Age cave, with ancient drawings like those found in caves in southern France. A sound and light show introduces the complexities of communication. There are four exhibit areas in the section on How We Communicate. Here youngsters can endeavor to communicate using antiquated techniques such as the Greek torch, African drum, Chappe semaphore and picturograms. This exhibit continues to expand on the development of coding and sending information by featuring computer games and sound tapes.

Another section, the Hall of Information, highlights the inventive techniques that have been used to store information. Old methods included paintings on hide and clay tablets, the use of knotted string, and wooden tally sticks. Today computer codes and punch cards retain pertinent facts. A peek through the museum's microscope shows an interesting comparison of the amount of information that can be stored on a disk, a semiconductor chip and in the human brain.

To reach the Mass Communication section of the exhibit, visitors walk through an arch with blinking lights. This is the façade of a 1906 nickelodeon, the last operational one in Washington. To illustrate graphically the vast difference the printing press has made in mass communication, an 18th-century print shop with working press is shown adjacent to a scriptorium. Visitors can use the press, make their own raised print blocks or try silk screen techniques. Contrasting this with old quill pens in the scriptorium makes even the youngest child appreciate the difference. A slide presentation provides more details on the history of print and type.

Satellites are represented by the five-meter dish on the museum grounds. Youngsters can practice positioning two small earth stations to receive satellite signals. A computer game called Orbit lets the operator simulate a satellite launch. This is only one of a number of computer games at the museum.

The importance of communication has not been forgotten in the second major exhibit area of the museum—International Hall. Here the museum's opening exhibit on Mexico continues to be a popular attraction. At the Marketplace children can don sombreros and serapes. One exhibit room re-creates a Mexican log cabin where visitors learn about daily life in Mexico while sampling a tortilla. Another room simulates a Mexican farm, complete with its resident goat, Rosie, who is a real crowd pleaser. Rosie has a friendly disposition and seems to enjoy being petted and fussed over.

Learning is fun in the Think Metric Room, donated by the Bureau of Standards, where kids can weigh and price fruits and vegetables using a metric scale. The long jump, calculated in centimeters, provides a more active learning opportunity. After exercising, children can weigh themselves on metric scales.

The City Room brings metropolitan life down to size—kid size. Manholes lead to a maze of underground pipes and circuitry that kids can explore. To get the feeling of a cross section of city jobs, children can try on a policeman's uniform, a mail carrier's jacket and pouch, a construction worker's hard-hat, or a motorman's cap and coin changer.

Adjacent to this exhibit is the Simple Machine Room. Hoists and pulleys, rope swings that can be balanced like scales, and other equipment encourage children to learn by doing.

There is so much to do that one visit will probably serve only to introduce this innovative and constantly expanding children's museum. Subsequent visits may make this a family favorite. On many weekends creative workshops and live performances by professional and amateur groups add another dimension to the day's outing. There is a gift shop, the Penny Exchange, and a cafeteria at the museum. The museum is open Tuesday through Saturday from 10:00 a.m. to 4:00 p.m. and on Sunday from 1:00 to 5:00 p.m. Admission is charged.

Directions: The Capital Children's Museum is located inside the Beltway at 800 3rd Street, N.E. just three blocks from Union Station.

CHRISTMAS TREES TO CUT
Tree-For-All

A nostalgic day-trip that will do much to dispel the over commercialization that is rampant around Christmas time is a family excursion to one of the numerous choose-and-cut Christmas tree nurseries in the area.

These tree farms have a wide variety of evergreens. You can choose from among acres of Scotch Pine, White Pine, Norway Spruce, Loblolly Pine, Blue Pine, Austrian Pine, White Spruce and Douglas Fir.

Not only will you be able to cut a fresher, healthier tree than you could purchase at the more centrally located stands, but it will cost you less. Prices, calculated so much per foot, will vary according to the tree size. At some farms you can buy trees pre-cut, or even balled and ready to plant. The more you have done for you, the more you will pay.

When deciding which tree farm to visit, keep in mind that it is probably best to pick the one closest to home. Hauling a tree in an open trunk or on top of your car for long distances can be a problem. Also, once you pick where you are going, call ahead to check their current supply because many places have limited selections that vary from one year to the next.

If you want to get an update on the choose-and-cut tree growers in Maryland and Virginia you can write for their annual guide. In Maryland, write Christmas Trees, Maryland Department of Agriculture, Parole Plaza Office Building, Annapolis, MD 21401. For the Virginia guide, address your requests to Virginia Department of Agriculture and Consumer Services, Division of Markets, P.O. Box 1163, Richmond, Virginia 23209.

The following is a list of Washington area tree-cutting sites.

MARYLAND

Anne Arundel County

Masque Farm
Robert C. Giffen, Jr.
Route 387, Spa Road
Annapolis, MD 21401
(301)757-4454 (no calls on weekends)
Open: December weekends
Selection: Scotch Pine, White Pine and Norway Spruce

Baltimore County

Johnson's Farm
John W. C. Johnson
1552 Glencoe Road
Sparks, MD 21152
(301)472-2882
Open: December weekends
Selection: Scotch Pine and White Pine

Carroll County

J.C.K. Christmas Tree Farm
John C. Kirby
Mayberry Road
Westminster, MD 21157
(301)837-2320, 346-7597
Open: December
Selection: Scotch Pine, White Pine, Austrian Pine and Norway Spruce
Special Comments: Wreaths and rope are available; free cookies.

Silver Run Tree Farm
E. & E. Trees, Inc.
Route 97
Westminster, MD 21157
(301)751-1237, 829-2799
Open: December
Selection: Scotch Pine, White Pine, Austrian Pine, Douglas Fir, Norway Spruce, Blue Spruce and White Spruce
Special Comments: Holly, wreaths and greens are available.

Montgomery County

Cider & Ginger Tree Farm
Barbara D. and Clinton F. Wells
17900 Elmer School Road
Dickerson, MD 20743
(301)349-5693
Open: December
Selection: Scotch Pine

Prince George's County

Tanner Farm
William H. Tanner
Bladen-Westwood Road
Brandywine, MD 20613
(301)579-2238 or (202)659-7528
Open: December weekends
Selection: Scotch Pine and Norway Spruce

VIRGINIA

Albemarle County

Ash Lawn
Route 795
Charlottesville, VA 22901
(804)293-9539
Open: December
Selection: Cedar

Fairfax County

James Thomas' Christmas Trees
1629 Beulah Road
Vienna, VA 22180
(703)938-0562
Open: Second and Third Weekend in December
Selection: Sheared Scotch, White Pine and Virginia Pine

Frederick County

Danny-Dayle Christmas Tree Plantation
Route 7, Box 259A
Winchester, VA 22601
(703)662-9026 or (304)229-2824
Open: Thanksgiving weekend and December weekends
Selection: Scotch Pine, Spruce and Fir
Special Comments: There is a Trim a Tree Shop with
imported handmade ornaments; pine wreaths and cones
are available.

Pinehill Christmas Tree Farm
Edward L. Christianson
Route 2, Box 95A
Winchester, VA 22601
(703)877-1643
Open: December
Special Comments: Scotch Pine wreaths and boughs are
available.

Scuttlebutt Christmas Tree Farm
Robert F. Dresel
Siler Star Rt., Box 307
Winchester, VA 22601
(703)888-3442
Open: December, Friday through Sunday
Selection: Scotch Pine and White Pine

Walnut Ridge Farm Nursery
Charles Leight
Rt. 1, Box 145
Clear Brook, VA 22624
(703)667-9537
Open: December weekends
Selection: Scotch Pine and White Pine

Loudoun County

Loudoun Nursery
Louis S. Nichols
Rt. 1, Box 346
Hamilton, VA 22068
(703)882-3450 or (703)327-6586
Open: Daily from Thanksgiving weekend
Selection: Scotch Pine

Rappahannock County

Chestnut Hills Farm
Frank P. McWhirt
Rt. 1, Box 770
Amissville, VA 22002
(703)937-5461
Open: December
Selection: Scotch Pine and White Pine

Parson Christmas Tree Farm
Nels A. Parson
Box 85
Washington, VA 22747
(703)675-3523
Open: Weekend before Christmas
Selection: Douglas Fir

Quail Call Farm
William J. Keim
Route 642
Amissville, VA 22002
(703)937-4696
Open: December
Selection: Scotch Pine, White Pine, Fraser Fir and
Colorado Blue Spruce

Yulelog Christmas Tree Farm
Ralph S. Woodruff
7308 Lois Lane
Lanham, MD 20706
(703)364-2811 or (301)577-4316
Selection: Blue Spruce, Norway Spruce, Scotch Pine,
Virginia Pine and White Pine

Warren County

Skyline Evergreen Farm
Jim Frith
4919 N. 14th Street
Arlington, VA 22205
(703)527-2743 or (703)635-4366
Open: December
Selection: Norway Spruce, White Spruce, Scotch Pine and
White Pine
Special Comments: The farm is near Front Royal, Virginia.

EPHRATA CLOISTER
It's Worth the Effort

A visit to the Ephrata Cloister in Pennsylvania is an experience in living history. The Cloister was built between
1735 and 1749 by a Seventh-Day Baptist sect formed by the
German Pietist mystic, Conrad Beissel. They and many other
sects came to Pennsylvania to build their churches and
make new lives under William Penn's benign policy of freedom of religion.
   This Seventh-Day Baptist religious community consisted
of three orders, a brotherhood and a sisterhood which practiced celibacy and a married order of householders. Still
standing today and open to visitors is the Saron, the sisters'

house, as well as a typical example of a householder's cabin. The Bethania, the brothers' house, was destroyed in 1908.

The austerity of the sisters' cells attests to the spartan nature of the order. The sisters slept on board benches with wood pillows. Even the way the buildings were constructed was intended to remind them of their religious vows. The narrow hallways were symbolic of the path they were to walk in life. Each time they had to bend to pass through the low doors they were reminded of their vow of humility.

Other restored buildings open to the public include the Saal, or chapel; the Almonry, an alms and bake house; founder Conrad Beissel's log house and two cottages. The original Academy building still exists, as does the Print Shop.

Special schools were established for teaching the religious precepts of the order and the hymns that were composed to exalt the mystical life. To sing these hymns properly, a particularly rigid diet had to be maintained in order to purify the voice.

The religious society numbered about 300 at its height in 1750. By 1800, the celibate orders were becoming extinct but the congregation of householders continued to use the chapel until 1934.

From late June through early September you can see a production of the musical drama, *Vorspiel*, which depicts life in the Cloister in the 1700s. There are Cloister tours from 6:30 to 8:00 p.m. that end in time for the performance at 9:00 on Saturday evenings. The drama illustrates the degree of religious fervor that was so much a part of the Cloister member's daily life. There is a $4.00 admission charge for *Vorspiel*.

The Ephrata Cloister can be visited from 10:00 a.m. to 4:30 p.m. Tuesday through Saturday and from noon to 4:30 p.m. on Sunday. It is closed on holidays. Admission is charged. For more information about the Cloister call (717)733-6600.

Directions: From the Beltway take Exit 22, the Baltimore-Washington Parkway, to the Baltimore Beltway. Go northwest toward Towson, then take I-83 north around York. Follow Route 30 east to Lancaster, Pennsylvania. At Lancaster take Route 222 north to the Ephrata Cloister on your right.

EXPLORERS HALL
Make Your Own Discoveries

Washington has many attractions for both the tourist and the native. One that you may have missed is Explorers Hall at the National Geographic Society. If you've ever enjoyed one of the Society's magazines you will enjoy a visit here.

The National Geographic magazine is known for its excellent photographs, and in Explorers Hall several displays capitalize on this artistry. An ever-changing collection called Windows of the World features six-foot color transparencies that emphasize the wonders of nature.

Nature and our world are put in perspective at Explorers Hall. The world's largest unmounted globe, 11 feet in diameter and 36 feet in circumference, slowly rotates to give you a view of the planet earth. The orrery, a working model of the solar system, shows the earth orbiting in space. Earth's journey of 584 million miles a year takes a mere 60 seconds on this model. Here you also can see the 3.9 billion- year-old moon rock brought back by the astronauts of Apollo 12.

Man, too, is put in perspective at Explorers Hall. A video program acquaints you with worldwide archeological discoveries relating to early man. Many of the expeditions were sponsored by or received research grants from the National Geographic Society. The Discovering Prehistoric People exhibit presents reconstructions of the precursors of modern man.

Prehistoric man in the southwestern portion of the United States is presented in the Cliff Dwellers display. On exhibit is a kiva, or ceremonial chamber, of the Wetherill Mesa cliff dwellers of Colorado. This was the center of community life for these early people who vanished from that region in 1290.

From Central America you will see one of the 11 huge stone heads discovered on a joint National Geographic Society–Smithsonian Institution venture that began in 1939. The giant basalt head, called the Olmec Head, was uncovered in Tabasco, Mexico. The lost Olmec civilization thrived between 2000 to 1500 B.C. before the Mayan and Aztec civilizations.

These are just some of the permanent exhibits; there are also constantly changing special displays at Explorers Hall.

And the Publications Desk has a collection of books, atlases and globes for sale.

Explorers Hall is open to the public at no charge from 9:00 a.m. to 6:00 p.m. weekdays, Saturday from 9:00 a.m. to 5:00 p.m. and Sunday from 10:00 a.m. to 5:00 p.m.

Directions: Explorers Hall in the National Geographic Building is inside the Beltway at 18th and M Street in northwest Washington.

FOLGER SHAKESPEARE LIBRARY
As You Like It

A visit to Stratford-upon-Avon may well evoke Elizabethan times, but that same feeling can be captured here at home. The Folger Shakespeare Library in Washington gives us a glimpse of the times of William Shakespeare. The interior of a great Elizabethan Hall is suggested by the Exhibition Gallery with its mellow oak paneling, vaulted ceiling and the Queen's own coat of arms carved over the door. The theatre, with its series of balconies, a trap door through which actors rise to "heaven" and an inner stage, is a recreation of the public playhouses of Shakespeare's day.

The Folger Theatre Group performs Shakespearean, Renaissance and other plays in the theatre from October to June. This is an exciting as well as an educational opportunity to see plays staged as they were in the days of the famous playwright.

The library contains one of the world's finest collections of Renaissance books as well as many constantly changing exhibits. There are walk-in tours that can be joined without making reservations Monday through Friday between 11:00 a.m. and 1:00 p.m. The Elizabethan Theatre and Exhibition Gallery are open from 10:00 a.m. to 4:00 p.m. Monday through Saturday and during the same hours on Sunday from mid-April to Labor Day. The theatre is, however, closed periodically for rehearsals. For more information you can call (202)544-7077. The box office number is (202)546-4000.

Directions: The Folger Shakespeare Library is located inside the Beltway at 201 East Capitol Street in southeast Washington.

GENERAL MOTORS PLANT TOUR
Rivets Your Attention

It is often said that Americans have a love affair with their cars. If that is true for you, you have an excellent opportunity to see the object of your affection as it progresses from a collection of parts to a finished product. A tour of the General Motors plant in Maryland will show you how cars are assembled and produced.

Car manufacturing has come a long way since Henry Ford's first assembly line. It is mind boggling to see the huge conveyors. They carry parts in a rainbow of colors for the many different car styles and consistently deliver the right part in the right color at the exact time the matching part is in front of a given worker.

The 1½-hour plant tour is a visual experience. It is also something of a physical workout because it covers 1¼ miles and entails climbing up and down a flight of 80 steps. Also, if you tour in the summer, keep in mind that no sandals or other open shoes are allowed because they are considered unsafe in the plant area. In fact, it is advisable to wear flat shoes to make the long walk more comfortable.

More than 30,000 visitors a year take this tour to discover exactly how a car is made. They see the seemingly random parts assembled into a finished product that is then painted and tested.

Visitors over the age of ten are welcome without charge Monday through Friday for tours at 9:00 a.m. and 12:30 p.m. There are no weekend or holiday tours. The tours are halted July 1 through September 30 so that competitors do not find out about General Motors' new models.

To make arrangements to be included on one of these tours, call (301)955-9508 or write Mr. I. P. Galliher, Baltimore Plant, P.O. Box 148, 2122 Broening Highway, Baltimore, Maryland 21203. Unfortunately, tours are filled a month or two in advance, but call anyway if your family is small and perhaps you can be fitted in with another group. If you write, include your name, phone number, which tour time you prefer, and the date you would like to tour. It is best to include several dates in case your first choice is already booked.

Directions: From the Washington Beltway, take Exit 22, the Baltimore-Washington Parkway, and go through the

Baltimore Harbor Tunnel. Take the first exit past the tunnel onto Holabird Avenue, then go right at the third traffic light on Broening Highway until you come to number 2122, the General Motors Baltimore Plant.

GODDARD SPACE FLIGHT CENTER
An A-OK Place

Dr. Robert H. Goddard is considered the "Father of American Rocketry." He dreamed of conquering space through the use of rocket propulsion and he, as much as anyone, is responsible for the dawning of the Space Age. On May 1, 1959, the National Aeronautics and Space Administration established the Goddard Space Flight Center, the first major scientific laboratory operating solely for the exploration of space.

The National Space Science Data Center is housed at Goddard Space Flight Center in Maryland. It contains one of the highest concentrations of computing capability in the world. The computers are the repository of data collected by scientific experiments in space.

Goddard is also responsible for the Delta launch vehicle that has boosted into orbit more than 50% of all NASA spacecraft. Fifteen hundred sounding rockets and 150 satellites including weather, communications and scientific satellites have been launched.

Goddard serves as the nerve center for NASA tracking and communications activities. Two large operational areas are NASCOM Message Switching Computer and NASCOM Voice Control. There, on massive phone banks that permit 400 people to talk simultaneously, Goddard scientists and technicians keep track of various space ventures such as the space shuttle. There are more than 3,000,000 miles of circuits in the NASCOM operation.

In the past Goddard hosted about 30,000 visitors a year, but since the Visitor's Center opened in May 1976, that figure has increased. The Visitor's Center makes family visits much easier as no prior arrangements are needed and the complex can be seen without having to join a touring group. Watch the signs carefully for the special gate leading directly to the Visitor's Center; a pass is necessary at the main gate. Surrounding the center you will see rocket models, weather satellites, a Delta launch vehicle, sounding rockets, scientific satellites and a scale model of a lunar vehicle.

Within the Visitor's Center itself you can explore the many worlds of the National Aeronautics and Space Administration and the Goddard Space Flight Center. Although there is a receptionist to answer questions, it is for the most part a do-it-yourself tour. Films, tapes, television cassettes, telephone messages and exhibits all offer you an insight into America's space activities.

Films will bring back memories of many of the exciting lift-offs you may have seen in years past. Other films show aeronautical experiments such as vertical take-offs. The video presentation includes many photos of the earth taken by orbiting satellites. You will also have the chance to see "real time" satellite weather pictures that are being transmitted directly as they are taken.

Displayed within the center is the first satellite the United States launched, Explorer I. Vanguard I, an early satellite the size of a softball; the LANDSAT satellite and other weather and communication satellites are also on exhibit. A hot line phone system delivers cassette messages about the many aspects of NASA's work. A do-it-yourself computer experiment gives the children a chance to get involved.

On Thursday afternoons at 2:00 p.m. a general tour takes visitors through the tracking, computer and communication nerve centers. On the average tour, a demonstration call is made from the switchboard to London, Madrid or Australia to show the quality and speed of the connections. You will be overwhelmed by the sheer number of computers available in this small section of the NASCOM Center. Goddard workers can be seen plugging into various switching stations around the world. On my visit they plugged into the London switching station and we heard Goddard's London associate describe his activities and give a weather report. The communications center is the last stop and by then you should have an excellent perspective on the work being done by the NASA scientists at Goddard.

On the first and third Sunday of each month, model rockets are launched from the grounds at 1:00 p.m.

The Goddard Space Flight Visitor's Center is open Wednesday through Sunday from 10:00 a.m. to 4:00 p.m. For additional information call the Public Affairs Office at (301)344-8101. There is no admission fee.

Directions: From the Beltway take Exit 22, the Baltimore-Washington Parkway, towards Baltimore. Stay in the far right lane so that you can take the next turn off onto Greenbelt Road. Turn left at the light onto Greenbelt Road and proceed one mile to the Goddard Space Flight Center on your left. A sign will direct you to the special gate for the Visitor's Center.

HILLWOOD MUSEUM
Old World Elegance

Marjorie Merriweather Post's Hillwood estate is not only a museum reflecting her lifelong love of French and Russian art, it is also a reminder of entertainment on a lavish and elegant scale rarely possible today.

In the French Regency paneled dining room, scene of many formal evenings, the table is set with one of the many services in Mrs. Post's collection. One of her favorites was a silver-gilt service for 36 which was made for the Emperor Franz Josef of Austria; she frequently used this with Sèvres porcelain. More casual hostesses will be amazed to learn that when the table was set at Hillwood the overhang of the tablecloth was carefully measured so it would be exactly the same on each side and each plate was precisely 16 inches from the next. While eating, guests could admire the many plaques and bronzes given by the French people to Czar Alexander I at the end of the Napoleonic Wars.

The drawing room is also decorated in the French style with lovely Beavais tapestries above the matching sofas. The sofas and 12 chairs were commissioned by Louis XVI and Marie Antoinette as a gift to Prince Henry of Prussia, the brother of Frederick the Great. Flanking a portrait of Empress Eugenie are wall cases filled with Sèvres porcelain.

The French motif continues in Mrs. Post's bedroom, which is done in pink and gold in the style of Louis XVI. Pictures, objets d'art and her collection of bloodstone pieces vie for space.

Although each room provides a setting for her vast collection of furniture and art objects, it is in the Icon, Porcelain and Russian Folk Art Rooms that the real scope of Mrs. Post's collection becomes apparent. Her collection is considered the finest array of Russian art outside the Soviet Union.

She acquired these treasures in 1937 and 1938 when she was in Moscow with her husband Joseph E. Davis, Ambassador to the Soviet Union. The Russians, on the 20th anniversary of Soviet rule, sold the contents of state storerooms filled with czarist works of art. Many of the objects were related to the Russian Orthodox Church and were sold for 50 cents per gram of silver content without any regard for their artistic worth. Included in the Russian collection are many fine chalices as well as creations by Fabergé, jeweler to the czars.

A visit to Hillwood offers more visual splendor if you plan your day to include time for a garden tour. Spring is the best season for exploring because the flowering dogwood, cherry and crab apple trees compete with the rhododendron and azaleas to bedazzle visitors. But you can appreciate the tranquil beauty of the Japanese garden and Moorish water canal year round. The two rose gardens provide enjoyment throughout the summer. At the estate greenhouse, in addition to enjoying the orchid collection, you can purchase plants.

While exploring the Hillwood grounds don't miss the one-room Russian dacha. This wooded cottage is like those used by the Russian aristocracy for weekend retreats. It contains additional pieces from the Russian collection.

A new museum added in 1983 features American Indian art and artifacts. Mrs. Post donated her extensive collection to the Smithsonian Institution, but a third of it is on long-term loan to the Hillwood Museum.

The 190 pieces include rugs, pottery, baskets, quillwork and feather headdresses. The exhibit is housed in a newly constructed log cabin, suggesting the Adirondack "camp" where the artifacts were originally on view. The museum and gardens are open from 11:00 a.m. to 4:00 p.m. daily, except Tuesday and Sunday. You can call ahead on the day you want to visit the Indian museum and gardens, but to tour the Hillwood Museum itself you will need advance reservations.

The mansion can be toured Monday, Wednesday, Thursday, Friday and Saturday at 9:00 a.m., 10:30 a.m., noon and 1:30 p.m. Admission is charged and reservations are necessary; to make arrangements call (202)686-5807. The tour of the house takes about two hours and is preceded by a film on Marjorie Merriweather Post's life.

Directions: Take Beltway Exit 33, Connecticut Avenue, into Washington. From Connecticut Avenue turn left on Tilden Street and then left on Linnean Avenue. Hillwood is located at 4155 Linnean Avenue.

KENSINGTON ORCHIDS
Floral Royal

During winter's cold grip it is particularly pleasant to visit an attraction that specializes in flowers; it reminds us that spring will eventually arrive.

A unique spot for such reminding is Kensington Orchids just off Connecticut Avenue in Maryland. Although this is a business, it is also a floral fun house. The overhead plants have such dangling roots that they obstruct the narrow passageways. Orchids bloom here in a wide spectrum of exotic hues. You will see orchid varieties that have never graced a florist shop. It's hard to resist touching them to see if they are indeed real.

Kensington Orchids has eight greenhouses open to the public at no charge and there are approximately 100,000 plants. The collection includes botanic orchids that cannot be seen elsewhere in this area, as well as numerous varieties of the more commercial Cattleya orchids.

Although you can't buy cut orchids at Kensington, you can buy plants—small pots for about $10, up to special hybrid orchids costing thousands of dollars.

Kensington Orchids is open daily from 8:00 a.m. to noon and from 1:00 to 5:00 p.m.

Directions: Take Beltway Exit 33, Connecticut Avenue, north to 3301 Plyers Mill Road. Turn right on Plyers Mill Road and watch for the Kensington Orchid sign.

LONDON BRASS RUBBING CENTRE
A Touch of Brass

From medieval times attempts have been made to turn base metals into gold. You can achieve this alchemy with unique brass rubbings that make "golden" gifts. Brass rubbings are a marvelous inflation-fighting holiday gift that you can make on a fun-filled day's outing to the London Brass

Rubbing Centre at the Washington Cathedral.

Interest in this age-old craft was kindled by American soldiers stationed in England during World War II. On their off-duty hours many soldiers made brass rubbings of the intricate commemorative plaques found on the walls and floors of English churches. The soldiers brought these rubbings home as gifts and mementos. After the war, travelers to England wanted to make their own rubbings. The handsome souvenirs were simple to make and provided inexpensive reminders of one's trip. The increased popularity of brass rubbings, however, threatened to destroy the details on irreplaceable medieval brasses.

Something had to be done to preserve the historically and artistically important originals. To that end the first Brass Rubbing Centre was set up in London in 1970. It provided casts of original brasses that could be rubbed for a modest fee. This achieved two objectives: the originals were preserved and a number of choices were made available in one location. These centres rapidly became popular and we are fortunate to have one here in the Washington area.

The director of the centre at the Cathedral, Richard Etches, came to Washington in 1977 with his wife, Ann. Both are on hand with their assistants to help you choose from among the more than 70 brasses at the centre. They regale visitors with fascinating asides about the dress and background of the individuals depicted on the brasses.

You will find brasses at the centre that span the years from the 1300s when the first commemorative plaques were commissioned to the early 1700s when marble effigies began to replace the brass memorials.

The very first brasses were life-size commemorations of the Crusador knights. A cast of the third oldest brass in England, done in 1302, can be found at the centre. This brass figure of a knight is 6 feet, 9 inches tall. When the practice of making brasses started, only the very wealthy knights and nobility could afford such testimonials. As the idea spread, wealthy middle class merchants also began to commission brasses, but on a smaller scale.

All the details of medieval costumes are depicted on the brasses. You can learn the difference between armor that knights wore into battle and the armor worn merely for ceremonial occasions. The ladies' dresses are so carefully reproduced that brocade patterns can be distinctly seen.

The "Lace Lady" is an attractive and popular brass at the centre. This memorial plaque to Margaret Peyton was made in 1484. She was the second Mrs. Peyton and was suspected by some of having murdered the first Mrs. Peyton, whose plaque can also be found at the centre.

You can spend as little as a half-hour or as long as an afternoon in this intriguing medieval-style crypt, where taped period music provides the proper ambience as you work. The reasonable cost of the rubbings—many are under $5—make them ideal holiday gifts. You can do several in a few hours' time. The centre has now expanded its offerings so that you can mat your rubbing when you finish. It can be hung as is, or popped into a frame.

Rubbings can be done on black, gold or white paper. The rubbing itself can be done in gold, silver, bronze or black wax. Even novices, if they work carefully, can master a difficult black-on-white rubbing. A more sophisticated effect can be achieved by combining silver, gold and bronze wax for a single rubbing, but that does get a bit tricky. The London Brass Rubbing Centre is open daily from 9:30 a.m. to 5:00 p.m.

If you have extra time for exploring after your brass rubbing is completed, there are several points of interest at the Washington Cathedral. Guided tours are conducted Monday through Saturday, both mornings and afternoons, and also on Sunday afternoons. The stained glass windows, particularly the rose windows, are considered to be some of the finest examples of the art in America.

If it is a clear day, you may want to pay the nominal charge to visit the Pilgrim Gallery. At 490 feet above sea level, you'll have a panoramic view of Washington, Maryland and Virginia. The glass enclosed observation gallery is open from mid-morning to mid-afternoon Monday through Saturday and on Sunday afternoons.

Finally, if the weather is not only clear but also mild, you might want to explore the medieval Bishop's Garden. The extensive plantings of boxwood, yew and ivy as well as the interesting additions of early Christian sculpture make this worth seeing at any time of the year.

Directions: The Washington Cathedral is inside the Beltway. It is located at the intersection of Massachusetts Avenue and Wisconsin Avenue just above Georgetown. Parking is available on the grounds.

NATIONAL CAPITAL TROLLEY MUSEUM
Streetcars You Will Desire

For adults who want to indulge in a little nostalgia and children who enjoy rail transport the Trolley Museum in Maryland is the perfect place. A group of enthusiastic streetcar buffs is responsible for creating this museum with its 14 cars, 1¾-mile track, Visitor's Center and carbarns. The streetcars depart every half-hour from the Visitor's Center which is built to resemble an old-time railroad station. A nominal fare is charged for the ride. At the end of the track a volunteer gives a talk about the trolley museum, answers questions and punches your ticket before your return trip.

The museum has cars from Germany and Austria as well as some of the early cars from Washington's own trolley line. The "Berliner" car is gayly decorated with flowers, as were all trolley cars in Germany on Flower Festival Day. The Austrian car has a measuring stick on the wall because they used to charge for children by age or height, whichever was the greater. How much would your child's fare be?

From Labor Day to Memorial Day the trolley museum is open only on Saturday and Sunday from noon to 5:00 p.m. During the summer the museum is open Wednesday from noon to 4:00 p.m. and on Saturday and Sunday from noon to 5:00 p.m. At least once a month the trolley museum schedules special programs: on the third Sunday in April and September there is a Trolley Car Parade. There are also musical programs, special movies and model car exhibits. For more information on the trolley museum and its special programs call (301)384-9797.

Directions: From the Beltway take Exit 28, New Hampshire Avenue, north for 5.4 miles. After the road narrows look for a Freestate station on the left. Turn left just before the Freestate station and go 1.9 miles to the trolley museum on your right.

NATIONAL SHRINE OF THE IMMACULATE CONCEPTION
Not Just for the Religious

Washington is noted for its many religious denominations and you can achieve the equivalent of having taken a course in comparative religion by spending some time visiting its various temples, mosques, cathedrals and churches. One that you will certainly want to see is the National Shrine of the Immaculate Conception. It is the largest Catholic church in the United States and the seventh largest in the world, but its enormous size merely emphasizes its innate grace.

No matter what your own religious affiliation may be, the shrine is well worth a visit. Like Medieval cathedrals it is built of stone, brick, tile and concrete. The church is a perfect blend of Byzantine, Romanesque and contemporary architecture.

Inside the shrine are two distinct areas, the Crypt Church which was opened in 1926 and the large Main Church which opened in 1959. The Crypt Church preserves the atmosphere of the ancient Roman catacombs. Religious artifacts and sculpture make it a living museum.

The Main Church with its towering walls and great dome supported by arches is an impressive sight. It contains many valuable mosaics, tapestries, glowing stained-glass windows and fine pieces of contemporary American sculpture, as well as objects donated by the Vatican.

The National Shrine of the Immaculate Conception is open free to the public from 7:00 a.m. to 7:00 p.m. from April through October and from 7:00 a.m. to 6:00 p.m. from November through March. There are guided tours Monday through Saturday from 9:00 a.m. to 4:00 p.m. and on Sunday from 1:30 to 4:00 p.m. Tours begin at Memorial Hall and last approximately 45 minutes.

The Great Organ of the Shrine can be heard at the Masses on Sundays and Holy Days. These Masses regularly bring together visitors and pilgrims from throughout America.

Directions: The shrine is located inside the Beltway at 4th Street and Michigan Avenue in northeast Washington. It borders on the Catholic University of America. Plenty of free parking is available. The shrine is a two-minute walk across the Catholic University campus from the Brookland Metro Station.

NAVY YARD MUSEUMS
Macramé, The Navy Way

Macramé may be enjoying a new popularity but it's been around a long time as you will see at the U.S. Navy Memorial Museum, in Washington. Among the more than 4,000 artifacts on exhibit is a collection of seamen's rope tying that would be a challenge to any macramé enthusiast.

History buffs will love the museum's large collection of ship models, such as the *Constellation*, *Constitution*, and Admiral Farragut's flagship *Hartford*; paintings by Anton Fisher of the Revolutionary War and lithographs from the Civil War period; weapons and personal memorabilia. The central part of the museum has a weapons display that includes torpedoes, mines, cannon, atomic bombs and guided missiles. Surely any young gunslinger will be awed and more respectful of weapons after seeing this display. The submarine room has three periscopes that visitors can use to view the waterfront and ordinance park. Also on display is Admiral Byrd's Antarctic hut.

Along the waterfront outside the museum is Admiral Willard Park. Here are displayed captured guns, early and unusual submersible objects, a battleship propeller and prototypes from the field of radar and guided missiles.

At the north end of the museum is Admiral Leutze Park with cannon trophies from the Tripoli War and the War of 1812 as well as a memorial to the *USS Enterprise*.

The U.S. Navy Memorial Museum is open to the public free of charge Monday through Friday from 9:00 a.m. to 4:00 p.m. and Saturday, Sunday and holidays from 10:00 a.m. to 5:00 p.m.

Also within the Washington Navy Yard is the Marine Corps Museum and Historical Center, a time tunnel that encompasses the more than 200-year history of the United States Marines. Artifacts and equipment are flanked by letters and personal mementos of the conflicts in which Marines have taken part from the American Revolution to Vietnam.

One rather different exhibit you might not expect to find in a military museum is the constantly changing display of combat art by or about Marines. Another artistic field represented at this museum is music. The display on military music features old scores, band uniforms and instruments.

The focal point of this display is the musical contribution of John Philip Sousa.

The Marine Corps Museum is open daily except Christmas. Hours are Monday through Saturday from 10:00 a.m. to 4:00 p.m. and Sundays and holidays from noon to 5:00 p.m. During the summer the museum stays open until 8:00 p.m. on Wednesday and 11:00 p.m. on Friday.

Directions: The Washington Navy Yard is inside the Beltway at 9th and M Street, southeast Washington. The U.S. Navy Memorial Museum is in Building #75 and the Marine Corps Museum is in Building #58.

OLD STONE HOUSE
Early Georgetown

The Old Stone House in Georgetown is thought to be the only surviving pre-Revolutionary building in Washington. The house was begun in 1764 by Christopher Layman, who built the ground floor as a shop for his cabinetmaking business. The house was acquired in 1765 at Layman's death by the Chew family who added the north wing in the 1770s.

The small middle class colonial building was used both as a home and as a commercial establishment. The town developed rapidly after a local warehouse was designated as the official tobacco inspection site. Georgetown grew to be one of the most important tobacco markets along the Atlantic seaboard.

When you visit the Old Stone House you will see six rooms carefully restored to represent a middle class dwelling in the late 18th century. The cabinet making shop and the kitchen on the ground floor were the main centers of daily life for the busy family. The heat from the kitchen fireplace encouraged the women to do most of their household work in front of its friendly warmth. On the first floor there is a decorated dining room with fine wood paneling, an inviting parlor and a servant's bedroom. The main bedroom space is in the attic. There is also a charming but small 18th-century English garden.

The Old Stone House is open Wednesday through Sunday from 9:30 a.m. to 5:00 p.m. It is closed on Mondays, Tuesdays and major holidays. There is no admission charged.

Directions: The house is inside the Beltway in Georgetown at 3051 M Street, N.W.

PAUL E. GARBER FACILITY
Smithsonian's Other Air Museum

Who is Paul E. Garber and why is there a fascinating museum named for him? As Garber is quick to point out, he's no relation to Greta (she's a Garbo) and he doesn't make baby food (Gerber does). Paul Garber started working at the Smithsonian on June 1, 1920 and immediately made the early years of aviation his special area of interest.

Because the air force decided not to open its own air museum, Garber was in on the ground floor as the Smithsonian began to acquire the foreign planes that came to this country as war prizes at the end of World War II. On August 12, 1946, less than a year after the war ended, President Truman signed into law the act which established the National Air Museum. But it wasn't until 1980 that the collection housed at the Silver Hill Museum in Prince George's County, Maryland, was renamed the Paul E. Garber Facility in recognition of Garber's many years of devoted service.

Winter is a good time to plan a visit to the Garber facility because it can be enjoyed regardless of the weather. Air enthusiasts will like the "no frills" display and the chance to see actual preservation work being done on the planes.

This museum is less well known and certainly less crowded than its larger companion museum, the National Air and Space Museum on the Mall. However, it does contain a considerable part of the Smithsonian collection. Of the Smithsonian's 280 aircraft, 76 are at the Mall location, and 92 are at the Paul E. Garber Facility. Others are on loan or are not currently on display.

For some, this behind-the-scenes look at aviation is even more intriguing than the polished displays offered by most air museums. In addition to the old planes in the 24-building facility you can also see an extensive collection of artifacts associated with our space program. There is even a kite display.

Tours are given at 10:00 a.m. Monday through Friday and at 10:00 a.m. and 1:00 p.m. on Saturday, Sunday and holidays. Advance reservations are necessary and there customarily is about a two-week wait. To make arrangements call (202)357-1400 or write to the National Air and Space Museum, Smithsonian Institution, Washington, D.C. 20560.

Directions: Take Maryland Beltway Exit 4, St. Barnabas Road, toward Suitland. Cross Silver Hill Road and take Old Silver Hill Road to the Paul E. Garber Facility adjacent to the Silver Hill Volunteer Fire Department.

PHILADELPHIA
Philadelphia, Here We Come!

Philadelphia, the city of "brotherly love," can entertain your entire family for one day or for a weekend. The historical sites are a good place to begin because at the time of the American Revolution Philadelphia was the largest English-speaking city in the world after London. On 48 acres in downtown Philadelphia, the Independence National Historical Park has 40 historic buildings and numerous 18th-century park areas that bring back those by-gone days. The buildings here are not merely old, they are closely associated with the men and events that Americans revere.

Independence Hall, site of the First and Second Continental Congresses, was the birthplace of the Revolution. The single most historic room in America is the Assembly Room where both the Declaration of Independence and the American Constitution were hammered out.

A brochure and map available at the Independence National Historical Park Visitor's Center will enable you to enjoy a walking tour that includes all the important sites—Independence Hall, the Liberty Bell Pavilion, Franklin Court, the Second Bank of the U.S., Library Hall, Carpenters Hall and the old houses in the park (Pemberton House, Bishop White House, Todd House and Graff House).

Philadelphia also has many fascinating museums. In fact, the wide Benjamin Franklin Parkway modeled after the Champs Élysées in Paris is called "museum row." At one end of the parkway is the Philadelphia Museum of Art, built like a Greek temple. This museum's collection of a hundred thousand works in 200 galleries is the third most important art collection in America. Skillfully arranged rooms permit visitors to stroll through a 17th-century Chinese palace, a

Japanese Buddhist temple and a 12th-century French cloister.

A short distance down the parkway is the Rodin Museum, housed in a chateau-like building with the masterful *The Thinker* outside the gates. This is the largest collection of Auguste Rodin's work outside of Paris. Farther down the street is the Franklin Institute of Science Museum. This do-it-yourself, push-button museum lets youngsters interact with the exhibits. Have you ever wanted to be an airline pilot, ship's captain or astronomer? Here's your chance to live your dreams. The institute also contains the Fels Planetarium where you can take a trip through the solar system.

Across the street you will find the Academy of Natural Sciences, which contains exhibits that span the ages from prehistory to the present. Thirty-five habitat groups give you the chance to explore the simulated environment of a Chinese panda or an Alaskan brown bear.

If you prefer your animals live, you'll be delighted with a visit to the Philadelphia Zoological Park—America's oldest zoo. The Safari Monorail will transport you through the park which houses more than 1,000 residents in a naturalized setting extending over 42 acres of land. Of special interest is the Hummingbird House, a tropical microclimate with free-flying birds.

Directions: Take Beltway Exit 27, I-95, north to Philadelphia. Follow it into the city where it will become Front Street. Turn left on Lombard Street and right on Broad Street and then left onto the Benjamin Franklin Parkway. At Kennedy Plaza you will see Philadelphia's Tourist Hospitality Center. For Independence National Historical Park turn left off Front Street at Walnut Street.

PRINCE WILLIAM FOREST PARK
Your Own Walden Pond

If you enjoy nature in its primeval state, this is the place to visit in Virginia. There are more than 35 miles of trails winding along streams and through Virginia pine, mountain laurel, holly, dogwood and many other of the 89 varieties of trees and shrubs in the park.

Prince William Forest Park encompasses the watersheds of the north and south branches of Quantico Creek. Many of the paths are so infrequently traversed that visitors often come upon white-tailed deer, red and gray foxes, beavers, racoons, opossums, squirrels, rabbits, wild turkeys and grouse. There are many spots where you can sit and enjoy the special tranquility that comes from being close to the quiet world of nature.

There are facilities within the park for picnicking and camping. Park naturalists provide conducted trips, illustrated talks and other programs but it is often nice just to set off on your own. The trails provide many picturesque spots with wooden bridges crossing and recrossing the creeks.

Much of this haven can be enjoyed by the handicapped. The paved Pine Grove Forest Nature Trail, the Nature Center building and the park's campgrounds are all accessible.

Directions: Take Virginia Beltway Exit 4, I-95, south to the Prince William Forest Park sign. From the Washington Beltway, it takes about 25 minutes to reach the park. For more information, call (703)221-7181 or write Prince William Forest Park, P.O. Box 209, Triangle, Virginia 22172.

RICHMOND
A Great Place to Visit Since 1607

Richmond is truly rich in history and the arts. Many famous people from America's past have left their mark on this city. Thomas Jefferson lived there when he served as Governor of Virginia from 1779 to 1781. John Marshall also made his home in Richmond, and it is now preserved as a National Historic Landmark. The city served as the capital of the Confederacy and was so grand in style that it was called "a miniature Paris." The monuments, hand-paved boulevards and many museums still call up parts of Paris.

The Richmond Information Center map provides for a suggested auto tour that clearly marks the most noteworthy historical and cultural sites. If you've had enough driving on your own, you can take a two-hour Richmond bus tour that stops at the major attractions in the city. Seeing Richmond is an all-day undertaking so be sure to give yourself plenty of time. There are no fewer than seven intriguing museums.

The Valentine Museum at 1015 East Clay Street is a complex of 19th-century residences. The most striking is the Wickham-Valentine House which was designed in 1812 by Robert Mills and is considered one of the architectural gems of America. The house was built for John Wickham, a lawyer whose most notorious client was Aaron Burr. The Valentine Museum has the third largest costume collection in America; a 1668 linen christening dress is the oldest item. Other notable exhibits are the Indian Collection, which includes artifacts dating back to 10,000 B.C., and the Pipe Collection of silver, ivory, meerschaum, briar and clay pipes. The Valentine Museum is open Tuesday through Saturday from 10:00 a.m. to 4:45 p.m. and on Sunday from 1:30 to 5:00 p.m. Admission is charged except for children under five. Children under 16 are admitted at no cost on Sunday.

The second museum, also located on Clay at 12th Street, is the Museum of the Confederacy. This classic building served as the White House for the Confederacy. From here for 3½ years Jefferson Davis tried to lead a new country. Mementos of the Confederate cause make this a fascinating place. The museum houses the largest collection of Confederate papers, uniforms, flags, firearms and personal items in the world. It is open Monday through Saturday from 9:00 a.m. to 5:00 p.m. and on Sunday from 2:00 p.m. to 5:00 p.m. Admission is charged.

The third museum is totally unimposing from the outside but inside you enter the world of Edgar Allan Poe's tortured mind. You will see the Enchanted Garden, a delightful alcoved retreat, the Raven Room and the Old Stone House, which was built in 1737 and is considered Richmond's oldest building. It was in these surroundings that Poe composed some of his most brilliant work. The Poe Museum at 1914 E. Main is open Sunday and Monday from 1:30 to 4:00 p.m. and Tuesday through Saturday from 10:00 a.m. to 4:00 p.m. There is an admission fee.

America's first state supported art institution is the Virginia Museum at Boulevard and Grove Street. It contains an outstanding art nouveau collection and a gorgeous array of Fabergé jewelry as well as many masterpieces of painting and sculpture. Classical and contemporary plays are presented regularly by the Professional Museum Theatre. It is open Tuesday through Saturday from 11:00 a.m. to 5:00

p.m. and Sunday from 1:00 to 5:00 p.m. Admission is charged for adults; children under 16 are admitted free.

The Science Museum of Virginia, housed in the restored 1919 train station on West Broad Street, features computers that talk, crystals that grow as you watch, a full-sized space capsule and the world's most advanced planetarium and space theater, Universe. Open 10:00 a.m. to 5:00 p.m. Monday through Saturday, and 1:00 to 5:00 p.m. Sunday, the museum offers many special events, exhibits and film programs. There is admission charged both for the museum and for the Universe planetarium. Universe programs are scheduled throughout the day and evening.

The Richmond Children's Museum, focusing on the 3-to-12 age group, is one place where youngsters are urged to put their hands on the objects displayed. Located at 740 North 6th Street, the museum includes a play area complete with environmental shapes to climb on. Admission is charged. The museum is open from 10:00 a.m. to 4:30 p.m. Tuesday through Friday, and 1:00 to 5:00 p.m. Saturday and Sunday.

The Spider Museum at 2401 Hartman Street, with its 27 spider varieties including wolf spiders, black widows, and common Virginia species, is giving spiders good press. Large photographs of spiders, artifacts, books and jewelry with spider motifs all help the professional staff to educate people about the beneficial environmental role of these arachnids. Hours are 9:00 a.m. to 4:00 p.m., Monday through Friday. Admission is charged.

Three other historical points of interest are located in the same area as the museums: the Marshall House, the Capitol and St. John's Church. John Marshall, the first and probably the most famous of the Supreme Court's Chief Justices, designed his house and it still contains most of the original furnishings and many of his personal possessions. In this house from 1802 to 1835 he wrote many of his famous decisions. The house at 818 East Marshall is open Monday through Saturday from 11:00 a.m. to 4:00 p.m. Admission is charged.

Close by is the State Capitol on Capitol Square. Jefferson, when he convinced the state to move the capital from Williamsburg to Richmond in 1780, helped design the Capitol in an area that was regarded as being "as handsomely built as any city of Europe." The statue by Houdon of George

Washington in the Rotunda is considered by many the single most valuable sculpture in America. The State Capitol is open Monday through Saturday from 9:00 a.m. to 5:00 p.m. and on Sunday from May through September from 1:00 to 5:00 p.m. On holidays it is also open from 9:00 a.m. to 5:00 p.m. There is no admission fee.

The last stop in this area is St. John's Church at 24th and Broad Street. The picturesque old church played a role in our nation's history because it was here during the fourth day of the Virginia Convention in 1775 that Patrick Henry said, "Give me liberty or give me death." His statement marked a definitive step toward revolution. You can visit this church at no charge from 10:00 a.m. to 4:00 p.m. Monday through Saturday. On Sunday it is open from 1:00 p.m. to 4:00 p.m.

After being inside so long you may want to take a leisurely drive up Monument Avenue where statues of Robert E. Lee, "Stonewall" Jackson and Jefferson Davis, among others, line the historic boulevard that was paved by hand more than half a century ago. Monument Avenue is the northern border of Richmond's noted Fan District where modern life goes on in classic Tudor and Victorian houses.

After exploring the Monument Avenue area turn right on Westmoreland Avenue to three more places of interest: Virginia House, Agecroft and Wilton. Virginia House at 4301 Sulgrave Road was built in Warwick, England, in 1125 and later dismantled and shipped to Richmond in the 1920s. It was painstakingly reconstructed brick by brick. Even the coat of arms of Elizabeth I, who once visited this English estate, was left intact. Virginia House is open Tuesday through Friday from 10:00 a.m. to 4:00 p.m. and on Saturday and Sunday from 2:00 to 5:00 p.m. There is an admission fee.

Agecroft Hall, built in England five centuries ago and reconstructed in Richmond during the 1920s, is an authentic example of a pre-Elizabethan half-timbered manor house. The atmosphere of an English country gentleman's residence is captured in the simple furnishings and formal, elegant gardens which include a rectangular sunken garden. Agecroft Hall and its gardens are open Tuesday through Friday from 10:00 a.m. to 4:00 p.m., except for legal holidays, and on Saturday and Sunday from 2:00 to 5:00 p.m. Admission is charged.

Wilton is also well worth a visit. This restored mansion once served as headquarters for General Lafayette and was owned by the Randolphs of Virginia. Both Jefferson and Washington were frequent guests. The stately home brings back the days of Virginia's colonial glory.

There is a great deal more you might want to do in Richmond. If you are interested in battlefields you will want to stop at the Richmond National Battlefield Park, Chimborazo Park, 3215 E. Broad Street, open 9:00 a.m. to 5:00 p.m. daily. At the National Battlefield Information Center you can get directions to nearby battle sites including Mechanicsville, Cold Harbor, Gaines' Mill, Frayser's Farm, Savage Station, Fair Oaks, Seven Pines, Malvern Hill and Fort Harrison.

Other parks in Richmond are worth a stop, most notably Maymont where you will find Dooley Mansion, delightful gardens and a wildlife exhibit. Bryan Park with its azalea gardens and Byrd Park with its Swan Lake are also appealing.

A final mention must go to Tobacco Row, which you probably observed as you drove into Richmond. Free tours of many of the plants can be taken Monday through Friday. The American Tobacco Company at 26th and Clay Street has tours from 8:00 a.m. to 2:00 p.m. The Phillip Morris Research Plant on Commerce Road has tours from 8:00 a.m. to 4:00 p.m.

Directions: Take Virginia Beltway Exit 4, Route I-95, south directly to Richmond. Driving time is approximately two hours. For the Tourist Information Center, take Exit 14 from Route I-95/I-64. Turn right on Boulevard and left on Robin Hood Road. The Center, 1700 Robin Hood Road, will be on your left.

SANDY POINT STATE PARK
Bundle Up for the Beach

Something that always provides a change of pace is to visit in winter a place one normally sees only in summer. Pick a pleasant day and take a 40-minute drive to the beach— Sandy Point State Park in Maryland on the Chesapeake Bay. Children will enjoy the unexpected opportunity to play in the sand along the water's edge. The unpopulated beach with its lapping water and swaying sea grass is peaceful and restorative.

Sandy Point is not often thought of as an area for birds, though it is considered the top spot for bird watching in Anne Arundel County. Visitors can often spot interesting shore birds and ducks because many spend the winter on the marsh ponds within the park. A walk along the shore provides you with the opportunity to discover a unique piece of driftwood or an unusual shell that the winter winds have washed ashore.

There is no admission to the park from December 1 through March 31. During the spring and fall there is a small automatic toll for entering the park; the entrance fee is higher in the summer.

Directions: From the Beltway take Exit 19, John Hanson Highway (Route 50), to the Chesapeake Bay Bridge. Immediately before reaching the toll booth turn right at the Sandy Point State Park sign.

UNITED STATES NAVAL OBSERVATORY
Star Light, Star Bright

If you've always known that winter's cold, crisp nights were good for something, it will not surprise you to learn that star-gazing is never better than on a clear winter's night. For a different scientific experience, take one of the United States Naval Observatory's night tours.

Two or three nights each month near the first quarter moon you can peer through the observatory's giant telescopes at celestial objects. Guides will direct your attention to double stars, nebulae, star clusters and the planets.

There are two telescopes used for this nighttime observation, the 26-inch refracting telescope and the 12-inch Alvan Clark refracting telescope. The 26-inch telescope is the observatory's largest; in fact, when it was completed in 1873, it was the largest refractor in the world. Its primary use is to observe multiple star systems. This telescope is mounted so that it compensates for the rotation of the earth and thus is able to follow celestial objects as they move across the sky. The 45- foot observatory dome can be rotated so that the desired portion of the sky is visible. The observatory floor also changes position. It can be raised or lowered to accommodate those using the telescope. The way the floor and ceiling move up, down and around always delights first-time visitors.

The second telescope nighttime visitors can use is the 12-inch refractor built in 1892 and restored to its original appearance by astronomy volunteers. This telescope has "star dials," no longer found on telescopes but once used to direct the telescope to the desired star. This is a working example of a 19th-century astronomical instrument.

On the night tours you will be able to see the displays and exhibits in the Main Building, learn about the work of the U.S. Naval Observatory and scan the skies. Although observations cannot be made on cloudy nights, these tours are conducted on schedule except during severe weather conditions.

You will discover that this is the only institute in the United States (and one of the few in the world) where the fundamental positions of the sun, moon and stars are continually observed. The astronomers work with a telescope called a Transit Circle.

The observatory regulates all Standard Time. It has a Master Clock for the United States as well as receiver equipment that monitors time signals from various navigational systems and commercial time reference stations. You will see an atomic clock on your tour. Researchers actually keep track of four kinds of time: Sidereal Time, based on the transit of the stars; Mean Solar Time, founded on the period of rotation of the earth on its axis; Ephemeris Time, determined by the position of the moon in relation to the stars; and Atomic Time, a very accurate recording of time measured by atomic cesium beam clocks, which use electromagnetic waves of a particular frequency that are emitted when an atomic transition occurs.

The observatory can handle only 110 visitors a night in its telescope domes so passes are handed out on a first-come-first-serve basis. Children under 14 are not permitted on this tour. There are always more visitors on sharp, clear nights when observation is best. From September through April the observatory gates are open from 7:30 to 9:00 p.m. From May through August hours are 8:30 to 10:00 p.m. Be sure to check the recorded message on the day you plan to confirm the time. The number to call regarding night tours is (202)653-1543.

Directions: The U.S. Naval Observatory is located inside the Beltway at 34th and Massachusetts Avenue, N.W. in Washington, D.C.

VILLA PACE
Diva Deserted Hollywood for Baltimore

Imagine trading the exciting life of a Hollywood personality for that of a suburban matron. In 1939 Rosa Ponselle gave up the glamour of practice sessions with Irene Dunne, Gloria Swanson and Joan Crawford for afternoon teas.

As she herself said in *Ponselle, A Singer's Life*, "I was sure all that Baltimoreans did was eat: the women had garden parties and luncheons in the middle of the day, and at night their husbands had dinner parties."

Rosa Ponselle grew to love Baltimore. She designed a gracious mansion, Villa Pace, where she lived until her death on May 25, 1981. The house, now open to the public, is a museum and center for the arts.

This legendary diva was considered by many to be the world's greatest dramatic soprano, earning her the title "the Caruso in petticoats." Unfortunately, differences of opinion with the management of the Metropolitan Opera forced her into an early retirement at age 39 after the 1937 Metropolitan Opera season.

She made Baltimore her home when she married Carle Jackson, the son of Mayor Howard Jackson. Rosa Ponselle threw herself into the planning of her home in Greenspring Valley. She designed it to reflect her own taste and her splendid career. Even the name Villa Pace (House of Peace) was taken from the aria "Pace, pace mio Dio" from *La Forza del Destino*. This was the opera in which she made her debut in 1918, fresh from the vaudeville stage.

As you enter the white mansion with its ornate iron grillwork and red tiled roof you will see that the interior is in the shape of a cross. The religious influence is evident also in the colors used in the entrance foyer. Red, blue, gold and ivory are the colors used to depict the Virgin Mary. Religious paintings, statues and carvings also reflect Rosa Ponselle's devotion.

A second important thrust of the decor was to showcase her own brilliant career. Paintings and porcelain figurines capture Rosa Ponselle in the many roles with which she was identified.

Many of the large pieces of furniture came from the Hearst estate and were obtained by Miss Ponselle at New York auctions. Villa Pace suggests a small-scale San Simeon. They both have a strong European flavor. The dining room is meant for serving in state. All the massive pieces were hand carved. The walnut coffered ceiling is similar to those seen in churches and palaces in Italy.

Across the foyer is the Music Room which was Miss Ponselle's favorite room. Its hand-painted cathedral ceiling provides the large wall expanse needed to show to advantage the beautiful 16th-century Belgian tapestry. In the corner is the custom-built Baldwin grand piano used for so many at-home musicales. RCA Victor came here to Villa Pace and recorded Ponselle in this room when she was nearly 60 years old.

In the downstairs library on Christmas Eve, 1979, a fire started that nearly destroyed the estate. The last years of Miss Ponselle's life were blighted, even as her house was, by the extensive damage caused by the fire. Repairs cost $250,000, equal to the cost of original construction in 1940.

The money to salvage Villa Pace came from the Rosa Ponselle Foundation, established in her will so that the insurance money could be used to rebuild her home and the Foundation could sustain it as a museum and center for the arts. The villa holds a definitive place in musical history. Not only was it Rosa Ponselle's home but it was also the place from which she launched such distinguished protégés as Beverly Sills, Sherrie Milnes, James Morris, Lili Chockasian, Adriana Maliponte, Spiro Malas and many more.

Mounting the grand staircase makes you feel like a character out of grand opera. Ponselle liked to greet her guests by appearing on the balcony and bursting into song. The stairway also gives you a closer look at the torch-like chandelier suspended by a reinforced velvet cord from the center of a sunburst-painted ceiling. It is a powerful and dramatic artistic statement.

Rosa Ponselle's personal suite is the most interesting of the upstairs rooms. Her bedroom, which has been completely restored to its original appearance, is decorated in carnation pink with mirrored and lucite furniture. Laid across one of the divans is a 30-pound costume, which although gorgeous with its spun gold thread, was actually too heavy to wear.

Additional costumes can be seen in the adjoining dressing room designed in the style of ancient Pompeii. Hand-painted figures adorn the deep red room. Docents open some of the custom-made closets and drawers to display gowns, costumes and shoes worn by Miss Ponselle in her many roles. Two mannequins are shown wearing costumes from Carmen. Off this room is an octagonally-shaped bathroom again in the Pompeiin style with hand-painted walls and a domed ceiling. The enormous black enamel tub is the room's centerpiece.

Tours are available Wednesday, Saturday and Sunday from noon to 4:00 p.m. Group tours with luncheons can be arranged on Tuesday, Thursday and Friday by appointment. You can also arrange Sunday afternoon group tours with a concert performance. For additional information, call (301)486-4616. Admission is charged.

Directions: Take Beltway Exit 27, I-95, to the Baltimore Beltway and head toward Towson. Use Exit 21, Park Heights Avenue. At the first traffic light turn right on Greenspring Valley Road and continue to the Rosa Ponselle Home and Museum, which is directly across the street from the Villa Julie College.

WASHINGTON DOLLS' HOUSE AND TOY MUSEUM
Lilliputian Land

A delightful miniature world that includes authentically furnished houses, shops, schools, churches and other Lilliputian buildings awaits you at the Washington Dolls' House and Toy Museum. The private collection of Flora Gill Jacobs, noted author of *Dolls' Houses in America* and *History of Dolls' Houses*, will fascinate young and old alike. Mrs. Jacobs began collecting antique dolls' houses after she began writing her first book. Thirty years later her enormous collection of houses and toys prompted her to open the museum.

After entering the chic Washington townhouse you pay your admission price at an antique post office window. The entire museum is charmingly arranged and there is so much to see you won't know where to look first.

Much of the display dates from the Victorian period. One prize is a six-story Victorian hotel complete with guest rooms and a grand stairway. Another winner is Bliss Street, a collection of gingerbread houses surrounding a town square that contains a functioning water fountain, an antique trolley, a knickered boy in a go-cart, and a piloted blimp rising above the square.

There are small replicas of five east Baltimore row houses with white front steps, a Victorian house complete with a "captains' walk," an 1800s general store from Zurich, a French turn-of-the-century villa with its original furniture still sewn in, a post-Civil War mansion, a one-room Ohio schoolhouse and an assortment of butchers', millinery, grocers' and other shops.

The collection also includes antique toys, games and dolls. Two are of special interest: a small replica of Mount Vernon with George and Martha Washington standing on the front lawn and an 1884 replica of the United States Capitol that contains a moveable strip of interior views behind its lithographed paper-on-wood facade.

At the museum shop collectors can purchase a whole world in miniature: doll houses and supplies to build their own, handcrafted furnishings and such items as miniature wallpaper, mini-samplers, tiny copies of the New York Times and sheet music for small pianos.

Parties for young and old can be arranged at the museum. At birthday parties children are served ice cream, cake and punch on antique glass-topped tables by staff members in Edwardian costumes. Noon lunch parties, showers and teas can also be planned. At all the parties, a number of the quaint old toys such as the performing bear and a carousel are wound up and set in motion. It is best to plan parties well in advance and on weekdays when the museum is less likely to be crowded.

The Washington Dolls' House and Toy Museum is open Tuesday through Saturday from 10:00 a.m. to 5:00 p.m. and on Sunday from noon to 5:00 p.m. It is located at 5236 44th Street, N.W., Washington, D.C. Additional information can be obtained by calling (202)244-0024.

Directions: From the Beltway take Exit 34, Wisconsin Avenue, south into Chevy Chase. The museum is near both Lord & Taylor and Neiman-Marcus.

WASHINGTON POST NEWSPAPER TOUR
The Inside Story

Most of us use many items daily that we tend to take for granted, and we rarely reflect on all the activities that had to be coordinated in order to produce them. It can be an eye opener to watch a daily newspaper being prepared.

On the *Washington Post*'s hour-long tour you visit the production and mailing rooms, the library where they have computerized the clipping file, and the advertising department to watch an artist compose an ad. Of particular interest is the newsroom. Your guide will explain how the wire services work. The *Washington Post* not only receives news but also sends it: as part of the *International-Herald Tribune* it wires daily reports to Paris and as part of the *Los Angeles Times–Washington Post* News Service it sends items around the world.

Tours of the *Washington Post* are available Monday through Friday from 10:00 a.m. to 3:00 p.m. Because the *Washington Post* is a morning newspaper, activity in the building picks up later in the afternoon. You are more likely to see reporters at their desks if you arrange an afternoon tour.

The *Washington Post* has switched from hot type to cold type. You should ask your guide if you are interested in seeing an example of the old linotype machine. The hot type method used the linotype machines whereas the cold type employs a photographic computer. When the enormous presses are running you can see them from the lobby windows.

Tours are available free of charge to anyone over 12; insurance regulations do not permit young children. For an appointment call (202)334-7969,-7970,-7971 or-7972.

Directions: The *Washington Post* is inside the Beltway at 1150 15th Street, N.W., Washington, D.C.

WINTER CALENDAR OF EVENTS

DECEMBER

EARLY

Christmas Open House & Bazaar—Carroll County Farm Museum, MD (301)848-7775
The Main House at this farm museum is decorated with garlands, wreaths and an old-fashioned Christmas tree. You can purchase handcrafted gifts and enjoy caroling and listening to Christmas music. Time: Noon to 8:00 p.m. on Saturday and noon to 6:00 p.m. on Sunday.

Traditional Christmas Celebration—Colvin Run Mill Park, VA (703)759-2771
Family celebrations of an earlier era are brought to life when you join in on the taffy pull, popcorn stringing, straw wreath making and singing of Christmas songs. St. Nick is on hand so children can visit with this guest of honor. Time: 7:00 to 9:00 p.m.

Annual Old Tyme Christmas Celebration—Harpers Ferry, WV (304)535-6610
Celebrate an old-time Christmas in an historic setting. Costumed workers, Christmas decorations, caroling and refreshments all add to the fun at this weekend-long event.

Child's Colonial Christmas—London Town Publik House, MD (301)956-4900
Elementary school children can participate in traditional holiday crafts and enjoy Christmas entertainment. Refreshments are served at this reservation-only event. Time: Noon to 4:00 p.m.

Christmas Candlelight Tours—London Town Publik House, MD (301)956-4900
The old ferry house at London Town is decorated with holiday greens. Music of the 18th-century will entertain you as you tour by candlelight. Holiday greens are also on sale. Time: 7:00 to 9:00 p.m.

Christmas Candlelight Weekend—Fredericksburg, VA (703)373-1776

Resembling a Currier & Ives picture, the streets of Fredericksburg echo with the sound of horse-drawn carriages and the long full skirts of the costumed docents brush against the sidewalks. The annual Christmas Walking Tour lets you explore a number of private homes as well as the many historic sites in Fredericksburg. Throughout Fredericksburg you will see Christmas decorations and hear holiday music and carolers. This is a weekend-long event.

Christmas Madrigal Evenings—St. Mary's City, MD (301)994-0779

A Medieval feast is served at long tables in the reconstructed state house. Madrigal singers, jesters and strolling musicians in the Renaissance and 17th-century style entertain and amuse diners at this family-style dinner. Wassail is served before dinner and the customary Yule log is burned. Everyone joins in as musicians play familiar Christmas favorites and the evening ends convivially as the holly is thrown into the burning fire. Time: 6:30 to 10:30 p.m. Reservations are necessary.

Herbal Christmas Shopping Weekend—National Colonial Farm, MD (301)283-2113

Special seasonal gifts are available at the National Colonial Farm's gift shop. Time: 10:00 to 5:00 p.m.

Christmas Celebration—Morven Park, VA (703)777-2414

Historic Morven Park is decorated for the Christmas season in the Victorian motif. Time: Saturday 10:00 a.m. to 5:00 p.m. and Sunday 1:00 to 5:00 p.m.

Scottish Christmas Walk—Alexandria, VA (703)549-0111

You're invited to join in this parade through Old Town Alexandria saluting the city's Scottish heritage. Taking part each year are bagpipers, Highland dancers, Scottish clans' members and eager onlookers. You can also purchase hand-crafted items and fresh heather. There are special children's events, music and refreshments. Time: 10:00 a.m. to 4:00 p.m.

Old Town Christmas Candlelight Tour—
Alexandria, VA (703)549-0205

Christmas decorations bedeck Alexandria's historic attractions. Costumed guides escort you through Gadsby's Tavern Museum, the Boyhood Home of Robert E. Lee, the Lee-Fendall House and Carlyle House. Tours begin at Ramsey House where maps of this evening walking tour are available. Period music, colonial dancing and light refreshments add to the festivities. Time: 7:00 to 9:30 p.m.

Candlelight Tour—Montpelier Mansion, MD
(301)779-2011

This colonial plantation house in Laurel, Maryland, is decorated for the holiday season and serves refreshments after the candlelight tour. Time: 5:30 to 9:00 p.m. Wednesday and Thursday and 11:00 a.m. to 3:00 p.m. on Friday.

Christmas in Waterford—Waterford, VA
(703)882-3243

The historic 18th-century Quaker village of Waterford features old-fashioned country decorations, and following the Loudoun tradition there are carolers on horseback. This is a weekend-long event.

Christmas Open House—Ladew Topiary Gardens,
MD (301)557-9466

The English manor house at Ladew is decorated with Christmas greens. You can buy wreaths and greens as well as handcrafted items. Holiday music will add to the Friday evening fun.

Festival of Music and Lights—Mormon Temple
Visitor's Center, MD (301)587-0144

Twinkling lights create a holiday atmosphere which is enhanced each night by a Christmas music program. Time: 9:00 a.m. to 9 p.m.

MID

Carols by Candlelight—Woodlawn Plantation, VA
(703)557-7881

In addition to touring this historic house by candlelight you can enjoy 19th-century decorations and Christmas madrigals. Time: Friday from 7:00 to 9:00 p.m. and on weekends from 3:00 to 5:00 p.m.

Christmas Display in Conservatory—Brookside Gardens Conservatory, MD (301)949-8230

Beginning on the second Thursday in December hundreds of poinsettias, two poinsettia "trees", ornamental peppers, cyclamen and other flowering plants make a floriferous Christmas display. Time: 9:00 a.m. to 5:00 p.m.

Candlelight Christmas Tours—Sully Plantation, MD (703)437-1794

Sully Plantation is decorated with 18th-century Christmas decorations and lit by candlelight. Refreshments from the same period include hot mulled cider and old-fashioned cookies. Time: 6:00 to 9:00 p.m.

Christmas Open House at Rose Hill Manor, MD (301)694-1650

The 19th-century comes alive with kitchen exhibits and weaving looms that children can handle and manipulate at Rose Hill Manor. At Christmas time children will enjoy the old-fashioned Christmas decorations and Santa Claus's visit. There are sleigh rides when the weather permits. Time: 10:00 a.m. to 4:00 p.m.

A Civil War Christmas—Fort Ward Museum, VA (703)838-4848

You can partake of a 19th-century Civil War Christmas along with costumed soldiers and their ladies at Fort Ward Museum. Music and light refreshments complete the day's festivities. Time: 1:00 to 5:00 p.m.

Christmas Candlelight Tours—Mary Surratt House, MD (301)868-1121

A Victorian Christmas tree and greenery decorate this historic old house. You can also see a collection of children's toys from this bygone era. Punch and cookies are served. Time: Saturday 4:00 to 9:00 p.m. and Sunday 6:00 to 9:00 p.m.

Special Christmas Celebration—Stratford Hall Plantation, VA (804)493-8038

A candlelight tour of this gracious colonial plantation house is augmented by the Christmas decorations. There is also caroling and refreshments are served. Time: 9:00 a.m. to 4:30 p.m.

Christmas at the Miller House—Hagerstown, MD (301)797-8782

At this Federal period townhouse Christmas has been rec- reated as it was celebrated over 100 years ago. A giant tree is decorated with rare antique ornaments and beneath it you will see toys from a bygone era. Time: 1:00 to 4:00 p.m.

Grand Illumination—Williamsburg, VA (804)229- 1000 ext. 2372

Fireworks begin the fortnight Christmas celebration at Colonial Williamsburg. Shops and historic buildings are decorated with period finery.

Christmas at the William Paca House—Annapolis, MD (301)267-8149

The William Paca House is decorated with greenery and resounds with traditional music for this annual celebration. There are colonial cooking exhibits and refreshments are served. Time: 10:00 a.m. to 4:00 p.m. Tuesday through Saturday and noon to 4:00 p.m. on Sunday.

Christmas Conservatory Display—Longwood Gardens, PA (215)388-6741

Thousands of poinsettias are on display in Longwood Gar- dens's 3½ acres of conservatories. You can also enjoy the continually changing orchid collection along with an assort- ment of spring bulbs that perfume the air. Time: 10:00 a.m. to 5:00 p.m.

Christmas Open House—Rising Sun Tavern, Fredericksburg, VA (703)373-1776

This is one of the best times of the year to visit this tavern built by George Washington's brother, Charles. There will be carolers, costumed hostesses, as well as hot spiced tea and gingersnaps. Time: 6:30 to 10:00 p.m.

Christmas Open House—Decatur House, Washington, D.C. (202)387-4062

Decorations at the Decatur House reflect two 19th-century periods. Downstairs you'll see decorations from 1819–20, the period of Stephen Decatur's residency. In years past handmade ships rode the Christmas tree boughs to sustain the nautical connection. Upstairs there are decorations of the 1870s, the Victorian era when the table top tree was popular. Time: Weekends noon to 4:00 p.m.

Christmas at the Woodrow Wilson House— Washington, D.C. (202)387-4062

At the Woodrow Wilson House you can see Christmas celebrated as it was in the 1920s. Trees were becoming more fashionable and German glass ornaments were in vogue. Novelty items of that time included Japanese-made lights in the shape of comic characters. Outdoor decorations like the Della Robia wreath on display also were introduced. Time: Noon to 4:00 p.m.

Christmas at the Octagon—Washington, D.C. (202)638-3105

If you can't schedule a Christmas visit to the White House, then plan instead to see the Octagon, where in 1814 at the nation's first temporary White House the Madisons celebrated Christmas. Period decorations capture this early era. You will see an elaborate fruit fanlight, a cone centerpiece of fruit, pine roping, garlands and a Victorian tree. Beneath the tree you'll see toys a youngster might have received on a Christmas morning in the early 1880s. Time: 1:00 to 4:00 p.m.

Maymont Christmas Open House—Richmond, VA (804)358-7166

At this many faceted Richmond park they will be celebrating a Victorian Christmas with strolling carolers, bell choirs and musicians, as well as light refreshments of hot wassail and gingersnaps. Time: 2:00 to 8:00 p.m.

LATE

Christmas Pageant—Washington National Cathedral, Washington, D.C. (202)537-6200

The Washington National Cathedral holds a Christmas Eve service for children in late afternoon as well as a later service in the evening. Times in years past have been 4:00 p.m. for the early service and 10:00 p.m. for the later one.

Christmas Candlelight Tours of the White House— Washington, D.C. (202)472-3669

This annual event lets you get a look at the Christmas decorations adorning the President's home. These tours customarily run from 6:00 to 8:00 p.m. They are also scheduled after Christmas for a two or three day period.

Scottish New Year's Eve, Hogmanay—Alexandria, VA (703)549-0205

Like its Scottish founders, Alexandria annually celebrates Old Year's Night with Scottish food and entertainment. The evening culminates with a traditional "first footing" ceremony at midnight. The fun begins at 10:00 p.m. and reservations are required.

Happy New Year—Baltimore Inner Harbor, MD (301)332-4191

Big band music and fireworks at the Inner Harbor provide a novel way to welcome the new year.

JANUARY

EARLY

January 1—Philadelphia Mummers' New Year's Day Parade, PA (215)864-1976

Every year since New Year's Day, 1901 the Mummers have paraded down Broad Street in Philadelphia. Each year in sequins and feathers thousands of marchers and string musicians take part in this 12-hour spectacular. It's a great way to start the year.

Winter Chores—Oxon Hill Farm, MD (301)839-1177 or (301)839-1176

Although most visitors stop at the Oxon Hill Farm during the growing season, it is also interesting to observe the winter farm chores being done on crisp January days. Farm workers are involved in repairing the farm tools, clearing the fields and preparing them for the spring planting, and grooming the animals. Farm hours are 8:30 a.m. to 5:00 p.m. daily.

MID

Religious Freedom Day—Fredericksburg, VA (703)373-1776

Every year at the Thomas Jefferson Religious Freedom Monument in Fredericksburg the drafting of the Statute of Religious Freedom is commemorated. Thomas Jefferson, who wrote this significant statement, asked that his tombstone inscription include the words, "Author of the Declaration of

Independence, of the Statute of Virginia for Religious Freedom, and Father of the University of Virginia." This bill,
written in Fredericksburg in 1777, was one of his most
famous single pieces of legislation. The commemoration
includes an honor guard and wreath laying ceremony at the
monument.

January 19—Robert E. Lee's Birthday—Stratford Hall Open House, VA (703)493-8371

The Lee family tree contains the names of many who influ-
enced the course of history. One of the first was the patriarch
of the family, Thomas Lee, who held the highest office in the
colony of Virginia as president of the King's Council. In
1720, Thomas Lee built the family estate, Stratford Hall, on
the cliffs overlooking the Potomac River. Thomas Lee's sons,
Richard Henry and Francis Lightfoot, were signers of the
Declaration of Independence. His great-nephew, "Light Horse
Harry" Lee, married Matilda Lee, who had inherited Stratford Hall. It was here at this family home on January 19,
1807, that Robert E. Lee was born. Each year this 20-room
mansion is open free on General Robert E. Lee's birthday.

LATE

Lee Birthday Celebrations—Candlelight Tours of the Boyhood Home of Robert E. Lee and the Lee-Fendall House, VA (703)548-1789 or (703)548-8454

Alexandria, which considers itself the Lee family hometown,
annually holds a dual Lee family birthday celebration at the
two Lee homes. The Lee-Fendall House is dedicated to "Light
Horse Harry" Lee, whose birthday falls on January 29. Harry
Lee never, in fact, resided at this house but it was here that
he wrote the moving farewell address to Washington from
the citizens of Alexandria. Costumed guides tell many interesting anecdotes as they escort visitors through the house.
Across the street at the Boyhood Home of Robert E. Lee,
music of the period is part of this annual celebration. Robert
E. Lee spent ten of his early years at this house, leaving at
age 18 to attend West Point. His upstairs room with its view
of the Potomac River has been carefully restored.

FEBRUARY

EARLY

Love Themes From Tudor England—London Brass Rubbing Centre, Washington, D.C. (202)244-9328

You can start thinking ahead in early February because the London Brass Rubbing Centre at the Washington Cathedral begins offering their collection of 12 brasses with romantic themes at half price to give you a chance to "rub" up something special for your valentine. You may choose a brass with a medieval knight presenting flowers to his lady or a "zodiac" brass. You can personalize your valentine by doing a rubbing of your loved one's sign. Hours are Monday through Saturday from 9:00 a.m. to 5:00 p.m.

MID

Victorian Valentine Display—Mary Surratt House, Clinton, MD (301)868-1121

At the Mary Surratt House's annual antique valentine display you can see more than 50 sentimental souvenirs from the 1840s through the 1890s. You can also watch fancy valentines being made with calligraphy and papyrotamia (deft paper-cutting). Reproductions of period valentines are for sale.

Revolutionary War Reenactment—Fort Ward Park, Alexandria, VA (703)549-0205

Recreated Revolutionary units annually reenact a typical Colonial and British clash at Fort Ward Park in Alexandria. Prior to the battle you can enjoy an interpretation of camp life. You will readily discern the differences between officers's and soldiers's tents. Activities include musket demonstrations and a chance to watch camp fire chores like sewing, cooking and weapon repairing.

George Washington Birthday Parade—Alexandria, VA (703)549-0205

On the Monday designated for celebrating George Washington's Birthday the nation's largest annual parade in honor of George Washington will wind through the historic streets of Alexandria. He may be the "Father of his Country" but in

Alexandria Washington is also a hometown boy who made good. Traditionally more than 100 units take part in this parade.

George Washington Birthday Celebration—Mary Washington House, Fredericksburg, VA (703)373-1569

Each year in Fredericksburg at the home of George Washington's mother a birthday celebration is held. A vignette capturing the pivotal role played by Mary Washington in her son's life is traditionally a part of this observance of his birthday. The Mary Washington House is open from 10:00 a.m. to 4:00 p.m. for this event.

February 22—George Washington Birthplace National Monument, VA (804)224-0196

What could be more appropriate than to spend the actual day of George Washington's birth at his birthplace. A yearly party lets you celebrate with refreshments and demonstrations of colonial crafts at Pope's Creek Plantation, as the place was called at Washington's birth. Time: 9:00 a.m. to 5:00 p.m.

SPRING

BALTIMORE AND OHIO RAILROAD MUSEUM
Birthplace of the American Railroad

Charles Carroll, one of the signers of the Declaration of Independence, said in 1828, when he laid the first stone for the Baltimore and Ohio Railroad, that he considered that act second in importance only to that earlier signature and perhaps even more important. Recognition of the part the railroad played in America's history and providing a home for the old equipment of the great railroading era are the purposes of the Baltimore and Ohio Railroad Museum.

The Baltimore museum is housed in the Mt. Clare Station which is believed to be the oldest railway station in the United States and one of the oldest in the world. In a sense, the station is the birthplace of American railroads, making its function as a museum singularly appropriate.

The Georgian architecture is reminiscent of the 1800s and the old passenger car roundhouse, with its round geometric shape and 22 separate tracks, provides an ideal display area. Among the historic locomotives and cars are the tiny "Tom Thumb" of 1829, the "Iron Mule" of 1945 and old Imlay coaches. The collection is one of the most extensive in existence. Neither railroad buffs nor "choo-choo" fans can resist the museum.

In addition to the tools and equipment of railroading and the cars themselves, other early forms of transportation, such as the Conestoga wagon, are represented. The museum is open Wednesday through Sunday from 10:00 a.m. to 4:00

p.m. It is closed Monday, Tuesday and all major holidays. Admission is charged. For more information call (301)237-2387.

Directions: From the Beltway take Exit 22, the Baltimore-Washington Parkway, into Baltimore and turn left on Lombard Street. Continue west to Poppleton and go left to the museum.

BELAIR MANSION AND STABLE MUSEUM
Lots of Horsing Around

Why is it that although we explore exotic ports of call with thoroughness and unflagging energy, we all too often ignore attractions in our own neighborhoods? Spring is a good time to remedy this oversight and get to know the attractions—historic and scenic—of one of Washington's largest bedroom communities, Bowie, Maryland.

Belair Mansion, "The Home of the Early Maryland Governors," was once a showpiece of colonial grandeur. Its history goes back more than 230 years. The central portion of the mansion was built in the 1740s by Benjamin Tasker, for his son-in-law Samuel Ogle, while he was honeymooning in England with Tasker's daughter, Anne. Ogle had raised colonial eyebrows when at age 47 he married the 18-year-old Annapolis belle.

In addition to planning the mansion house Benjamin Tasker, between 1752 and 1760, planted an "avenue of tulip trees" starting at the mansion entrance and continuing down the hill to Old Annapolis Road. Actually the trees at Belair Mansion have their own history. In addition to the tulip poplars, one of which is older than 200 years, there are other noteworthy specimens. A magnolia acuminata, or cucumber tree, is the National Champion—the largest of its kind in the nation. Another tree, the ailanthus, is the State Champion.

As part of the free mansion tour you will see the interior styling of the central portion of the house that was done by Benjamin Ogle II about 1810. Although most historic homes open to the public have undergone substantial restoration, that is not true of this five-part Georgian mansion. Much is yet to be done at Belair. It is a great place for the interested citizen to get involved and play a meaningful role in restoring the past.

In addition to its distinction as the property of five Maryland governors, Belair Mansion is also known as "The Cradle of American Racing." At the Belair Stable Museum, listed on the National Register of Historic Places, you can enjoy another free tour covering over 200 years of American thoroughbred racing. It began during the colonial period when Samuel Ogle brought some of the most valuable horses in racing from England to Belair.

When Ogle returned from his honeymoon he brought with him two horses—a stallion, Spark, and a filly, Queen Mab. Frederick, Prince of Wales and father of George III, had given the stallion to Charles Calvert, the fifth Lord Baltimore. Calvert, in turn, gave Spark to Governor Ogle.

Another famous British horse, Selima, was brought to the Belair stables by Benjamin Tasker, Jr. when he took over the management of the Belair estate. Selima was a champion racehorse in her day. When William Woodward purchased the Belair Mansion in 1898 he placed a plaque on the stable wall honoring Selima and her equally famous offspring, Selim.

It was William Woodward who added the hyphen and wings to the mansion, giving it the exterior appearance it has today. Woodward also added the stone stables and continued the tradition of horse racing at Belair. Three great horses would be stabled at Belair during the Woodward era—Gallant Fox and Omaha, both winners of the Triple Crown, and Nashua, one of the great money-earners of his day.

While touring the historic sites of Bowie don't miss scenic Allen Pond. During the summer boats are available; youngsters can fish from the banks while families enjoy a picnic. Well-placed benches invite visitors to just sit and enjoy the day. Be sure to walk as far as the gazebo and watch the swallows sweeping and gliding by.

The Belair Mansion is open the second Sunday of the month from 2:00 to 4:00 p.m. and Wednesdays from 10:00 a.m. to 1:00 p.m. The Belair Stable Museum is open on Sundays from 1:00 to 4:00 p.m. in May, June, September and October.

Directions: Take Beltway Exit 19, Route 50, to Bowie. Then take Collington Road to Route 450 and make a right. Take Route 450 to the light immediately past Bowie High

School. At the light make a right on Belair Drive. The stables are on the left. To reach the mansion turn right on Tulip Grove Drive and you will see it on your left.

BELTSVILLE AGRICULTURAL RESEARCH CENTER
Uncle Sam Has a Green Thumb

There are excursions to be taken at the Beltsville Agricultural Research Center that will leave you a walking compendium of little-known facts.

While stopped at the concrete feed lot to observe the beef cattle you will discover that their diet can be made up, in part, of newsprint or phone directories, excluding the comic sections or yellow pages. This information derives from studies on developing feed that did not compete with human diets. Sixty-five percent of beef cattle in the U.S. are fed by this method. The concrete feed lots do not permit cattle to exercise, which means the beef has a higher percentage of fat and the meat is of better quality.

At the oldest part of the research center, the dairy section, you can watch the cows being milked. The herd was established here in 1918.

Most visitors are surprised to learn that the pig is considered the smartest animal on the farm. Pigs are often used to duplicate medical research applicable to human medical problems because they metabolize food very much like humans.

But animals are only one aspect of the research conducted at this center which is the largest and most complex agricultural center in the world. The second major thrust is plant research. It is fascinating to see a field that is monitored by the Landsat satellite. This satellite takes pictures from space and can determine what crop is growing and whether or not it is healthy. This information provides a basis for preliminary crop reports. Fertilization and irrigation projects can also be observed by satellite. During the spring and summer months you can see the outdoor plant research plots. At other times you can see the greenhouses where extensive research is being done. There are four greenhouse areas: the fruits and vegetables, the ornamental flowers and shrubs, the economic crops, and a problem center handling national concerns like pesticide degredation.

The two-and-a-half-hour tours are conducted at no charge from 8:00 a.m. to 4:00 p.m. Monday through Friday. The tours are by appointment only; call (301)344-2483. It is possible, but not as instructive, to obtain a map at the Visitor's Center and then explore the research center on your own.

Directions: Take Beltway Exit 25, U.S. 1, to Powder Mill Road, Route 212. Turn right and proceed to the Visitor's Center, marked Tour Route Stop 1.

CHADDS FORD
Wyeth Not?

If you think you must head for a big city to enjoy a one-day outing that includes art, history, nature crafts and a Colonial inn, think again. Chadds Ford in Pennsylvania, only a two-hour drive from Washington, offers just such a mixture.

The rolling hills and farmlands make the ride itself a pleasure. This is the area that inspired the Wyeths, one of America's most prominent families of artists, and three generations of Wyeths have their work on display at the Brandywine River Museum. The museum is in a renovated 19th-century grist mill that boasts a glass tower through which visitors see the Brandywine River and a meadow as they climb from floor to floor.

The gallery not only displays work in the Brandywine tradition but also sells prints, framed or unframed, in a wide range of prices. The museum shop offers an excellent assortment of books on art and conservation, as well as wildflower seeds. Art is only one of the concerns of this museum, the second being the conservation of natural resources.

A mile-long nature trail begins at the museum and meanders along the river. Elevated walks cross marshy sections and helpful trail markers broaden one's appreciation of the plants and natural features encountered along the way.

A visit in spring is particularly enjoyable because wildflowers bloom along the woodland trail. Volunteers of the Brandywine Conservancy have also planted wildflowers around the museum. Blue flowers predominate in the spring, yellow in summer and fall. The museum is open daily from 9:30 a.m. until 4:30 p.m. and admission is charged.

For a change of pace, the village of Chadds Ford offers a quaint collection of craft shops. Each of the Chadds Ford Barn Shops has a specialty and all feature handcrafted items.

At Chadds Ford Inn, where Washington's troops once dined, lunch is served during the week from 11:30 a.m. until 2:00 p.m. and dinner from 5:30 to 10:00 p.m. On Friday and Saturday evenings dinner is from 5:00 to 10:30 p.m. The Inn does not open on Sunday until 2:00 p.m. and dinner is served until 8:00 p.m. Though reservations usually are not necessary for lunch, they are a good idea for dinner. Call (215)388-7361.

For an economical outing, at Brandywine Battlefield Park, a mile south of Chadds Ford, benches and picnic tables are available. It was at Brandywine Battlefield on September 11, 1777, that the English won the battle that enabled them to go on to capture the Colonial capital of Philadelphia. Faulty intelligence contributed to the American defeat, although Washington might have felt "intelligence" wasn't the right word for the information he received about the British troops.

General Howe had landed in Maryland with 15,000 men and had begun the long march toward Philadelphia. First reports indicated Howe had divided his force. Thinking the British therefore could be outnumbered, Washington sent 14,000 men under General Greene to attack. A second report came in—Greene faced the entire British force. Washington ordered a quick retreat across the Brandywine River. Still a third report was received: the British force was divided. Washington accepted the second message, unfortunately incorrect.

Misinformation, ammunition shortages and British superiority—numerically and in terms of experience—led to their victory. Thus the English wintered in comfortable quarters in Philadelphia while the Americans were consigned to the misery of Valley Forge.

At the Brandywine Visitor's Center, maps and displays give a detailed account of the events of this battle and put the encounter at Brandywine into historical perspective. The park contains the restored headquarters of General Washington and those of his aide, General Marquis de Lafayette. They are open weekends only from October to May from 10:00 a.m. to 4:30 p.m. During the summer months they are open daily from 10:00 a.m. to 5:00 p.m. and on Sunday from 12:00 to 4:30 p.m. No admission is charged.

Within a 15-minute drive of Chadds Ford you will also find Longwood Gardens and Star Rose Gardens. A somewhat longer drive, but one still easily included in your trip to Chadds Ford, will bring you to Winterthur, Nemours or the Hagley Museum and Eleutherian Mills. Between Longwood Gardens and the Star Rose Gardens, going south on Route 1, you will pass Phillips Mushroom House on the right. A stop here will give you the opportunity to purchase fresh or preserved mushrooms. This area is the mushroom capital of the world.

A good place to enjoy lunch or dinner is the Red Rose Inn near the Star Rose Gardens. This colonial restaurant was founded in 1704 and paid an annual rent of one red rose to King George. The inn is open during the week, except Monday, from 11:30 a.m. to 2:30 p.m. and for dinner from 5:00 to 9:00 p.m. On Friday and Saturday evenings it is open 5:00 to 10:00 p.m. and no lunch is served on Saturday. A buffet brunch is served on Sunday from 11:00 a.m. to 2:00 p.m. and dinner is from 3:00 to 8:00 p.m. For reservations, call (215)869-3003.

Directions: Take Beltway Exit 27, I-95, to the Wilmington, Delaware area. Exit on U.S. Route 202 and continue to U.S. 1. Go left on Route 1 for a short distance to the Brandywine Battlefield Park on the left. One more mile will bring you to Chadds Ford with the Brandywine River Museum on your right and the Barn Shops on your left. If you wish to avoid the tolls or vary your route and don't mind a slightly longer ride, just continue south on U.S. 1 and it will take you back to Baltimore where you will have to go through the Baltimore Harbor Tunnel to get to Washington.

COLVIN RUN MILL AND SULLY PLANTATION
Everything is Grist to the Mill

A long-term project involving the painstaking full-scale restoration of an old merchant mill in Fairfax County, Virginia, now provides a most rewarding excursion. The old Colvin Run Mill was built in 1794, according to tradition and the date on the mill's east wall, but architectural historians believe that it was built around 1810. The mill, located near Difficult Run on the Leesburg Turnpike, stands on what was a major artery connecting the rich farming valley of the Shenandoah to the busy port of Alexandria. Colvin Run was a merchant mill engaged in buying and selling grain as well as grinding.

Oliver Evans was an early American inventor whose book, *The Young Millwright and Miller's Guide*, revolutionized milling. We know designs from that book were used in the restoration of Colvin Run Mill because the ruins of the mill showed many similarities to Evans's plans. Originally all the jobs except turning the millstone were performed by hand. Evans redesigned mills so that each floor served a specific function. A canvas belted elevator carried the grain from floor to floor. When the new arrangement was completed, a miller's duties were reduced to weighing the grain, checking the equipment, starting the waterwheel and receiving money.

The old building has been very carefully and completely restored; the American Institute for Architects awarded Colvin Run Mill first prize for excellence in historic architecture. On your visit you can see the grain being ground into flour and cornmeal. Samples can be bought at the Country Store.

Situated on a hill just above Colvin Run Mill is the Miller's House. It too has been restored and serves as a museum for local artists and craftsmen. On weekends Colvin Run is the center of an active crafts program, with a variety of special events scheduled throughout the year.

Colvin Run Mill is open 11:00 a.m. to 5:00 p.m. daily except Tuesdays, Thanksgiving and Christmas. It is closed January 1 to March 16. Tours are given every half-hour until 4:30 p.m. Admission is charged.

Not far from Colvin Run Mill there is a second Fairfax County site you should explore—Sully Plantation. This house, built by Richard Bland Lee in 1794, is interesting because it combines two distinct architectural styles. It uses the popular Georgian colonial plantation style favored in Virginia and the Philadelphia- style frame exterior Lee learned to like while serving as northern Virginia's first congressman.

The plantation house along with the kitchen-laundry, smokehouse and stone dairy have been restored. The house is furnished with antiques from the Federal period. Sully Plantation is open daily except Tuesdays, Thanksgiving and

Christmas, from mid-March through December. Hours are 11:00 a.m. to 5:00 p.m. with tours on the half-hour until 4:30 p.m. Admission is charged.

Directions: For Colvin Run Mill take Beltway Exit 10W, Route 7, west for five miles; the mill is on the right. For Sully Plantation take Beltway Exit 9, Route 66, to Route 50 west and proceed for 5.5 miles to Route 28. Bear right and proceed three-fourths of a mile to Sully Plantation.

CYLBURN ARBORETUM, SHERWOOD GARDENS AND *USS CONSTELLATION*
Baltimore Beckons

Washingtonians and their visitors are lucky to have the diverse sites and activities of two major cities to fill their weekends. During spring one should see either or both of two Baltimore gardens; they can easily be added to a visit to the the popular Inner Harbor.

At Cylburn Arboretum there are 12 nature trails. They are not laid out for extended hiking but are short, well-marked, inviting trails with a wide variety of native trees, shrubs and wildflowers. Special plantings and feeders have encouraged a large bird population. In fact, the arboretum is now designated as a bird sanctuary and over 100 species have been sighted there.

One very special trail is the Garden of the Senses designed for the visually impaired and wheelchair visitors. Plants are labeled with braille signs and have been chosen for their interesting texture and aromatic appeal.

The arboretum is open daily during daylight hours. Cylburn Mansion, a nature museum located within the park, is open Monday through Friday from 8:00 a.m. to 4:00 p.m.

Just a 15-minute drive from Cylburn is the second city garden, the seven-acre Sherwood Garden. On what was once a private estate in the elegant Guilford section of Baltimore, this garden is noted for its thousands of azaleas and tulips that open its flowering season in mid-May.

Any youngsters who weary of seeing nothing but flowers will appreciate a stop at the Inner Harbor to see the *USS Constellation*. It was the first official ship of the United States Navy and it is the oldest ship still afloat. The frigate was launched at Fell's Point in 1797 and has had an adventure-filled history.

The *Constellation* saw action against the pirates at Tripoli in 1802, the British in 1812 and the South during the Civil War. In World War II it was the flagship of the Atlantic Fleet.

The *Constellation* was constructed of wood, necessitating much restoration and renewal through the years. In fact, there are those who feel that it has been so extensively rebuilt it is no longer the original vessel. The restored fittings provide an exact picture of the way it used to look.

The *Constellation* is open daily from 10:00 a.m. to 8:00 p.m. from mid-June to Labor Day. From Labor Day to mid-October and from mid-May to mid-June the hours are 10:00 a.m. to 6:00 p.m. Hours the rest of the year are from 10:00 a.m. to 4:00 p.m. Admission is charged.

Directions: For the Cylburn Arboretum, take Beltway Exit 27, I-95, to the Baltimore Beltway; go left towards Catonsville. Then take the Greenspring Avenue Exit south from the Baltimore Beltway and follow this to 4915 Greenspring Avenue and the well-marked arboretum entrance on the left.

To find Sherwood Gardens take Greenspring Avenue to Cold Spring Lane and follow it east past Jones Falls to Underwood. Turn right and continue on to Highfield Road. Turn right again and the gardens will be on the left at Highfield Road and Greenway.

For the *Constellation* return to Cold Spring Lane and turn west to Jones Falls south. Then follow Guilford Avenue straight to the Inner Harbor.

To return to Washington from the harbor turn right on Pratt Street and go straight for nine blocks; then turn left on Greene Street. This will lead into Russell Street and the Baltimore-Washington Parkway.

DEEP CREEK LAKE
Dam Fun

Your position on the Beltway will determine how much time you can spend at this delightful lake resort area. In fact, if you are too far removed from the northwestern end of the Beltway it would be unwise to plan this as a one-day affair. It is amazing how many people are unaware of the unspoiled charm of this man-made attraction begun with a dam erected in 1923–25 for a hydroelectric project. Deep Creek Lake is the largest freshwater lake in Maryland.

Deep Creek State Park has a beach area, picnic facilities and a trail up the southern slope of Meadow Mountain—well worth the climb for the panoramic view from the summit. Depending on the amount of time you have available you might want to consider renting a boat from Bill's Marine Service, which is located directly across the lake from Deep Creek State Park. You can also rent water-ski equipment; contact Bill's at (301)387-5536. As there is no road that follows the water line around the entire lake, the only way you can really explore the many irregular inlets is by boat.

Also in this area is Swallow Falls State Park. If you continue on Route 219 towards Oakland you will be able to follow the signs to this park. There are three falls and many woodland trails to explore. Along the bank above the 64-foot cascading Muddy Creek Falls, Henry Ford, Harvey Firestone and Thomas Edison used to enjoy camping together. Both Parks are open daily at no charge.

This area is a treat in any season. Spring and summer let you enjoy fishing, boating and water sports; autumn offers the spectacle of fall foliage; skiing and snowmobiling make it a popular retreat in winter.

Directions: From the Beltway take Exit 35, I-270, past Frederick to Hancock, where you will continue on Route 40 and 48 to Keyser's Ridge, Exit 14 off Route 48, the intersection of 40 and Route 219. Take Route 219S into Deep Creek Lake State Park.

DUMBARTON OAKS
A Blooming History Lesson

From August to October, 1944, world leaders met at Dumbarton Oaks in Washington to lay the groundwork for the United Nations. Their plans, submitted at the San Francisco Conference in April, 1945, evolved into the United Nations Charter.

Dumbarton Oaks is more than a historical footnote: it is a beautiful estate surrounded by one of the handsomest gardens in or around Washington. The ten acres of gardens were landscaped beginning in 1922 by Beatrix Farrand and consist of a number of small gardens and a tree-fringed lawn around the house.

One feature you will enjoy is the Pebble Garden. Its vari-colored pebbles are arranged in a massive geometric pattern. There are other specific areas such as the Urn Terrace with ivy, the Rose Garden, Camellia Circle, Crabapple Hill, Lover's Lane Pool and fountains. The Orangery and Ellipse offer their own attractions and in the spring daffodils and other flowering bulbs make the woodland walks particularly enticing.

The estate is now a research center owned by Harvard University. Collections of Byzantine and early Christian art, Pre-Columbian art, as well as paintings, fine furniture, and tapestries are on public view.

Spring and fall are the best times to visit Dumbarton Oaks. The gardens are open daily from 2:00 to 6:00 p.m., except for bad weather. There is an admission charge of $1 from April through October. The collections are open from 2:00 to 5:00 p.m. and there is no charge to visit them. Both collections and gardens are closed on national holidays.

Directions: Dumbarton Oaks is located inside the Beltway at 32nd and R Streets in Georgetown.

FIRE MUSEUM OF MARYLAND, INC.
A Flaming Success with Small Fry

Most of us are familiar with modern fire fighting equipment but we have little idea of how it got that way. A trip into the past at the Fire Museum of Maryland, Inc. in Lutherville, Maryland, fills in some of the missing pieces. The museum was founded in 1971, and houses a permanent collection of 40 pieces of fire equipment as well as a number of others on loan. It is the second largest fire museum in the United States. All who ever yearned to be firemen will enjoy themselves enormously here.

One of the vintage pieces, an 1888 Clap and Jones horse-drawn steam pumping engine, was used to fight the Baltimore fire of 1904 that razed a great portion of the downtown area. Other pieces include a 1908 American La France aerial ladder, an 1897 American steamer and a 1905 Hale Water Tower. One thing you will discover at this museum is that fire equipment is neither strictly utilitarian nor all red. Many companies have special parade equipment. Some of the engines and trucks are white, green, or maroon, and even an all-blue ladder wagon is on display.

The museum contains smaller equipment such as hand lanterns that burned kerosene or whale oil, brass trumpets that were used to call the men to a fire and old fire buckets. A Wells Fargo safe, old fire alarm telegraph equipment and an 1882 music box are also part of the memorabilia. In addition, two movies are shown free to visitors: one on fire safety and the other on fire fighting history.

The Fire Museum is a private collection, nonprofit, and manned by volunteers. It is open Sundays from 1:00 to 5:00 p.m., April through October. Special tour groups can visit by appointment only. A nominal admission is charged. For more information, call (301)321-7500.

Directions: From the Washington Beltway take Exit 27 to I-95 north to the Baltimore Beltway (I-695) and go west toward Towson. Get off at Exit 26 of I-695 and go north on York Road (Rt. 45), just two blocks. You will see on your right the Heaver Plaza Office. The Fire Museum is located directly behind that building.

FORT WASHINGTON
Torchlight Tattoo

Fort Washington brings alive the ghosts of the past as volunteers re-create camp life by torchlight. The Torchlight Tattoo ceremony is held from May through October at 8:00, 9:00, and 10:00 p.m.

Visitors are briefed so that they can ask questions pertinent to the Civil War period, as if they had come down from Washington during those tense days to check out the defenses protecting the capital. By torchlight you can watch volunteer soldiers walking post, polishing equipment, mending uniforms and telling tales around the campfire.

These night programs are only a part of the activities at Fort Washington. Every Sunday afternoon from 12:00 to 5:00 p.m. living history demonstrations can be seen at the fort. Soldiers in uniforms demonstrate weapons and re-create fort life. At 4:00 p.m. the brass cannon is fired. There is even a laundress working in one of the lower casements.

A slide program introduces you to this fort. Built in 1824, it was the earliest fort to be constructed to protect the capital. It is a notable example of the early 19th-century coastal defense system. You learn that this is actually the second fort to stand here and that there is quite a story associated with the fall of the first—Fort Warburton. When the British approached the fort in August 1814, Captain Samuel Dyson blew up his own powder magazine and retreated. Though there had been a confusion in orders, he was subsequently court-martialed. The fort was rebuilt after the War of 1812 and renamed Fort Washington.

You'll enter Fort Washington by crossing a drawbridge over a dry moat. The fort is 140 feet above the Potomac River. Two half-bastions face the water above and below the fort. Guns could be fired at passing vessels from three levels: the water battery, the casement positions and the ramparts. While at the fort you will see the officers' quarters and the soldiers' barracks. Although the fort did not see action during the Civil War, troops were quartered here.

Fort Washington is open daily from 7:30 a.m. until 5:00 p.m. September through April. From May through August the fort does not close until 8:00 p.m. On nights when the Torchlight Tattoo is held it closes even later. Picnic tables are available and there is a splendid view of the Potomac River with Mount Vernon visible across the water.

Directions: Take Maryland Beltway Exit 3, Route 210 (Indian Head Highway), south for five miles to Fort Washington Road. Turn right and go three miles to the fort.

FREDERICKSBURG FORAY
Original Americana

Founded in 1727, Fredericksburg from its earliest days has figured prominently in our nation's history. Many well-known figures of our past lived along these tree-lined streets: James Monroe, John Paul Jones, Fielding Lewis and George Washington. Later, during the Civil War, the Fredericksburg area was the scene of some of the most devastating battles. Some 100,000 men lost their lives in the battles of Fredericksburg, Chancellorsville, the Wilderness and Spotsylvania Court House.

To begin your journey into the past, stop at the Bicentennial Visitor's Center at 706 Caroline Street for a free audio-visual orientation. If you plan to visit all of the five major historic sites buy a block ticket; it costs less than paying the individual admission charges. The five sites, all within walking distance of one another, are the Hugh Mercer Apothecary Shop, the Rising Sun Tavern, the James Monroe Museum and Memorial Library, the Mary Washington House and Kenmore.

Follow the map provided at the Visitor's Center down Caroline Street to the Hugh Mercer Apothecary Shop which is open daily. In colonial days the practice of medicine and the mixing of prescriptions were not separate professions. Dr. Mercer practiced medicine in this shop from 1771 to 1776 when he left to fight in the Revolution. He died at the Battle of Princeton. His office and the sitting room, where his friend George Washington used to conduct business when in Fredericksburg, have been restored to their original appearance.

Just a few more blocks down Caroline Street you'll find the Rising Sun Tavern. This spot, like much of the town, has a connection with the Washington family: the youngest brother, Charles, built the tavern in 1760. It was a popular haunt of the early patriots—Patrick Henry, the Lee brothers, Thomas Jefferson, George Mason, John Marshall and, of course, the Washingtons.

Spiced tea is served by costumed tavern wenches who'll give guests the recipe for such 18th-century favorites as "stewed quaker."

Follow the map next to 908 Charles Street and the James Monroe Museum and Memorial Library, which is open daily except Christmas from 9:00 a.m. to 5:00 p.m. It was in Fredericksburg that our fifth President began the practice of law in 1786. The furnishings in the museum were the first to be used in the White House after it was burned by the British during the War of 1812. They were purchased in France in 1794 when Monroe served there as Minister and were used during his eight-year tenancy of the White House. The Monroes brought them back to Fredericksburg to furnish their own home and here they remain.

At 1200 Charles Street sits the Mary Washington House. Although his mother was reluctant to move from nearby Ferry Farm into the city, George feared for her safety during the tumultuous struggle he believed was coming, and he bought this town house for her in 1772. She spent the last 17 years of her life here. She planted part of the English garden before she died in 1789. Mary Washington is buried in Fredericksburg and there is a monument at her gravesite on Washington Avenue.

Just down the street at 1201 Washington Avenue you'll find Kenmore, the house of Betty Washington Lewis, George's only sister. It is a beautiful Georgian manor house built for his bride in 1752 by Colonel Fielding Lewis. Because Lewis went bankrupt trying to supply weapons to the Revolutionary Army the furniture is not original, but it has been selected to match inventories of the household items before debts forced their sale. Two rooms in this mansion are included in the book *The 100 Most Beautiful Rooms in America.* Kenmore is open 9:00 a.m. to 5:00 p.m. except during the winter months when it closes at 4:00 p.m. It is closed December 24, 25, 31 and January 1.

Those are only the main stops on your walking tour; there are others and you might simply like to amble along the historic streets. Anyone interested in the Civil War will certainly want to plan a stop at the Fredericksburg Battlefield Visitor's Center on Lafayette Boulevard.

Directions: From the Beltway take Virginia Exit 4, I-95, south to Fredericksburg. Exit on Route 17 and follow the well-marked signs to the Bicentennial Visitor's Center. It is 50 miles from the Washington Beltway.

HAGLEY MUSEUM AND ELEUTHERIAN MILLS
Museum, Mansion, and Mills

The Hagley Museum in Delaware is located on the site of the original du Pont powderworks, built in 1802 by E. I du Pont. The purpose of the museum is to preserve and interpret this historic site.

In the main exhibit building, an 1814 textile mill, are models and dioramas of early industry along the Brandywine River—mills, waterwheels, and the inventions of Oliver Evans. A talking map introduces the Brandywine region. The story of the du Pont family establishing their home and powder works completes the first floor exhibits. The second floor contains displays that represent growing industry in an expanding nation; the third floor features changing exhibits.

One wing of another building, a restored 19th-century machine shop, houses models that demonstrate the steps in the manufacture of black powder. In the other wing is a fully operable, late-1800s machine shop where visitors can see demonstrations.

On the museum's 232-acre property are millraces, many distinctively shaped granite powder mills, also picnic grounds. Walking tours of the Hagley Yard are offered, and a jitney bus transports visitors on a three-mile round trip along the Brandywine River. The nominal charge for the unlimited jitney rides is included in the general admission.

Outdoor exhibits include a turbine operated roll mill, a wooden waterwheel, a rare 1870s steam engine, a quarry, a working hydroelectric plant and more.

Eleutherian Mills, the residence built in 1803 by E. I. du Pont, is a three story Georgian-style home overlooking his powderworks on the Brandywine. He built his house in the French tradition and shared the danger of explosions with his workmen. His office was in his home and he was able to oversee the manufactory from there. The home was damaged by explosion several times, the most severe occurring in 1890. The extensive damage discouraged the family from rebuilding.

The house was restored in 1923 by Henry A. du Pont for his daughter, Louise Crowninshield, who lived there only a part of each year. At the time of her death in 1958, Eleutherian Mills became a part of the Hagley Museum. The furnishings in the eight rooms open to the public span the lifetimes of five generations of du Ponts. You can see a restored 19th-century garden; the stone Barn filled with 19th-century vehicles including a Conestoga wagon, farm tools and weather vanes; a cooper shop; the first office of the du Pont Company built in 1837; Lammot du Pont's workshop from the period 1831 to 1884 and the restored 1803 gardens of E. I. du Pont.

Eleutherian Mills and Hagley Museum are open year-round from 9:30 a.m. to 4:30 p.m. on Tuesday through Saturday and from 1:00 to 5:00 p.m. on Sunday. They are closed on major holidays. Admission is charged. For additional information you can call (302)658-2401.

The Hagley Museum and Eleutherian Mills are located three miles north of Wilmington and a little more than a two-hour drive from the Washington Beltway.

Directions: From the Beltway take Exit 27, I-95, and continue north to Wilmington. Take the Route 52N Exit and go north to Route 100. Follow Route 100 to Route 141 and make a right. Stay in the left lane on Route 141 because the Hagley Museum is only a few hundred feet down this road on the left.

HISTORIC PLANTATIONS
From Mary Washington's to Carter's Grove

If your mental images of the plantations of the South are based on *Gone With the Wind*, why not get out and explore the real thing? Within little more than a hundred miles of Washington are six plantations that will give you a variety of new insights into life in the Old South. Take Route 301 from Beltway Exit 7 through one of the main tobacco centers in Maryland. From mid-April to mid-July on weekday mornings loose leaf tobacco auctions are held in Upper Marlboro and La Plata. Across the Potomac River past the weapons center at Dahlgren, Routes 301 and 3 split; continue on Route 3 to the intersection with Route 214, then go left for a short distance to Stratford Hall.

As you approach Stratford Hall imagine the time two centuries ago when the two Lee brothers used this same road. Not only was Stratford Hall the family home of two signers of the Declaration of Independence, but it is also the birthplace of Robert E. Lee. It is still a working plantation with thoroughbreds in the stables; the fields supply grain for the mill, and the large waterwheel still grinds wheat, barley and oats that are sold at the Stratford Store. The large H-shape house evokes a more gracious age. Coaches of the late 18th and 19th centuries that might once have brought guests to the elegant rooms can be seen in the Coach House. Stratford Hall is open daily, except Christmas, from 9:00 a.m. to 4:30 p.m. There is an admission charge.

Resume your journey down Route 3 to Epping Forest in the Northern Neck region. Built in 1680, Epping Forest was the home of Mary Ball Washington, the mother of our first President. Not as grand as other plantations you will see, it claims a special place in our country's history. Epping Forest is open from 9:00 a.m. to 5:00 p.m. daily from April 1 to December 1. Admission is charged.

Continue on Route 3 to Route 17, then cross the York River into Yorktown. After crossing the bridge follow the signs on the right to the Yorktown Victory Center, which is open daily, except Christmas and New Year's Day, from 9:00 a.m. to 5:00 p.m. Admission is charged. This exciting new center will refresh your memory of the background and events of the American Revolution. You start with a walk down "Liberty Street" which re-creates the sounds, sights and architecture of colonial America. You see a reproduction of Washington's campaign tent and the offices of the *Tidewater Gazette*, a colonial newspaper. In the fascinating Gallery of the Revolution hang rotating collections from the colonies and from the settlers' mother countries. And a 28-minute movie, *The Road to Yorktown*, completes your mini-course on the Revolution.

From the Victory Center you can continue on to the next plantation and make the big circle back to Washington, or you might prefer to spend more time in Yorktown. After you explore Yorktown, you can retrace your steps to Washington and save the remainder of the plantations for another trip.

If you opt to stay in Yorktown continue on to the National Park Service's Yorktown Battlefield Center which is open at no charge from 8:30 a.m. to 5:00 p.m. daily except Christmas. It's a good idea to see the 12-minute film on the historic Yorktown surrender before braving the battlefields. Yorktown itself is of interest because of the restored Customhouse, Grace Church and several historic homes, including that of another Declaration of Independence signer, Thomas Nelson, Jr. Don't miss the cave where Cornwallis took refuge.

Farther down the Colonial Parkway towards Williamsburg, worth a trip of its own any time, lies Carter's Grove Plantation on Route 64. Built in 1750 by Carter Burwell, a member of the Virginia House of Burgesses, it is considered by some the "most beautiful house in America." Legend has it that in one room both Jefferson and Washington had their proposals of marriage rejected. The house commands a magnificent view of the James River. It is open 9:00 a.m. to 5:00 p.m. from mid-March to the Sunday after Thanksgiving. Admission is charged.

The nearby towns of Williamsburg and Jamestown need no explanation. You can, if you are so inclined, by-pass these major sites and continue on to some lesser known plantations on the James River. From Carter's Grove take Route 5 out of Williamsburg towards Richmond. After 18 miles you will come to Sherwood Forest, the home of President John Tyler. The house was built in 1730 and is furnished with a mixture of family heirlooms and additional period pieces of the 18th and 19th centuries. The garden has more than 80 varieties of century-old trees, many of them not indigenous to the area. In fact, the gingko was brought back to America by Admiral Peary when he reopened the trade route to the Far East. Sherwood Forest is open daily except Christmas from 9:00 a.m. to 5:00 p.m. Admission is charged and reservations are necessary. Call (804)829-5377 or write Sherwood Forest, Charles City County, Virginia 23030.

Continuing up Route 5 you will come to Berkeley, the site in 1619 of the first official Thanksgiving. Berkeley was built in 1726 by Benjamin Harrison, whose son and namesake was one of the signers of the Declaration of Independence. It was the home of two of our country's Presidents, William Henry Harrison and Benjamin Harrison, a distinction it shares with the Adams family home in Massachusetts. It's a beautifully restored plantation and a living monument to a large portion of American history. Berkeley is open daily from 8:00 a.m. to 5:00 p.m. Admission is charged and includes a slide talk.

One last fine home before you reach Richmond is Shirley Plantation, just five miles up the road from Berkeley. This 800-acre estate, built in 1723, is still owned and operated by the Carter family. They are the ninth descendants of the original owners. The family portraits, original furnishings and old English silver give you a feeling of what this stately home has witnessed. Shirley is open daily, except Christmas, from 9:00 a.m. to 5:00 p.m. Admission is charged.

You can return to Washington by following Route 5 to Richmond and taking Interstate 95 to the Beltway or you can reverse the trip and start down Route 95, stopping when you have seen enough to absorb in one day.

Directions: Either take Maryland Exit 7 (Route 5) or Maryland Exit 11 (Route 4) to Route 301-3 or take Exit 4, Interstate 95, to Richmond and then pick up Route 5.

LONDON TOWN PUBLIK HOUSE AND GARDENS
A Publik House Not Known to the Public

The London Town Publik House, a National Historic Landmark, is all that remains of a once thriving port in Anne Arundel County, Maryland. From the 1680s to the mid-1700s, sailing vessels brought European and East Indian goods to the colonies and departed with Maryland's popular export, tobacco. Thomas Jefferson mentions in his diary crossing the South River on the ferry at London Town in 1775. Colonial travelers, heading to and from Philadelphia and Williamsburg, passed through London Town and often stopped at the London Town Publik House.

On your visit you will see, still shaded by the largest willow tree in the state of Maryland, the same building they frequented and the same tranquil view of the South River. The Publik House was constructed by William Brown, a ferry master and cabinet maker, about 1760. The inn is furnished with mid-to-late 18th-century antiques.

The old inn has many distinctive architectural features; of special note is the unusual way that the bricks were laid in an all-header pattern instead of the normal lengthwise fashion. The thickness of the brick wall explains why the doors are deeply inset. Several first floor rooms are raised one step for some inexplicable reason. A plausible explanation is that the builders were trying to deflect drafts from the four large doors.

The basement public rooms boast beautiful beam ceilings and brick arched doorways. All exterior doors, woodwork, hardware and most of the glass windows are original.

The 8½ acres of rolling countryside surrounding the inn have been developed into a series of natural woodland gardens. In the springtime sailboats burst upon the South River like flowers along the paths. There are natural groupings of holly, camellias, dogwoods and other Virginia plants.

The London Town Publik House and Gardens is open Tuesday through Saturday from 10:00 a.m. to 4:00 p.m. and on Sunday from noon to 4:00 p.m. It is closed Mondays, Thanksgiving and Christmas Day and the months of January and February. The Visitor's Center has a gift shop with many attractive handmade articles. Admission is charged. Phone: (301)956-4900.

If you're sailing or cruising in a motorboat you may want to break up your day on the water with a stop at London Town. It's a captivating trip up the South River from the Chesapeake Bay to the John O. Crandall Pier. There is no dockage fee and boats of all sizes can be accommodated. The wide lawns and garden area will give the kids a chance to stretch their legs.

If you want to extend your day continue on into Annapolis when you reach Route 450 on your return trip. This will take you into the heart of Annapolis and you can easily follow the signs down to the City Dock. At the end of the dock area is Market House which was built in 1859 and has recently been restored. Shop around for some lunchtime snacks and then walk down to the waterside benches and enjoy your lunch alfresco as you watch the endless harbor activity.

After lunch the children may want to take the hour-long trip on the *Harbor Queen*. It leaves the dock hourly on weekends during the summer months and at noon, 2:00, 4:00, 7:00 and 8:00 p.m. during the week. If you still feel energetic, pick up a walking tour guide booklet for Annapolis at the Kiosk across from Market House and explore the town.

One of the "must" stops on any tour of Annapolis is the William Paca House and Gardens on Prince George Street. This 37-room Georgian mansion has been painstakingly restored. It was built by William Paca, a signer of the Declaration of Independence and Governor of Maryland during the Revolutionary War. The furnishings, though not original, reflect the decor of the decade before the war. Behind the house, lost for almost a century, are the two acres of restored gardens. A central path or "grand allée" leads through descending terraces to a pond. The garden is designed with separate sections or "parterres." These parterres feature roses, boxwoods, holly and seasonal flowers, making the garden pleasant year-round. The house and gardens are open Tuesday through Saturday from 10:00 a.m. to 4:00 p.m. and Sunday from noon to 4:00 p.m. Admission is charged.

Directions: From the Washington Beltway take Exit 19, the John Hanson Highway. Take Route 450 at the Annapolis-Parole Exit. Continue down Route 450 to the second light, then turn right on Route 2 to Edgewater. Turn left at the traffic light at Lee Airport onto Route 253, Mayo Road.

Continue to the well-marked intersection with Londontown Road, a little more than one mile. Turn left on Londontown Road and go to the end where you will find the London Town Publik House and Gardens. It's about a 45-minute drive from the Beltway.

LONGWOOD GARDENS
Finest Gardens on the North American Continent

Where would you expect to discover the finest garden estate in North America? Sunny California? Florida? Wrong. It is Longwood Gardens in Pennsylvania, only a two-hour drive from the Washington Beltway. Visit this 1,000-acre garden estate and you will understand why experts feel it is unequaled outside of Europe.

Spring is a particularly enjoyable season at Longwood. Daffodils bordering the lake cast soft yellow reflections on the water. As you wander along the woodland path you will pass large groups of rhododendron and azaleas. Formal plantings of tulips, foxglove, pansies, peonies and Canterbury bells are grouped in harmonious arrangements of purple, pink and yellow along wide sidewalk paths.

The Italian Water Garden, based on the design of the garden at Villa Gamgeraia near Florence, Italy, is always popular. It features sets of fountains in blue-tiled pools, a rock cascade and a water staircase. There is another set of fountains where lighted water displays may be seen from mid-June to Labor Day on Tuesday and Saturday evenings at 9:15.

Another delight is the rock garden built on a hillside dominated by a splashing waterfall. You can climb a stepping stone path through the rock garden up to and across the top of the waterfall to the Chime Tower. Be sure to bring your camera.

Do not neglect the conservatories where more than 3½ acres of flowers and plants are displayed. Inside the glass houses you have the opportunity to see plants rarely, if ever, seen in this area and certainly never in such lush form. In the spring you find striking groups of six-foot delphiniums in white, indigo, pastel blue, lavender and deep violet, also eye-catching orchids, salpiglossis, Easter lilies and columbine.

The conservatories are open daily from 10:00 a.m. to 5:00 p.m. and the outdoor garden from 9:00 a.m. to 6:00 p.m., but only until 5:00 p.m. in the winter months. The fountain displays are from mid-June to Labor Day on Tuesday and Saturday. Admission is charged for all but children age 5 and under. The Terrace Restaurant, with seating both indoors and out, is open every day as well as those evenings when special holiday displays, fountain shows and theatrical performances are held. For more information write Longwood Gardens, Kennett Square, Pa. 19348 or call (215)388-6741.

Directions: From the Washington Beltway take Exit 27, I-95. Once you are in Delaware watch for Route 141 north to Newport. Follow this north and exit at Route 52 North. Continue north on Route 52 into Pennsylvania until it intersects U.S. Route 1. Turn left, south, on Route 1. Longwood's exit ramp is about one mile away. Longwood is three miles northeast of Kennett Square, Pennsylvania. If you wish to avoid the tolls and don't mind a slightly longer return trip continue south on U.S. 1 for an alternate route to Washington.

MORVEN PARK AND OATLANDS
Two Colonial Garden Estates

Just 40 minutes from the Beltway in Leesburg, Virginia, are two magnificent colonial estates—Morven Park and Oatlands. Spring is a particularly good time to plan a visit to Morven Park because the two nature trails on this 1,200-acre estate abound with wild flowers. There is also a formal garden with large, dense boxwoods. Youngsters will enjoy Morven Park's Carriage Museum with its 75 horse drawn vehicles. The display also includes sleighs, miniature models and liveries offering a mini visual history of transportation in colonial times.

The mansion itself was begun in 1781 and includes a variety of architectural styles such as a Greek Revival facade, Renaissance Great Hall, Jacobean Dining Room and French Drawing Room. The mansion served as a home for two governors, Westmoreland Davis of Virginia and Thomas Swann of Maryland.

Morven Park estate is open from April through October, 10:00 a.m. to 5:00 p.m.; Sunday from 1:00 to 5:00 p.m. It is closed on Monday and Tuesday. Admission is charged.

You may wish to include a stop at Oatlands, a meticulously preserved early 19th-century Georgian mansion, on your itinerary. The gardens at Oatlands were planned by the estate's founder, George Carter, and contain, among other things, giant boxwoods that are into their second hundred years, massive stone terraces and enormous magnolias which are particularly handsome in the spring.

Oatlands is open from 10:00 a.m. to 5:00 p.m. six days a week and on Sunday from 1:00 to 5:00 p.m. April through November. There is an admission fee.

While in Leesburg stop at the Loudoun Museum at 16 West Loudoun Street. It was to Leesburg that President Madison and his cabinet fled with 22 wagonloads of government papers when Washington was burned during the War of 1812. The museum will provide maps and brochures for a walking tour of Leesburg or a driving tour of the county. Also featured is an audio-visual documentary of the area. The museum is open Monday through Saturday from 10:00 a.m. to 5:00 p.m. and on Sundays from 1:00 p.m. to 5:00 p.m. No admission charge.

Directions: From the Washington Beltway take Exit 10, Route 7, to Leesburg. Turn south on Route 15 and go six miles to Oatlands. Morven Park is about ten minutes farther down Route 15 on the western edge of Leesburg. Signs will indicate both estate entryways.

NATIONAL ARBORETUM
Blossoms and Bonsai

Washingtonians can be classified many ways but one distinction is between those who have never been to the National Arboretum and those who are regulars.

Once the arboretum is discovered it becomes a seasonal treat throughout the year. It is in spring, however, that the arboretum is most floriferous. With 80,000 azaleas in bloom it becomes nature's own theme park—Azalealand. The wooded hillside paths are flanked with multi-hued azaleas. Although this spring show needs no supporting cast, the blooming rhododendrons and dogwoods are also abundant.

The azaleas are probably the single most popular collection in the arboretum but an earlier spring showing, the daffodils near Fern Valley, has its own fans, probably because it signals the end of winter. Another early bloomer, the camellia, has suffered from the harsh Washington winters and the arboretum's collection is severely curtailed.

Late spring and early summer is the ideal time to explore the National Herb Garden, which was begun in 1980 and is still changing. One of the three sections in this two-acre garden is the Historic Rose Garden. From the trellised overlook you can enjoy an overview of this garden. Even at that distance you will quickly discover that the Historic Rose Garden is also designed as a Fragrance Garden. The two other areas of interest are the 16th-century English Knot Garden and the Specialty Garden, which actually includes ten individual sections. Each section has plants arranged by use—Plants in Medicine, Dye Garden, Industrial Garden, Culinary Garden, Beverage Garden and others.

Fall brings autumn foliage to the many trees in the arboretum plus bright berries and fruit. Winter respite can be found in the National Bonsai Collection, the Holly Collection and the Gotelli Dwarf Conifer Collection.

The National Bonsai Collection, Japan's $4.5 million bicentennial gift to the United States, is located in the Japanese Garden and Viewing Pavilion on Meadow Road. The 53 bonsai plants range in age from 30 to 350 years. A 180-year-old Japanese Red Pine is the prize of the collection. It is the first specimen from the Imperial Household of Japan ever to leave that country.

Another less familiar feature of the collection are the *suiseki*, or viewing stones. Their names reveal why they are prized by the Japanese: Chrysanthemum Stone, Puddle Stone and Quiet Mountain Stone.

Outdoor display area with holly and evergreen provide eye-pleasing displays even on crisp, cold days.

The National Arboretum is open daily, except Christmas. There is no admission charge. Hours are 8:00 a.m. to 5:00 p.m. during the week, 10:00 a.m. to 5:00 p.m. on weekends. The National Bonsai Collection, however, is open only from 10:00 a.m. to 2:30 p.m.

Directions: The National Arboretum is inside the Beltway at 24th and R Street, N.E. There is an entrance off New York Avenue and another off Bladensburg Road.

NEMOURS
Tres Chic

Many elegant homes of the well-to-do give visitors a glimpse of the gilded life, but few so successfully create the illusion that you have joined that special circle as does Nemours, outside Wilmington, Delaware.

Nemours is just about ten minutes from the interstate at the Wilmington exit, little more than a two-hour drive from the Washington Beltway. Your gracious reception will quickly erase all the anxieties of turnpike travel. After receiving a flower from the hostess you can enjoy juice on the terrace as you hear about the history of the du Pont family and the building of this fairytale estate. The main house and all the dependencies are tinted light pink. Nestling among the 300 acres of woodland and landscaped gardens, they blend perfectly with the light pastels of spring—dogwood, azaleas, tulips and lilacs.

The patriarch of the du Ponts, Pierre Samuel du Pont de Nemours, fled from France after the Revolution. As a member of Louis XVI's cabinet, his future in France was problematic. He emigrated to America in 1799. Although he returned briefly after Napoleon's defeat and became part of the provisional government, he left again in 1815 when Napoleon returned to power.

It was his great-great-grandson, Alfred Irénée du Pont, who built this modified Louis XVI French chatêau in 1909–1910. Throughout the 77-room house you will see reminders of Pierre Samuel du Pont and his association with Louis XVI and Marie Antoinette. Several of the decorative pieces in the house either belonged to the French King or were gifts to the du Ponts from the King. The French chandeliers in the formal dining room once hung in Schönbrunn Castle, Marie Antoinette's girlhood summer home in Vienna. The hall clock that plays a number of musical selections also once belonged to her.

To tour Nemours is to become acquainted with Alfred Irénée du Pont, a man of incredible scope and brilliance. He had over 200 inventions under patent, was an avid hunter and sportsman, composed music and interested himself in a multitude of projects. Your tour lets you see the informal side of his life at Nemours. There is an exercise room, billiard room, bowling alley and a photographic laboratory. Spring water was pumped to another room where, at his direction, he had the water bottled as Nemours Silver Spring. This tour even shows you the boiler room, where there are two boilers and two hot water heaters, just in case the first should malfunction. The personal side of life revealed at Nemours makes this tour endlessly fascinating, and the formal side makes it unforgettably impressive.

Add to these two aspects the garden tour, and Nemours becomes an excursion you won't want to miss. The gardens extend for a third of a mile from the château. Designed in the manner of Versailles with 12 lakes flowing into one another and oversize sculpture and colonnades, the scene is breathtaking, and made even more appealing in the spring by the addition of 58,000 tulips.

On your return to the Reception Center where the two-hour tour ends you will stop at the Garage and Chauffeur's House to see a collection of du Pont cars. There is a 1912 Cadillac with a 1934 chassis and a second Cadillac with a 1924 body and a 1934 chassis. On the latter there was no front door and the chaffeur had to enter at the back seat and climb over the front seat. There is also one, of only ten made, in the 1951 Silver Wraith Rolls Royce series, a 1960 Phantom V Towncar, and a 1933 Buick Roadster.

If you have time after your visit to Nemours, just ten minutes away is the Hagley Museum and Eleutherian Mills where E. I. du Pont de Nemours and Company established a gunpowder mill and the family fortunes began. You can also combine a trip to Nemours with a visit to the other nearby du Pont estates, Longwood and Winterthur. Excursions to these sites are described elsewhere in this book.

Nemours is open from May through November and reservations are necessary. All visitors must be over 16. Tours are given Tuesday through Saturday at 9:00 and 11:00 a.m. and 1:00 and 3:00 p.m. Sunday tours are at 11:00 a.m. and 1:00 and 3:00 p.m. There are a number of steps to be negotiated on the tour, so wear comfortable shoes. Admission is charged for this tour. To make reservations write giving date and time you are requesting plus an alternate suggestion to Nemours Mansion and Gardens, Reservation Office, P. O. Box 109, Wilmington, Delaware 19899. You can also call (302)651-6912.

Directions: Take Beltway Exit 27, I-95, north to Wilmington. Take Exit 8 off I-95 at Wilmington. You want Route

202, the Concord Pike North ramp. On Route 202 get in the left lane so that you can turn left at the intersection with Route 141. Continue up Route 141 to the second light, Rockland Road. Turn left at Rockland Road and continue for a short distance until you see the sign for the Nemours entrance on the right. Signs will direct you to the parking area and Reception Center. To reach Hagley Museum return to Route 141 and turn left, then continue for a short distance to Hagley which is on the right and clearly marked by signs.

NORFOLK
Sailors, Scenery and Seashore

One of the oldest cities in the nation, Norfolk, Virginia, is rapidly gaining a reputation as one of the area's most diverse day-trip destinations.

Norfolk's heightened popularity is due in large measure to The Waterside, a multi-million dollar festival marketplace which opened in 1983. This complex embraces more than 100 unique places to shop, dine and browse. There is also a park in the Town Point waterfront complex.

The new project is only part of the fun in Norfolk. Historical and cultural points of interest abound on the self-guided Norfolk Tour. Most of the tour's attractions are contained within the one-square-mile downtown area. Here is St. Paul's Church, which survived the British bombardment of Norfolk in 1776. A cannonball fired during that siege is still embedded in the southeastern wall of the church. Admission is free and the church is open 10:00 a.m. to 4:00 p.m. Tuesday through Saturday and 2:00 to 4:00 p.m. on Sundays.

Nearby is the MacArthur Memorial, an 11-gallery museum, which houses the General's tomb. A collection of World War II memorabilia includes the General's famous corncob pipe, the surrender documents that ended the war and MacArthur's staff car. There is no charge for this museum open 10:00 a.m. to 5:00 p.m. Monday through Saturday and 11:00 a.m. to 5:00 p.m. on Sunday.

Historic houses on the Norfolk Tour include the oldest brick house in America, the Adam Thoroughgood House. The Willoughby-Baylor House has an Early Norfolk Room where you'll see a doll-size replica of Norfolk in the 1790s. This will give you an overview of Norfolk's history. The third home, the Moses-Myers House, was built after the American Revolution by one of the young country's "merchant princes." It will give you a look at the life-style of the rich of an earlier era. The three houses are open from 10:00 a.m. to 5:00 p.m. Tuesday through Saturday and noon to 5:00 p.m. on Sunday. Admission is charged at each house.

One of the top 20 museums in the country, the Chrysler Museum, is centrally located in the city and features exhibitions ranging from 2500 B.C. Chinese bronzes to the paintings and sculpture of the 1980s. The Chrysler Institute of Glass is noted for its extensive collection of Tiffany glass. This museum is open 10:00 a.m. to 4:00 p.m. Tuesday through Saturday and 1:00 to 5:00 p.m. on Sunday. No admission is charged.

Farther from the center of the city, but right off Route 337 is the Hermitage Foundation Museum, a riverside mansion which contains a large collection of Oriental and Medieval art. The home is surrounded by 12 acres of wooded gardens which are open to the public during museum hours. Admission is charged and the museum is open 10:00 a.m. to 5:00 p.m. Monday through Saturday and 1:00 to 5:00 p.m. on Sunday.

Continuing down Route 337 from the Hermitage you will find one of the most popular attractions on the Norfolk Tour—the Norfolk Naval Station. This is the largest Naval installation in the world. It is the home of both the Atlantic and Mediterranean fleets, which include aircraft carriers, nuclear submarines and destroyers. Visitors are permitted to board selected ships from 10:00 a.m. to 4:00 p.m. on Saturdays and Sundays. You can also arrange a bus tour of the base April through October.

Spring is the best time of the year to visit the next attraction, the 175-acre Norfolk Botanical Garden, also called Gardens-By-The-Sea. The gardens are at their peak during the vibrant azalea season and are accessible by footpath, trackless trains and canal boats. There is an admission charge to the gardens and the boat and train tours cost extra. The gardens remain open seven days a week from 8:30 a.m. to sunset. Many day-trippers enjoy viewing this garden from the water, and during the summer months there are a number of different harbor cruise vessels that provide that vantage point.

The best place to begin your tour and obtain additional information is the Visitor's Information Center in Ocean View Beach located near the east end of the Hampton Roads Bridge Tunnel.

Directions: Take Virginia Beltway Exit 4, I-95, south. Then just north of Richmond take I-64 east, which will take you directly to Norfolk.

PATUXENT RIVER PARK
Trade Your Wheels for a Pontoon

A marshland ecology tour awaits you aboard the Patuxent River Park's pontoon boat, *Possum*, at Patuxent River Park in Croom, Maryland. A trained naturalist will acquaint you with the birds, animals and plants that flourish in this marsh and river area.

All the boat tours are relaxed and informal and they are organized around different themes. There is one designed specifically for bird watchers; another is an aquatic study; and a third is especially for photographers who like to capture nature through their lenses. The *Possum* holds 12 adults (no one under 13 is allowed) and there is no charge for the tour which lasts approximately 50 minutes. Tours begin in April and continue through October on a reservation basis only; call at least 10 days in advance, (301)627-6075.

The pontoon rides are only one feature of the Patuxent River Park outdoor programs. Young children six and up may accompany their parents on guided nature walks through the Black Walnut Creek Nature Study Area. The hikes take 45 minutes and are free. A variety of ecological subjects are discussed by the guides such as marsh animals and identification of marsh plants. A marshland photography blind is available for camera buffs. It is necessary to call (301)627-6075 in advance to arrange for the hikes. The park also has special primitive camping facilities for backpackers.

Also unique are the canoe trips which, like the pontoon tours, also require reservations. The canoe trips can be taken Tuesday through Saturday from mid-April to the end of October. You can rent a canoe to explore Mattaponi Creek or Jug Bay. The Jug Bay area can also be explored by canoe on Sundays. A five-hour, 18-mile downriver trip from Hardesty to Jackson's landing can be reserved for more experienced canoeists.

Another popular park feature is Patuxent Village which is open for informal visits on weekends year-round. This is an historical interpretative exhibit featuring a smokehouse, tobacco stripping and packing barn, log cabin, hunting and trapping exhibits and dugout canoes.

Added to the park in 1983 was the W. Henry Duvall Memorial Tool Collection, open without advance reservations from 1:00 to 4:00 p.m. on Sunday afternoons. Call for updated information on Saturday hours: (301)627-6075. A carpenter's workbench is surrounded by the tools of that trade. Other trades represented are the cobbler and wheelwright. There is the chair and tools of a country dentist, R. Early Baden, who traveled throughout southern Maryland for 56 years. An old-fashioned kitchen display provides a glimpse of how significantly labor-saving devices have improved the once time-consuming job of food preparation. William Henry Duvall collected more than 1,200 antique tools and farm implements, shedding light on many 19th-century activities.

Patuxent River Park is only 35 minutes from the Washington Beltway. Before heading home you should plan to make one more stop at nearby Merkle Wildlife Management Area, just one mile farther down Croom Road. During the migratory season you will see large concentrations of Canadian geese, a wide variety of ducks and an occasional bald eagle or hawk. Be sure to bring your high-powered binoculars because there are no observation facilities here, only a parking lot overlooking the protected fields of this wildlife sanctuary.

Merkle's proximity to Washington makes it possible for you to observe the birds in the early morning when they leave to forage and continue their migratory flight or at dusk when they flock to the refuge for the night.

Directions: Take Maryland Beltway Exit 11, Pennsylvania Avenue, for 7.9 miles, then take the southern turn onto Route 301 and continue 3.8 miles to Route 382, Croom Road (do not make the mistake of taking the earlier Croom Station Road). Turn left onto Croom Road and continue 3.8 miles to the sign for Patuxent River Park, Jug Bay Natural Area and turn left. For Merkle Wildlife Management Area continue on Croom Road for another mile, then turn left on St. Thomas Church Road until you see the sign for Merkle on the left.

REMINGTON FARMS AND CHESTERTOWN
Shooting Permitted With Cameras Only

Wildlife centers are usually the domains of the state or federal government but occasionally a private company establishes one. You can see how well one company has performed this function by a visit to Remington Farms, a wildlife management area operated by the Remington Arms Company. Remington Farms is located in Kent County, Maryland, near Chestertown, and is open free of charge to the public.

The 3,000-acre research and demonstration area can be visited daily from dawn to dusk. During hunting season, mid-October through January, the wildlife habitat tour is closed, but the waterfowl sanctuary, which harbors Canadian geese and numerous species of ducks from October through March, is open year-round. Remington Farms satisfies the four basic needs of wildlife: food, water, shelter and living space.

While serving the needs of wildlife, parts of this acreage are farmed. The corn not only helps feed the more than 10,000 Canadian geese that winter here but also provides income for the maintenance of the farm. Other wildlife that need have no fear for provisions at Remington Farms include squirrels, deer, red foxes, rabbits, game birds and songbirds. The untamed creatures can be spotted from the tour route that runs through the Farms.

There are 26 fresh-water ponds within the compound ranging in size up to 50 acres. One of the ponds most frequented by the geese is located ¼ mile south of the main entrance and adjacent to St. Paul's Lake. Other birds often sighted include the blue goose, snow goose, whistling swan, pintail duck, shoveler, widgeon, wood duck, ruddy duck and black duck. Nearly 20,000 mallards winter each year at Remington. For the bird watcher this diversity is a definite plus. Be sure to bring your binoculars for a better view.

While in Kent County you should also spend some time exploring Chestertown, a town that seems suspended in time. Gracious Georgian and Federal homes along Water Street overlooking the Chester River were built in pre-Revolutionary times by the rich merchants of Chestertown. Most of the homes can only be seen from the outside. One exception is the Moore-Geddes-Piper House, normally open May through August on Sundays from 1:00 to 4:00 p.m. It was here that William Geddes lived. He owned the brigantine, *Geddes*, which was boarded on May 23, 1774 by irate townspeople infuriated over the high tea tax. They threw the tea on board into the Chester River in what came to be known as the Chestertown Tea Party.

The Moore-Geddes-Piper House is handsomely furnished with 18th-century pieces and has a fine collection of Chinese export teapots. The house is on Church Alley off Queen Street. A short stroll will bring you to High Street where you will find the White Swan Tavern. You can stop here for a cup of tea and have a look at this inn where George Washington often visited. Tea is served Wednesday through Sunday from 4:00 to 6:00 p.m.; tours of the tavern take place at 2:00 p.m. The tavern now offers bed and breakfast but advance reservations are a must.

The best time to visit Chestertown is the last weekend in May when the annual Chestertown Tea Party Festival is held. The dramatic re-enactment of the tea party is just part of the fun. Music, crafts and a wide variety of food complement the historic walking tours and vignettes.

Directions: From the Washington Beltway take Exit 19, Route 50, to the intersection with Route 301. Go north on Route 50-301 until it crosses the Bay Bridge, then continue on Route 301 when it branches to the left. Follow Route 301 until it intersects with Route 213. Turn left on 213 and go to Chestertown. At the third traffic light in Chestertown, turn left and travel about one mile to juncture with Route 20. Bear right on Route 20 for eight more miles and look for "Remington Farms—Wildlife Management Area" sign on the right, 1.2 miles beyond the Arco gas station.

SOTTERLEY
Hollywood Matinee

Why not head for a real-life Hollywood matinee at Sotter-ley? All the ingredients of an exciting movie can be found at this picturesque working plantation in St. Mary's County, Maryland.

Even the story of Sotterley's restoration contains elements of drama. Like a Gothic novel it deals with two families—the Platers and the Satterlees. During the War of the Roses in England, the Satterlees lived at Sotterley Hall in Suffolk, England. They were Lancastrians, supporters of the Earl of Warwick and therefore enemies of Edward IV. Upon Edward's victory he dispossessed them of their family estate. The Platers were given Sotterley Hall in 1771 in return for their loyalty to Edward.

In 1910 when Herbert Satterlee purchased the gracious Georgian plantation in St. Mary's which was the home of four generations of Platers, the circle was complete. The Satterlees once again controlled Sotterley, albeit in Maryland not England.

There is another tale that stems from the residency of George Plater V. In what was called Madame Bowles' drawing room, which is painted a vibrant red, there is a card table. Gambling was to have a profound influence on Sotterley because, as the costumed docents explain, "George Plater V had a taste for gambling but not the skill." In 1822 this gentleman, already deeply in debt, lost his family home in a dice game with Colonel William Somerville. All George Plater took with him when he left was a table and a bed. Both are now back at Sotterley.

The drawing room is interesting for other reasons as well. If a movie were ever made, this could be a pivotal set for there is both a secret compartment that was used to receive messages from Confederate sympathizers, and a secret passage to an upstairs bedroom.

It is fun to speculate on why this hidden passage was built. One explanation offered is that with the danger of pirates anchoring at Sotterley's wharf and threatening the house it was a quick way to hide the family silver. There is a story that pirates indeed did stop at Sotterley and that two were killed in a fight and are buried in the field between the house and the river. It is said that a pirate captain and two mates were seen from the window advancing on the house. Quick action by the Platers cost two of the pirates their lives and repulsed their foray.

The windows overlooking the flagstone veranda present yet another story for visitors as they explore the formal drawing room, or Great Hall, included in Helen Comstock's listing of the *Most Beautiful Rooms in America*. It was on a window in this room that Governor Plater's daughter, Elizabeth, having received a beautiful diamond ring from her fiancé, Philip Barton Key (the uncle of Francis Scott Key), tested its quality by writing "Key" on the window.

The drawing room is also architecturally interesting; all the wood was hand carved by Richard Bolton, an indentured servant. He also made the mahogany Chinese Chippendale trellis staircase. In the drawing room he raised the ceiling two and one-half feet, creating a bit of a problem for the upstairs bedroom, but providing a spacious drawing room. On each side of the fireplace he built carved shell alcoves.

Sotterley is exquisitely furnished. Particular pieces to notice are the partners' desk, the staircase clock so positioned that it could be read from the doorway of any of the upstairs bedrooms, and the 11-piece toilet set—a more complete assortment than is usually seen. Be sure to see the picture of George Washington floating on a cloud and crowned with a halo. Don't miss the angel's faces; each has George Washington's face.

In addition to taking the 45- to 60-minute house tour, you can explore the grounds where there are several dependencies and a charming garden. One of the most interesting is the old slave cabin, one of nine that formerly stood along the "rolling road" down which hogsheads of tobacco were rolled to waiting ships. There is also a smokehouse where hams are still smoked for sale at the Sotterley Gift Shop. Two gate houses flank the original entrance and one is furnished to represent an old-fashioned schoolroom.

Sotterley is open June through September from 11:00 a.m. to 5:00 p.m., with the last tour at 4:00 p.m. Admission is charged. You can visit during April, May, October and November by appointment; call (301)373-2280. Groups of 15 or more can arrange a luncheon on the veranda, a picnic on the lawn or an 18th-century candlelight supper. Weddings are frequently held at Sotterley. Like a good movie, Sotterley can be seen more than once.

Directions: Take Maryland Beltway Exit 7, Route 5, south to Mechanicsville. Take Route 235 to Hollywood and make a left turn on Route 245; continue three miles to Sotterley.

SUSQUEHANNA STATE PARK
Scenery, History and Fishery

Robert Louis Stevenson said ". . . it was called the Susquehanna, the beauty of the name seemed to be part and parcel of the beauty of the land for that shining river and desirable valley."

Stevenson's description of the Maryland countryside where the Susquehanna meanders into the Chesapeake still holds true. The park itself encompasses 2,200 acres and at its heart is the Rock Run area which remains as it was in the 1800s.

In 1794, Rock Run Mill, a water powered gristmill, was constructed. The mill structure has been completely restored and the essential gears and pulleys are now functioning. A house overlooks the mill, and it and the barn and icehouse have also been restored. One other building of the period that has been completely reconstructed is an old tollhouse.

In 1978 the Steppingstone Museum was moved to Susquehanna State Park. This museum recreates a turn-of-the-century country home. The rural arts of the 1880–1910 period are displayed and demonstrated at this living history museum.

Rural chores you can observe include carding, spinning and weaving wool and mealtime preparations on the old wood burning stove. Skilled craftsmen such as the blacksmith, leather worker, broom maker, woodworker, tinsmith, cooper, slater and mason can also be observed. The museum also has a collection of hand tools from our past. In the barn you'll see larger farm equipment.

Three yearly festivals provide an extra incentive to visit Susquehanna State Park. On the third weekend in June an oldtime arts and crafts fair is held. The Child Games Day on the third Sunday in August lets children play games their grandparents once enjoyed. The last Sunday in September is the Fall Harvest Festival and marks the end of the Steppingstone season.

The Steppingstone Museum is open weekends in May through September from 1:00 to 5:00 p.m. Admission is charged. For additional information on special programs you can call (301)939-2299. You can also write to the Susquehanna State Park, 801 Stafford Road, Havre de Grace, Maryland 21078.

These reminders of the past are not the only attraction of the park. During April, shad run up the Susquehanna and they, along with pike, perch and bass, make the River one of the best fishing areas on the East Coast. Susquehanna State Park is open free of charge during daylight hours year-round and is located about 35 miles from Baltimore. A visit to this area can be augmented by a stop at the Conowingo Dam. This dam is an enormous source of electrical power and visitors are welcome.

Directions: Take Beltway Exit 27, I-95, north to Exit 6 at Havre de Grace. Follow Route 155 towards Bel Air. After ¼ mile make a right turn onto Earlton Road and proceed for ½ mile. Then at Qualer Bottom Road turn left for the Steppingstone Museum. For park headquarters continue to Rock Run Road and turn right; you'll see the sign on the right after only a short distance.

TURKEY RUN AND THE CLAUDE MOORE COLONIAL FARM
A History Lesson Kids Gobble Up

A short drive around the Washington area allows you to see reproductions of what life was like on three different levels of society in the 18th century: Mount Vernon represents the plantation farm of the prosperous; National Colonial Farm is a re-creation of a freeholder's farm; and Claude Moore Colonial Farm, formally Turkey Run Farm, is a reproduction of a dirt farmer's homestead.

Claude Moore is a "living history" farm run the way it would have been two centuries ago. It is easy to believe that you have stepped back in time when the guide, dressed as a farmer, explains that his work in the fields prevented him from putting in the board floor they needed. The woman of the house sweeps the dirt floor with a hand-bound straw broom and says she hopes to get the board floor in soon. The one-room cabin is surrounded by fields of tobacco and corn (which the farmer plants and works) and livestock such as chickens, hogs, and horses. Although the farmer and his wife only come in by the day, they present a masterful illusion that they actually live there and that you have stepped into a time machine and have gone back to the Colonial Era.

Just inside the entrance to the Claude Moore Colonial Farm several picnic tables invite you to sylvan spots. The farm is open Wednesday through Sunday from 10:00 a.m. until 4:30 p.m. It is closed December through March and Thanksgiving Day. Admission is charged. For more information call (703)442-7557.

Directions: From the Washington Beltway take Exit 14 onto the George Washington Memorial Parkway; drive toward McLean. Take Exit 123 off the Parkway to Old Georgetown Pike, Route 193, and turn right at the sign for the Claude Moore Colonial Farm.

WINTERTHUR
Ignore the Name and Visit in the Spring

Despite its name the best time to visit Winterthur is in the spring, summer or autumn when the gardens are at their best. Garden paths wind for 2½ miles through meadows and forests, past creeks and ponds in the delightful wonderland at Winterthur. The Henry Francis du Pont Winterthur Museum and Gardens in Delaware are only two hours from the Washington Beltway. A day-trip to Winterthur is well worth the time.

The museum consists of 196 period rooms all furnished with articles made during the colonial period or during the first years of the New Republic. It is hard to choose which pieces best reflect the scope of this collection. Special items include six silver tankards made by Paul Revere; a pair of sofas owned by John Dickinson, who was known as the "penman of the American Revolution"; pewter by Philadelphian William Will; and a portrait of George Washington at Verplanck's Point painted by John Trumbull. There are excellent examples of domestic architecture, furniture, silver, pewter, paintings, textiles and ceramics.

The 200 landscaped acres in the garden area comprise only a small part of this 963-acre estate. The self-guiding tour map highlights 13 points of interest within the garden.

Plantings include almost every flower, tree and shrub that will grow in Delaware. It takes about 1½ hours to enjoy the 2½-mile tour of the gardens. One of the most popular areas is the Quarry Garden with hundreds of primroses, daffodils and wild flowers blooming among the rocks. Winterthur's gardens are also noted for their spring azalea display. In early May you see banks of azaleas and rhododendron along the woodland paths.

On an autumn visit, in addition to the colorful fall foliage, you will be likely to spot migratory waterfowl from the hillside overlook with its view of several interconnecting ponds. Actually, a wide variety of birds make their home year-round at Winterthur. Benches at scenic spots throughout the gardens give you a chance to sit quietly so that you can spot these sometimes elusive residents.

From mid-April through early June, the 16-room tour normally seen only by reservation, the 18-room American Sampler Tour, and the gardens are featured on an unreserved basis for Winterthur in Spring. The American Sampler Tour is a one-hour chronological exploration of the progression of the decorative arts in America from the 17th-century to the Empire period.

From early June through late September you do not need reservations to enjoy the American Sampler Tour and the gardens as part of Winterthur in the Summer.

Beginning on the last Sunday in September and extending through mid-November, Winterthur in Autumn offers the American Sampler Tour plus special seasonal floral arrangements in selected museum rooms. Garden tours are also still available. For those who have difficulty walking there is a motorized tram which runs through the gardens from spring through fall.

A combination of the American Sampler Tour and the Garden Tour is available from mid-November through early April as part of Winterthur in Winter. There is a special holiday exhibit for Yuletide at Winterthur running from late November through December.

Reserved tours are offered year-round except during Winterthur in Spring and the Yuletide celebration. Call or write the Reservations Office, Winterthur Museum, Winterthur, Delaware 19735, (302)654-1548. Children under 12 are not admitted on regular reserved tours; children between 12 and 16 are charged half-price; those under 12 are admitted free for all non-reserved tours.

Directions: Take Beltway Exit 27, I-95, to Wilmington. Go left, northwest, on Route 52. Winterthur is six miles from Wilmington on Route 52.

SPRING CALENDAR OF EVENTS

MARCH

EARLY

Needlework Exhibit—Woodlawn Plantation, VA (703)557-7880
More than 1,500 pieces of embroidery, canvas work, pillows, coverlets, quilts, wall hangings, counted thread work and crewel work are displayed at this annual event. Woodlawn Plantation is open daily 9:30 a.m. to 4:30 p.m.

MID

Maple Syrup Demonstration—Cunningham Falls State Park, MD (301)271-7574
Each year for several weekends in mid-March at this state park maple syrup demonstrations are held to acquaint visitors with this old American practice. The Park Rangers start boiling the sap at about 10:00 a.m. It takes about five hours before they can scoop out the syrup and give visitors samples. There are trees that are being tapped and a movie on syrup making at the Visitor's Center. Demonstrations are from 10:00 a.m. until 3:30 p.m.

Tavern Days—London Town Publik House & Gardens, MD (301)956-4900
In the 18th century the tavern was the social center of community life. Itinerant craftsmen would ply their trade while stopping at the tavern. For Tavern Days craftsmen will again be in residence. A wide range of activities will recreate the atmosphere of a colonial ferry tavern. Open Tuesday through Saturday 10:00 a.m. to 4:00 p.m., Sunday noon to 4:00 p.m.

Camellia Show—Norfolk Botanical Gardens, VA
(804)853-6972
Now that severe winter weather has badly damaged Washington area camellia gardens it's necessary to go farther south to enjoy these beautiful harbingers of spring. Each year the Norfolk Botanical Garden has a special show dedicated to the camellias. Open daily 8:30 a.m. until sunset.

Kite Festival—Gunston Hall Plantation, VA
(703)550-9220
Each year a 200-year old Mason family kite flying tradition is recreated at Gunston Hall. Children under 16 are admitted free to this day-long event featuring kites, puppets and pony cart rides. Open 9:30 a.m. to 5:00 p.m.

LATE

Flapjack Day—Colvin Run Mill, VA (703)759-2771
This popular program is a good way to get acquainted with the historic 19th-century Colvin Run Mill. You can actually sample freshly made flapjacks prepared with whole grain ground at this water-powered gristmill. These old-fashioned pancakes are cooked over an open fire, along with grits and hoecakes. If you come prepared with your own frying pan you can enter the annual "Flapjack Flipping on a Griddle Contest." This event is from 11:00 a.m. to 5:00 p.m.

Easter Conservatory Display—Longwood
Gardens, PA (215)398-6741
Delphiniums, daffodils, tulips, azaleas and a splendid array of flowering plants make a yearly visit to this annual show a popular area excursion. There are four acres of conservatories to explore, as well as the extensive outdoor display. Time: 8:00 a.m. to sunset; conservatories 11:00 a.m. to 5:00 p.m.

Loudoun County Day—Oatlands, VA
(703)777-3174
On Oatlands's 261 acres music, dancing, an equestrian exhibition and a children's dog show mark this festive occasion. Garden and house tours will complement the fun. This event is scheduled from noon to 5:00 p.m.

Spring Flower Display—Brookside Gardens, MD (301)949-8230

Fuchsias, hydrangeas, azaleas, lilies and many other spring flowering plants are regular favorites at this spring flower showcase. Open daily 9:00 a.m. to 5:00 p.m.

Maryland Day—St. Mary's City, MD (301)994-0779

Why not attend this annual birthday celebration? Just don't expect 350 plus candles on the cake. This party at the site of Maryland's first capital includes craft demonstrations, a water craft display and country cooking. Square dancing and music add to the fun. There is also the Symbolic Session of the General Assembly in the Old State House. Time: 11:00 a.m. to 5:00 p.m.

APRIL

EARLY

George Washington Visit—Boyhood Home of Robert E. Lee, VA (703)548-8454

Music, colonial refreshments, costumed docents and vignettes recreate the occasion when George Washington visited Colonel William Fitzhugh on April 3, 1799. Activities are customarily scheduled from 11:00 a.m. until 4:00 p.m.

Wildlife Art Show—Chincoteague, VA (804)336-6122

At this annual festival art runs the gamut from photography and decoy carving to glass etching and painting, all with themes from nature. Artists and craftsmen demonstrate their work from 10:00 a.m. to 5:00 p.m.

Spring Festival—The Claude Moore Colonial Farm at Turkey Run, VA (703)442-7557

Martial music and the First Virginia Regiment bring life to this farm that depicts life for the common farmer in the years between 1770 and 1775. This spring reopening is always a festive affair. Time: Usually 1:00 p.m. to 3:00 p.m.

White House Easter Egg Roll—South Lawn, Washington, D.C. (202)456-2200

The place for children to go on Easter Monday is the White House where a wide variety of entertainment, games and special events lend an air of excitement to this normally formal Presidential residence. Visits by both the President and the Easter Bunny please young and old. If you time your arrival for an hour after the event begins you can avoid a lot of the early crowding; you may miss the First Family, however, as they tend to put in an early appearance.

Cherry Blossom Festival—Tidal Basin, Washington, D.C. (202)426-6700

When nature and the calendar are in harmony and the cherry trees along the Tidal Basin bloom during this festival, it is a glorious sight. A parade with bands and princesses from all 50 states mark this yearly celebration.

MID

Blacksmithing Days—Colvin Run Mill, VA (703)759-2771

During Blacksmithing Days you can learn the importance of the blacksmith to an 18th-century community, watch blacksmiths from the East Coast demonstrate their skill, and attend an auction and bid on items made at this festival. Hobbyists and full-time blacksmiths make tools, ornamental ironwork and fireplace pieces. Both modern and traditional methods of forging and welding are used. Music and homemade food add to this event. Hours are noon to 5:00 p.m.

Daffodil Show—London Town Publik House and Gardens, MD (301)956-4900

While the London Town Gardens each spring has a delightful showing of daffodils along the woodland path, once a year the show moves indoors as well. A juried Daffodil Show offers the opportunity to see many exotic varieties of daffodils as well as beautiful flower arrangements. Time: Saturday from noon to 5:00 p.m. and Sunday noon to 4:00 p.m.

Farm Day—National Colonial Farm, MD (301)283-2113

Farming and the domestic arts are featured at this spring festival as this middle class tobacco plantation recreates our colonial past. Hours are 10:00 a.m. to 5:00 p.m.

Azalea Festival—Norfolk Botanical Garden, VA (804)853-6972

Each year since 1954 during the third week in April, Norfolk has hosted the International Azalea Festival to salute the North Atlantic Treaty Organization. Two acres at the Norfolk Botanical Garden are set aside exclusively for azaleas. There is also a parade, the coronation of the Azalea Queen and an air show.

John Wilkes Booth Escape Tour—Mary Surratt House, MD (301)868-1121

The Surratt Society sponsors a trip each spring and fall that retraces John Wilkes Booth's steps after he assassinated Lincoln at Ford's Theatre. Historical footnotes will fill in the details of this dramatic escape attempt that ended with the death of Booth in a barn on what is now Fort A.P. Hill military base. Reservations are required for this all-day event.

Trolley Car Spectacular—National Capital Trolley Museum, MD (301)384-9797

This program includes all 14 of the museum's operable cars in action or on display. This is a good time to photograph these American and European trolley cars. Hours are 1:30 to 3:30 p.m.

Bluebell Week and Bluebell Walk—Bull Run Regional Park, VA (703)278-8880

Nature lovers particularly enjoy this annual guided walk through the largest stand of bluebells on the East Coast. The walk is customarily scheduled at 2:00 p.m.

LATE

Historic Garden Week—Virginia (804)786-4484

Over 35 areas in Virginia open 250 historic gardens, estates and privately owned homes in the largest and one of the oldest Garden Weeks in the United States. Special events scheduled at many of these sites include luncheons, candlelight tours, teas and tours of private homes usually closed to the public.

Maryland House and Garden Pilgrimage— Statewide (301)821-6933
Homes of historic and architectural interest throughout Maryland open their doors to visitors during the last week of April and the first week of May. Garden lovers may get some ideas for their own landscaping. Hours are 10:00 a.m. to 5:00 p.m.

Coaching Days—Stratford Hall Plantation, VA (804)493-8038 or (804)493-8039
The greensward in front of the manor house at Stratford Hall seems to cry out for a coach; once a year that cry is answered. A parade of restored early American and British coaches grace the grounds of this colonial plantation. Competitive driving events are also scheduled during this one-day event.

Civil War Encampment—Mary Surratt House, MD (301)868-1121
Civil War units set up camp, provide demonstrations of black powder firings, exhibit military equipment and uniforms and answer questions for curious onlookers. Costumed docents as usual provide tours of the house. Hours are noon to 4:00 p.m.

Maryland Kite Festival—Fort McHenry, MD (301)377-5081
Free lessons and demonstrations of kite flying, kite battles and competitions to determine the highest kite, the one with the best train, the most beautiful kite, the most amusing, the largest and the smallest and the one with the best maneuverability all lend an air of frivolity to this yearly event. Hours are 9:30 a.m. to 3:00 p.m.

Spring Open House and Plant Sale—Woodend, MD (301)652-9188
A large selection of flowers, trees, shrubs and herbs are on sale at this spring event. Garden equipment, decorative planters, bird baths, and books on gardening, plants and birds are also available. The Woodend Mansion designed in 1920 will be open with displays of nature-related art and exhibits. There is a self-guided nature trail on this 40-acre estate. Hours are 10:00 a.m. to 4:00 p.m.

Shakespeare Birthday Celebration—Folger Shakespeare Library, Washington, D.C. (202)544-7077

Attend a rather different birthday party at this Elizabethan open house. No need to worry, the cake will not have the requisite number of candles.

Spring Candlelight Tour—Old Town Alexandria, VA (703)549-0205

What better way to see the historic houses and sites of Alexandria than by candlelight. The feeling of stepping back into the past is heightened by the soft flickering candles. Refreshments are served at several of the houses and visitors get a real feel for this city's renowned hospitality. Period music and military encampments often add to this event.

Annual Azalea Garden Festival—Landon School, MD (301)320-3200

On this wooded campus there are over 25,000 azaleas and rhododendrons which make a striking showing each year. You can enjoy a do-it-yourself garden tour and then purchase plants from the azalea stock. Other plants and garden equipment are for sale. Art is displayed and entertainment provided.

MAY

EARLY

Mother's Day Tribute—Mary Washington House, Fredericksburg, VA (703)373-1776

The last time George Washington saw his mother was on March 12, 1789, as he headed for New York to be inaugurated as America's first President. Each year on Mother's Day weekend this farewell visit is dramatically recreated at the Mary Washington House. Open 9:00 a.m. to 5:00 p.m.

Spring Open House Tours—Philadelphia, PA (215)864-1976

Special Philadelphia neighborhoods like the Old City, Washington Square, Society Hill, Southwark, Victorian University City and the Portico Row area are explored during Open

House walking tours. There are also guided bus tours of Germantown, the Main Line and Chestnut Hill.

Cylburn Market Day—Cylburn Arboretum, MD (301)396-0180

This annual fair features the sale of herbs, flowers, shrubs and trees. Arts and crafts are demonstrated, displayed and sold. Musical entertainment is provided and refreshments are available. Time is normally 9:00 a.m. to 4:00 p.m.

Spring Festival—Ellicott City, MD (301)992-2344

A May Day Festival has juried and non-juried displays of handmade arts and crafts. You can even enjoy an old-fashioned Maypole dance. Held in downtown Ellicott City from noon to 5:00 p.m.

Reenactment of the Battle of New Market—New Market Battlefield Park, VA (703)740-3101

Booming cannons, cracking muskets and "rebel yells" add to the color and excitement when uniformed members of reactivated Civil War units stage this 1864 battle. Young boys will find the scene particularly interesting as cadets from nearby Virginia Military Institute, many barely 15, had been called out to take part in this important battle which gave the Confederacy its last victory in the Shenandoah area.

Spring Festival—Montpelier Mansion, VA (301)776-2805

Entertainment for young and old is a tradition of this annual free festival. Cultural and artistic events figure prominently in this one-day event. Studios in the Montpelier Cultural Arts Center are open to visitors. There are also tours of the mansion. Time: Noon to 6:00 p.m.

May Day Tour of Private Gardens—Annapolis, MD (301)267-8149

Private gardens in historic Annapolis are open for this special tour. Following an old-fashioned tradition many of the houses are bedecked with baskets of fresh flowers. Time: 10:00 a.m. to 5:00 p.m.

Armed Forces Open House—Andrews Air Force Base, MD (301)981-4511

Equipment from all branches of the service will be on display, including more than 50 aircraft. Aerial shows are held throughout the day. Special aircraft are demonstrated. Various military musical groups perform. Time: 9:00 a.m. to 5:00 p.m.

Jamestown Day—Jamestown Colonial Historical Park, VA (804)359-0239

This event commemorates the landing of the colonists at Jamestown and the establishment of the first permanent English-speaking settlement in the New World. There is a religious observance on Jamestown Island near the only remaining 17th-century structure at Jamestown, the brick church tower.

Spring Farm Festival—Hard Bargain Farm, MD (301)292-5665

This activity-oriented farm tour provides a once yearly opportunity for families and individuals to visit this educational farm. Hay rides, sheep shearing, guided nature walks and participatory farm chores are all part of the fun. Time: 11:00 a.m. to 4:00 p.m.

MID

Market Square Fair—Fredericksburg, VA (703)373-1776

Following a tradition that began in 1738, each spring the square in Fredericksburg is decorated with flags and colorful canopies for a combination country fair and bazaar. Artisans demonstrate their wares and costumed hostesses sell homemade baked goods. The event is held from 9:00 a.m. to 5:00 p.m.

Plantation Daily Life—Sully Plantation, VA (703)941-5008

Each year Sully Plantation brings back the picturesque plantation days of the 18th and 19th century. Old-fashioned cooking techniques, crafts, country dancing and games illuminate life on a southern plantation. Time: 11:00 a.m. to 5:00 p.m.

Cavalier Days in Calvert County—Prince Frederick, MD (301)884-2144

Pageantry, music and fun are part of this "fair of the 1780s." Vignettes of colonial history, dueling, colonial games and old-fashioned crafts are all part of the fun. Time: 11:00 a.m. until 6:30 p.m.

Bowie Heritage Day—Belair Mansion, MD (301)262-6200

Free tours of the Belair Mansion and Stable Museum, displays of early American crafts and music, as well as refreshments mark this annual event. Time: 2:00 to 5:00 p.m.

Market Day—Claude Moore Colonial Farm at Turkey Run, VA (703)442-7557

Colonial crafts, music and country dancing along with the Virginia Militia Company add up to a fun fair. Time: 10:00 a.m. to 4:30 p.m.

Great May Pop Music Festival—Berrywine Plantation, MD (301)662-8687

Each year at the height of the May wine season at Berrywine Plantation there is a free musical celebration. The concert is traditionally at 4:00 p.m.

Folk Fest—Mercer Museum, PA (215)345-0210

At this country crafts fair in Bucks County you can see more than 50 masters of 18th- and 19th-century arts and crafts demonstrating and selling their wares. Continuous entertainment includes militia drills, old time medicine shows, folk dancing, sheep-shearing, wagon rides and juggling. An assortment of food is for sale. There is also an old time picnic basket auction. The event is held from 10:00 a.m. to 5:00 p.m.

Roses and May Flowers Day—William Paca House and Gardens, MD (301)267-6656

An exhibit of historic roses, 18th-century flower arrangements and opportunities to have your own roses identified are all part of this special day. Time: 10:00 a.m. to 7:00 p.m.

Fort Frederick Rendezvous—Fort Frederick State Park, MD (301)842-2504

The Maryland Forces, which were active during the French and Indian War, demonstrate frontier skills and ranger tactics. Other military units will participate in this rendezvous. Time: 1:00 to 4:00 p.m.

Virginia Hunt Country Stable Tour—Middleburg Area, VA (703)592-3343

Once a year Virginia's elegant thoroughbred horse farms open their stables and grounds to the public. The Middleburg Training Track is also open along with the adjacent Equine Swim Center. Time: 10:00 a.m. to 5:00 p.m.

Chestertown Tea Party Festival—Chestertown, MD (301)348-5755

On May 23, 1774, in sympathy with their compatriots in Boston, a group of Chestertown, Maryland, protestors boarded the brigantine *Geddes* and dumped the dutiable tea into the Chester River. This escapade is duplicated each year as part of the Chestertown Tea Party Festival. Streets are closed to traffic in this historic old town and craftsmen demonstrate and sell their wares at colorful booths. Militia demonstrations, music, dancing and a wide variety of refreshments round out this event. A sound and light presentation captures Chestertown's historical past. Hours are 10:00 a.m. to 10:00 p.m. on Saturday and noon to 4:00 p.m. on Sunday.

SUMMER

ALBERT POWELL TROUT HATCHERY
See the Small Fry

Fishermen, children and nature lovers will enjoy a visit to the Albert Powell Trout Hatchery in Maryland. Each year approximately 300,000 eggs are received from trout egg suppliers. When the eggs arrive, they are placed in hatching trays in a flow-through incubator. In two to three weeks, the eggs will begin to hatch and the resulting trout fry will then be moved to indoor tanks. The trout will grow in these tanks for two to three months until they reach fingerling size. The hatchery's water supply comes from a limestone spring that is very beneficial to their growth.

When the trout reach two inches in length, they are placed in outdoor raceways. The goal of the hatchery is to raise 120,000 adult rainbow trout that average 10 to 11 inches 15 months after hatching. The hatchery holds 15,000 of these trout for an additional year until they range from 15 to 18 inches in length and will provide a bonus to fishermen. When a year's production exceeds the 120,000 trout capacity, the extra fish are stocked in suitable waters where natural growth can occur. The normal stocking season begins in March of each year and the hatchery fish are stocked to satisfy fishermen in Maryland.

The Albert Powell Hatchery may be visited daily from 9:00 a.m. to 4:00 p.m. There is no admission charge.

Directions: From the Beltway take Exit 35, Route 270, to Hagerstown, Maryland. Exit on Route 66 and travel north 200 yards to the hatchery entrance on the left.

ASSATEAGUE ISLAND NATIONAL SEASHORE AND VIRGINIA BARRIER ISLANDS
Sand, Surf and Stallions

If the commercial development along the Atlantic Coast from Rehoboth Beach, Delaware, to Ocean City, Maryland, makes you yearn for an unspoiled beach, try visiting Assateague Island only six miles from Ocean City. Its 37-mile beach and the gently sloping ocean bottom and lack of undertow lure swimmers and fishermen alike.

Assateague is a wildlife preserve and if you are observant and lucky, you may catch a glimpse of a Sika deer, fox, racoon, a water bird or one of the famous wild ponies. The "pony penning" which is exciting to watch (see the Chincoteague Island selection) occurs every year on the Virginia side of the island during the last week in July.

Going to Assateague Island from the Maryland side you come to a Visitor's Center on the mainland side of the Sinepuxent Bridge. Here you will find printed information on both the ecological and anthropological history of Assateague, plus the legends and lore of this island's 6,000-year existence. It's said that Blackbeard the pirate once kept a wife hidden in one of the island's pine groves.

Optimists still like to believe that ten ironbound chests are buried somewhere on the island. The chests were valued at more than 200,000 pounds sterling in 1750; their worth today would be almost uncountable.

The Visitor's Center has daily schedules for swimming, fishing, clamming, crabbing, hiking and boating. You can explore Assateague by canoe or other shallow draft boat. Hike-in and canoe-in camping are available by reservation. Fees are charged during summer months, but the island is open year-round during daylight hours.

If your outing to Assateague leaves you wanting something even more unspoiled and out-of-the-way, then consider a day-trip along the Atlantic's last frontier—the Virginia Barrier Islands.

Sponsored by the Nature Conservancy, 25 to 30 boat tours are scheduled each season along the 18 islands that stretch below the Maryland–Virginia border to the mouth of the Chesapeake Bay. The Virginia Coast Reserve encompasses 35,000 acres of sandy islands and salt marshes. One of the principal pleasures of these cruises is the variety of waterfowl and migratory birds to be seen. The islands provide breeding grounds for numerous species of nesting birds: geese, loons, ibises, egrets and hawks, including the rare peregrine falcon. Keen-eyed passengers may also spot some of the islands' abundant wildlife.

These trips, lasting from 8:00 a.m. until 3:30 p.m., are for the hardy. There are no facilities on board nor on the unpopulated islands. The open boat provides maximum visibility for the meandering ride through the tidal marshes, but that also means maximum exposure to the elements. The boat leaves from Brownsville, Virginia. Reservations must be made well in advance; call (804)442-3049 or write the Virginia Coast Reserve, Brownsville, Nassawadox, Virginia 23413.

Directions: Take Beltway Exit 19, Route 50, all the way to the outskirts of Ocean City. Take a left on Route 611 to the Visitor's Center and Assateague. For the Virginia Barrier Islands take Route 50 to Salisbury, then take Route 13 south to Nassawadox and over to the Virginia Coast Reserve headquarters.

BARGING ON THE C&O CANAL
Mule Skinner's Special

On July 4, 1828, two events occurred that irrevocably changed transportation in America. In Washington, President John Quincy Adams turned the first shovel of dirt beginning work on the Chesapeake and Ohio Canal. In Baltimore, the sole surviving signer of the Declaration of Independence, Charles Carroll, laid the first stone for the Baltimore and Ohio Railroad. Things would never be the same.

You can experience canal life during its heyday in the 1870s at Great Falls, Maryland. From mid-April to mid-October the *Canal Clipper* plies the water.

The ride gets off to a fascinating start as passengers observe the "locking through" manuever. The barge enters a lock in front of the Great Falls Tavern. The lock then is closed and a valve opened, which permits water to raise the level of the barge eight feet in five minutes. When the water is even with the higher level the "upstream" lock is opened and the barge is hitched to the mule team for the rest of the journey.

Watching this complex operation makes one appreciate the accomplishment of the canal builders. This particular canal, which covers the 185 miles from Georgetown to Cumberland, has 74 locks that raise the water level a total of 605 feet.

The barges no longer make the long journey to Cumberland but the hour-and-a-half ride will give you a glimpse of what it must have been like. The costumed crew usually includes the captain, his wife and at least one assistant to walk the mules. In an average day the barge used to cover about 40 miles.

Many women ran the canal boats, although they operated under their deceased husbands' names because they were not permitted to own barges in their own right. Few of the canal families could educate their children beyond third grade. Youngsters would often begin walking the mules in their early teens; they were paid four cents a day.

Water travel was a more sociable way to journey than by wagon. This conviviality can be appreciated even today, as everyone on the barge rides is encouraged to join in the singing of old favorites. Barge crew members lead the singing and play along with fiddle, banjo and harmonica. A very special instrument is used by the captain when he approaches a lock: the great lock horn lets the lock tender know that a barge is waiting.

It used to cost 37½ cents to travel the length of the canal. Now you'll have to pay a bit more for a much shorter trip. Barge rides are given Wednesday through Sunday at 10:30 a.m., 1:00, 3:00 and 5:00 p.m. Tickets go on sale two hours before each ride with the exception of the 10:30 a.m. trip when they go on sale at 9:00. On weekends rides are sold out early. The best times are the afternoon rides during the week. For more information on the *Canal Clipper*, call (301)299-2026.

After you get your ticket you can explore the Great Falls Tavern Museum which now serves as a Visitor's Center. It is open 9:00 a.m. to 4:30 p.m. seven days a week. There are displays and an audio-visual presentation on the history of canals.

There is now a second canal barge, *The Georgetown*. Tickets for this barge trip are available at the Chesapeake and Ohio Canal National Historical Park Visitor's Center at The Foundry in Georgetown, located between 30th and Thomas

Jefferson Streets in Washington, D.C. The hours are the same as the Great Falls barge trips; in fact, everything is the same except the passing scenery. For more details on Georgetown barge trips call (202)472-4376.

During the winter months don't forget another popular canal activity, ice skating. Very cold spells can cause the canal to freeze over and Park Service Rangers will open the canal to ice skating when they feel it is safe. You can check to see if the ice is suitable for skating by calling (301)299-2026. If it isn't, you get no answer.

Directions: For Chesapeake and Ohio National Historical Park at Great Falls take Beltway Exit 40, the Cabin John Parkway, to Great Falls, Maryland. The park is at the end of MacArthur Boulevard in Potomac, Maryland. Signs will direct you.

BATTLE CREEK CYPRESS SWAMP SANCTUARY AND CALVERT MARINE MUSEUM
Neither Fish nor Fowl

The names Battle Creek and Marine Museum suggest a military or historical foray but actually these two offbeat destinations in Calvert County, Maryland, concern themselves with the ecology and natural history of southern Maryland.

Even many long-time explorers of the Maryland countryside are not aware that the northernmost stands of bald cypress in North America are right here in Calvert County. These 50- to 125-foot giants from an earlier age amaze first-time visitors. The swampy terrain hasn't changed much from the time 70,000 to 120,000 years ago when the bald cypress looked down not on tourists but on prehistoric mammoths and crocodiles. Today the animals you may spot are considerably less exotic but still interesting to urban adventurers—whitetailed deer, muskrats, oppossums, frogs and turtles.

A quarter-mile platform trail takes you through the swamp into close proximity with the trees. You can get a good look at the cypress "knees". These ungainly rootlike protuberances are believed to stabilize the cypress tree in the mud or, alternatively, they may furnish oxygen to the tree.

The Nature Center has displays about the mammals, birds and reptiles that make their home here, including some live specimens. There are also guided walks, lectures, nature films, field trips and craft demonstrations. For more information call (301)535-5327.

The Battle Creek Cypress Swamp Sanctuary is open April through September on Tuesday through Saturday from 10:00 a.m. to 5:00 p.m. and on Sunday from 1:00 to 5:00 p.m. From October through March the area closes at 4:30 p.m. It is closed on Mondays and on Thanksgiving, Christmas and New Year's Day.

Farther down the road, in fact as far down as you can go on this peninsula, is the Calvert Marine Museum on Solomons Island. This quaint fishing town is built around one of the world's deepest natural harbors. The museum aims to show visitors the local maritime history, the paleontology of Calvert Cliffs, and the biology of the Patuxent River and Chesapeake Bay.

An actual shipbuilder's lean-to gives you an idea of the many and varied tools used when three shipyards flourished here more than 50 years ago. In the Life of the Watermen Hall you will also see the tools of the oyster dredging trade.

Frequent demonstrations of ship carving take place in the Woodcarving and Model Shop. After viewing the miniature wooden masterpieces you can move into Maritime Hall where you will see a much larger carved specimen, a log canoe once commonly seen on bay waters.

In the Paleontology Room fossils from Calvert Cliffs are displayed. The Miocene fossils date back 12 to 15 million years. On display is a jaw from a prehistoric crocodile that may once have swum beneath the forebears of the giant cypress that you can see today at Battle Creek Cypress Swamp.

The Calvert Marine Museum is an indoor-outdoor complex and on the grounds you will see the small craft shed, the 1883 Drum Point Lighthouse and an old oyster bugeye, the *Wm. E. Tennison*, built in 1899. You can take an hour's cruise on this, the oldest certified passenger-carrying vessel on the Chesapeake Bay. It is an excellent way to explore Solomons Harbor and is sure to be a hit with the kids. For more information call (301)326-3719.

The Calvert Marine Museum is open Monday through Saturday from 10:00 a.m. to 5:00 p.m. and on Sundays from 1:00 to 5:00 p.m.

If any time remains you may want to explore several nearby Calvert County attractions such as the Drum Point Lighthouse, one of the three remaining screwpile cottage-style lighthouses from the 45 that once protected Bay waters, or the Cove Point Lighthouse, one of the last of the tower lighthouses. Visitors are not allowed to climb the tower but you can get an excellent view from here of Calvert Cliffs. Access to Calvert Cliffs is at Calvert Cliffs State Park. A picnic and playground area is available as are trails to the cliff area, first described by Captain John Smith in 1608. If you explore this area in mid-summer be sure to be well covered because ticks abound. Although digging at the cliffs is not allowed you can scavenge for shells or fossils.

One last stop you may want to make is the Calvert Cliffs Nuclear Power Plant Museum. A converted tobacco barn, it has dioramas and automated exhibits about the cliffs. You can also observe the nuclear power plant from an overlook; taped messages explain the installation and operation of this facility. The museum is open at no charge daily from 9:00 a.m. to 5:00 p.m. except Christmas.

Directions: Take Maryland Beltway Exit 11, Route 4, south into Calvert County. Your first stop off what becomes Route 2/4 is just south of Prince Frederick. You'll turn right onto Sixes Road. There will be a sign indicating a left turn on Gray's Road for Battle Creek Cypress Swamp Sanctuary. Back on Route 2/4 you continue all the way down to Solomons and make a left turn before the Solomons Bridge. The Calvert Marine Museum is 200 yards from the bridge on the left.

To reach the museum by boat you need to enter the mouth of the Patuxent River from the Chesapeake Bay. Then stay to the right and enter Solomons Harbor. The museum is on the west shore of Back Creek.

If your next stop is Cove Point Lighthouse go back up Route 2/4 and make a right on Route 497. Access to Calvert Cliffs and the power plant is directly off Route 2/4.

BURKE LAKE
A New England Lake in a Southern State

O ne of the most enjoyable aspects of one-day excursions in the Washington area is their great diversity. If you like the Adirondacks of upstate New York you can find a close facsimile at Burke Lake, Virginia. Only a ten-minute drive from the Beltway, Burke Lake transports you in spirit hundreds of miles north. Along the lake's irregular shoreline, Fairfax County Park Department has provided woodland trails for hiking, cycling and bird watching.

Those who want to get out on the 218-acre lake can rent a boat at Burke Lake Marina or launch their own for a nominal fee. Because the boats can't be reserved in advance, on weekends they are rarely available after 7:00 a.m. without a long wait. The marina opens at 6:00 a.m. Boats are available on weekdays from 6:30 a.m. If you bring your own, bring canoe or kayak only; gasoline motors and sailboats are not allowed. For additional information, call (703)323-6600.

If you bring children, you are sure to need money for the miniature train and the carousel. Both operate on summer weekdays from noon to 5:30 p.m. and on weekends year-round from 11:00 a.m. to 7:00 p.m. The train winds through the forest and a small tunnel, puffing smoke and whistling smartly. You can count on the kids to locate the carousel a short way from the Burke Lake Station.

Not all the joys are for children. There's an 18-hole golf course and a driving range, rustic picnic sites and a 163-site campground.

Directions: Take Beltway Exit 5, follow Braddock Road west and turn left on Burke Lake Road, Route 645. Proceed 5 miles to the left on Ox Road, Route 123, to park entrance on left.

CASTLE HILL AND MOORMONT ORCHARD
Treat Yourself Royally

M any gardens are modeled after the fabulous gardens on the grand estates of France and Italy, but Castle Hill's gardens are believed to have been planted with actual cuttings from the Tuileries, obtained by Judith Walker Rives when her husband, William Cabell Rives, was ambassador to France. Most of the major sections of the garden were planned by Mrs. Rives, the granddaughter of the builder of Castle Hill. The slipper-shaped garden with its terraces and fragrant old trees attracts many birds and is a delightful pastoral setting.

The original section of Castle Hill was built in 1765 by one of Thomas Jefferson's four legal guardians, Dr. Thomas Walker. In 1781, Colonel Banestre Tarleton, on his way to arrest Jefferson at Monticello, stopped at Castle Hill to arrest Dr. Walker. Tradition holds that Walker lavishly entertained the British enemies, giving Thomas Jefferson enough time to make his escape.

A section of the house was added in 1824 by the Riveses, so you will see both the early colonial clapboard section and the more elaborate Federal section. On the grounds in addition to the garden there are outbuildings associated with the 18-century plantation. Castle Hill is open March through November from 10:00 a.m. until 5:00 p.m. Admission is charged.

While in the area you might want to stop at Moormont Orchard where you can pick and picnic. From late June until mid-September you can pick your own peaches. Eleven varieties of peaches are grown at Moormont, as well as Damson plums, table grapes, and summer and autumn apples. The view from the top of Clark Mountain, elevation 1,100 feet, provides a scenic vista of eight counties. In April when the peach trees bloom it is a joyful sight for winter-weary eyes.

Directions: Take Beltway Exit 8, Route 50, to Route 29-211 south past Warrenton to Culpeper. Take Route 15 through Orange to Gordonsville. From there, take Route 231 south for eight miles to Castle Hill on the right.

For Moormont Orchard return via Route 321 from Castle Hill to Orange. At Orange take Route 615 east for approximately five miles. Then turn right on Route 627 and go 2 miles. Next make a left on Route 697 and go to the top of Clark Mountain for the orchards. To return to Washington take Route 615 into Culpeper and pick up Route 29-211 which will bring you back to the Washington area.

CEDARVILLE NATURAL RESOURCES MANAGEMENT AREA
On the Trail of the Lonesome Hiker

Hikers, fishermen and naturalists love the Maryland state park at the Cedarville Natural Resources Management Area. There are 14 miles of well-marked foot trails, a small fishing pond, charcoal kilns where briquettes once were made, and a variety of interpretive programs. Tame deer that are sometimes penned near the playfields will come to the fence to be petted or fed. There are more than 50 picnic tables as well as grills for use at no charge. Of particular interest is the mile-long self-guided nature trail.

Cedarville has a long history. It is said that an Indian burial ground is hidden in the forest because this was where, according to legend, the Piscataway Indians made their winter camp. Some 250 years ago the Zekiah Swamp overflowed. The land still remains wet and boggy despite efforts to reclaim it. John Wilkes Booth fled through this forest after assassinating President Lincoln and he stopped at Dr. Mudd's farm.

Dr. Samuel Mudd's farm house opened in 1983 as an historical site. Guides costumed in the fashion of the 1860s tell visitors about John Wilkes Booth's hurried stop here to have his broken leg set by Dr. Mudd, a medical service for which Dr. Mudd was sentenced to life imprisonment. After four years President Andrew Johnson pardoned Dr. Mudd and he returned home to resume his medical practice. The house is open on weekends from 12:00 to 4:00 p.m., except during the winter months. Admission is charged. The house is located outside Waldorf. From Route 5, turn left on Route 382, Mattawoman-Beantown Road. Markers direct visitors to the house. (For additional information on this pivotal time in American history see the description of the Mary Surratt House.)

Cedarville offers a variety of summer programs and social events, such as the Piscataway Indian Festival.

From the park you can easily drive to the Amish market at Charlotte Hall. At this flea market the determined shopper can find anything from plants, used furniture and old records to antiques, jewelry, clothes and bedding. Neighborhood farmers also sell their produce, home baked bread, preserves and other local favorites. The Farmer's Market at

Charlotte Hall is held every Wednesday and Saturday from 7:00 a.m. to 5:00 p.m.

Directions: From the Washington Beltway take Maryland Exit 7A South on Route 5, Branch Avenue, approximately 15 miles until you see the sign directing you to Cedarville Natural Resources Management Area. Turn left onto Cedarville Road. The Park entrance is about four miles down on the right.

CHESAPEAKE BAY MARITIME MUSEUM
History on the Shore

If the word "museum" conjures up an image of a dark cluttered building for you, you must see the Chesapeake Bay Maritime Museum at St. Michael's, Maryland. The museum has indoor and outdoor exhibits, including boats both in and out of the water. Best seen at a leisurely pace, the museum has expanded from its original building which opened in 1965 to a 16-acre complex. Its growth is but one measure of the fine job it does in conveying the Bay's history and heritage.

Boats to be seen at the museum include a skipjack, a restored log-bottom bugeye, a racing log canoe and other small craft. The skipjack, the *Rosie Parks*, ended her Chesapeake Bay oyster-dredging career in 1974. The Bay tradition of boat building, commercial fishing, yachting, waterfowl hunting and navigation are all part of the story told here.

You also can see the Hooper Strait Lighthouse, an example of the Bay's screw-pile lighthouses that stood on steel piles shaped like giant screws in order to anchor them firmly into the muddy Bay bottom.

The Waterfowl Building, which houses the museum's exhibit of waterfowl hunting on the Chesapeake Bay, tells the story of the Atlantic Flyway. You can learn about the birds that spend the winter on this Maryland peninsula, the decoy makers, and the spectacular if infamous days of market hunting and the outlaw gunner. There are also exhibits on the old-time guns and today's hunter.

Don't miss the Eagle house where you see boating implements and models including scale replicas of the steamboats that used to travel the Bay.

The museum is open daily from 10:00 a.m. to 4:00 p.m. during winter. It stays open an hour longer during the summer. In January, February and March it is open only on weekends. The museum is closed on Christmas and New Year's Day. An admission is charged.

Directions: Take Beltway Exit 19, Route 50, to Easton, Maryland. From there take Route 33 to St. Michael's. In St. Michael's turn right on Mill Street for the museum located at the end of the street at Navy Point.

COLLEGE PARK AIRPORT MUSEUM
Air Fare

The birthplace of aviation in this country, as we all know, is Kitty Hawk, North Carolina. But few know that College Park Airport is viewed as "the cradle of American aviation." The story behind this title can be explored at the College Park Airport Museum.

In 1908, attempting to sell their idea for a flying machine to the Army, the Wright brothers demonstrated their aircraft at Fort Myer, Virginia. The trials showed that the Wright plane met Army standards. The Army wanted a flying machine that could carry two people aloft for at least an hour, travel at least 40 miles an hour and land undamaged. On August 2, 1909 the Army Signal Corps accepted the Wright plane as Signal Corps Airplane No. 1.

The next step was to train two military officers to fly the plane. An aerial balloon was sent aloft to find a location for the flying school. A field near the Maryland Agricultural College in College Park was chosen and became College Park Airport. Previously, a crash at Fort Myer had resulted in the first air casualty and an injury to Orville Wright, so only Wilbur came to College Park in October 1909 to train the officers.

From the beginning, College Park was the scene of a succession of aviation firsts, dramatic events captured in photographs displayed at the College Park Airport Museum. At College Park on October 26, 1909, Lt. Humphreys became the first U.S. military officer to fly. The next day a friend of Katherine Wright's went up with Wilbur to become the first woman passenger.

In November of 1909, the first U.S. Naval Officer to fly in a U.S.-owned plane, Lt. George C. Sweet, took off from College Park. Later that month, the plane was severely damaged. After the mishap, it was crated and sent to Fort Sam Houston in Texas, ending, for a time, Army use of the College Park field. But civilian use kept the airport in service. College Park Airport is considered the world's oldest continually operated airport.

In 1910, Rexford Smith worked here, perfecting a biplane he had designed. He was joined the following year by the National Aviation Company which provided instruction on Wright, Curtiss and Bleriot airplanes. The government appropriated money for aviation in 1911 and work began again at the new Signal Corps aviation school at College Park in June that year.

This led to another flurry of firsts. The first bomb-dropping device was tested by Riley Scott, its inventor, who went on to win acclaim at the Paris Exposition of 1912. There was an amusing footnote to the first "long cross-country flight" on August 21, 1911. Returning after their flight from College Park to Frederick, Maryland, the pilots became "disoriented" or, more accurately, lost. They had to land to ask directions to College Park. When the plane stalled as they tried to take off again, the craft was damaged and the chagrined pilots ended up taking the train home.

Despite the successful first firing of an airplane-mounted machine gun in June of 1912, the War Department insisted that the airplane would be useful to the military only for reconnaissance missions. Later in 1912, the College Park Signal Corps operation ended although civilian operations continued.

The government resumed activities there in 1918, when the Post Office began the first regularly scheduled air mail service in the United States. The museum displays one of the early flying suits and goggles used on these flights as well as a display of early air mail stamps.

During the years 1927 through 1935 the U.S. Bureau of Standards used College Park Airport as the site of their experiments with "blind" or instrument landing systems. On September 5, 1931, the first blind landing in the history of aviation was made at College Park.

In 1973, the Maryland National Capital Park and Planning Commission purchased College Park Airport. It has been preserved both as an historic landmark and as an operating airfield. The museum is open Friday, Saturday and Sunday from noon until 4:00 p.m. Nearby the museum a restaurant, the 9th Aero Squadron, is slated to open in 1984. It will be housed in a reproduced French farmhouse, continuing the aviation theme with memorabilia of the World War I era.

Directions: The College Park Airport Museum is inside the Beltway, just off Kenilworth Avenue at Beltway Exit 23. Turn left onto Calvert Road and proceed to the street immediately before the railroad track. As the sign indicates, the museum is on the right on Captain Frank Scott Drive.

FLYING CIRCUS AERODROME
The Red Baron Flies Again

Barnstorming was once a popular source of thrills and adventure, and the Flying Circus Aerodrome near Warrenton, Virginia, is one of America's last vestiges of that form of entertainment. You will see vintage biplanes, 40-year-old Stearmans flying aerial formations, dogfights and the chilling spectacle of a wing walker standing atop a plane as it loops and rolls through the sky. Parachute stunts, hot air balloons, clowns and comic passes lighten the tension of the more dramatic moments.

The Flying Circus Aerodrome is run by a group of aviation enthusiasts: airline pilots, military personnel and hobbyists. There is a small museum of aviation artifacts in a wooden hangar reminiscent of the 1920s. You can purchase models of your favorite aircraft or take a ride in one of the old planes.

The Flying Circus Aerodrome is open every Sunday from May through October and showtime is at 2:30 p.m. Admission is charged.

During the season there are special events such as the annual Balloon Festival in mid-August, the model airplane competition and antique car meets. For information about the special events call (703)439-8661. There are picnic facilities and a concession for cold drinks and snacks.

Directions: The Flying Circus Aerodrome is a 45-minute drive from the Beltway. Take Virginia Exit 4 toward Richmond and Fredericksburg. The Aerodrome is located 22 miles north of Fredericksburg just off Route 17 in Bealeton.

You can also take Route 66 and 29 from Washington to Warrenton, Virginia, then go south on Route 17 to Bealeton.

FRANCISCAN MONASTERY
A One-Stop Trip to the Holy Land

If you can't get to Rome and would like to come close to experiencing one of the most interesting tours available in that city, try the Franciscan Monastery in northeast Washington. This unusual mission has re-created the sub-terranean passages known as the catacombs of Rome. It was in the narrow underground walkways of the catacombs of Rome that Christians gathered for prayer and funeral rites during the period of religious persecution. In Rome, the 600 to 900 miles of catacombs interweave beneath the city and the surrounding countryside. The walls of the catacombs are niched and served as graves for the Christian martyrs. In Washington, the catacombs contain chapels with murals and religious sculpture. Before leaving the catacombs you will see the Grotto of Bethlehem, a copy of the Grotto of the Nativity in Bethlehem and Mary's home at Nazareth.

The monastery itself is also of considerable interest. Its exterior resembles the early Franciscan missions in California. It was built in 1898 and redecorated in 1949. Within the monastery are reproductions of a number of the sacred shrines in the Holy Land, such as the Holy Sepulchre and Calvary.

Surrounding the monastery are rose gardens that are at their best in late May and June. The grounds also contain an accurate copy of the Grotto of Lourdes and the Grotto of Gethsemane in Jerusalem, the site of Jesus's betrayal. Holy Week takes on special meaning here.

The Franciscan Monastery is open daily to visitors for guided tours from 8:30 a.m. to 4:00 p.m. Monday through Saturday and from 1:00 p.m. to 4:30 p.m. on Sunday. Admission is free but donations are gratefully accepted. Sunday masses are celebrated at 7:00, 8:30 and 10:30 a.m. and noon and 4:30 p.m.; Saturday evening at 5:00 p.m.

Directions: The Franciscan Monastery is inside the Beltway at 1400 Quincy Street in northeast Washington.

GLEN ECHO PARK AND CLARA BARTON HOUSE
A Modern Chautauqua

To those who remember Glen Echo's days of garish glory, the brilliantly lit midway and the plummeting roller coasters, the old amusement park looks as exciting today as a faded scrapbook. But there is a cultural revival taking place here.

In the 1890s, an enthusiasm for the concept of democratic education swept the country. Called the Chautauqua Movement, this program sought to combine religious and educational instruction for the masses. Glen Echo was conceived as a part of that movement. With Victorian-style stone castles overlooking the Potomac, it was to be America's greatest center of general culture. An unfortunate malarial fever epidemic doomed the project. The only thing that remains is the old Chautauqua Tower where bells once summoned the students to classes.

The spirit of Chautauqua lives on, however, and the desire to put culture and education within the reach of everyone. In the derelict buildings the National Park Service offers workshops and classes for children and adults in ceramics, enameling, spinning and weaving, photography, drawing, painting, batik, leathercraft, picture framing, sculpture, silkscreen, drama, dance, music, yoga, natural foods, ecology and many other fields.

Since 1971, more than 140 artists, craftsmen and instructors have worked, taught and demonstrated their media at Glen Echo. The emphasis is on participation by the visitors. Informal workshops are also popular, such as the free children's "paint-in" every Sunday, May 15 through September 25 from 1:00 to 5:00 p.m. at the Cuddle Up Pavilion. Special festivals are held during the summer months; you can call (301)492-6282 for additional information.

The only structure remaining from the heydays of the amusement park, which lasted from 1911 until 1968, is the carousel. This hand-carved merry-go-round was constructed in 1922. Folk art specialists say it was created by the company responsible for the finest carousels in America. It still operates in summer months and is as glorious as ever to ride.

Another park feature designed especially for children is Adventure Theatre located in the old Penny Arcade. Its shows range from fairy tales to folk legends and old ballads. Also a number of marionette companies perform in the park during the summer.

The Glen Echo parking lot off Oxford Street also serves the Clara Barton House. Miss Barton was actively involved with the Glen Echo Chautauqua project. She is mainly remembered for her relief work during the Civil War, for which she was called the "Angel of the Battlefield." She also founded the American Red Cross; her home served as headquarters from 1897 until 1904.

Her home itself has an interesting history. In 1889, as part of its aid to the victims of the Johnstown flood, the Red Cross erected a hotel for the homeless. When Clara Barton and the volunteer relief workers had finished their work she had the hotel taken down and shipped to Washington. It was reconstructed in Glen Echo, Maryland, as her house and a Red Cross base.

When you visit you will see two furnished Red Cross offices complete with roll-top desks, 1890s typewriters and Red Cross ledgers. The house has 72 concealed closets to store equipment, including large wheelchairs. Visitors are always intrigued by the suspended room, a Victorian eccentricity, that appears to hang at the top of the house overlooking the floors below.

The Clara Barton House offers tours at no charge seven days a week from 10:00 a.m. to 5:00 p.m. Throughout the year there are numerous special programs; many are planned for Sunday afternoons. Be sure to see the 20-minute movie about Clara Barton's life before you tour the house.

Directions: Take Beltway Exit 40, the Cabin John Parkway, to Glen Echo. Exit at MacArthur Avenue and turn left. Proceed on MacArthur Avenue to the signs indicating Glen Echo and the Clara Barton House on your right. While you are on the Cabin John Parkway you will pass the parking lot for Lock 7 of the C&O Canal. This is an excellent place for a hike in nice weather.

HERSHEY
How Sweet It Is

When you arrive in Hershey, Pennsylvania, a sign welcomes you with the message "Come for the Chocolate—Stay for the Fun." Well-marked signs guide you throughout "Chocolate Town, U.S.A.," to a wide variety of attractions. The sign at the junction of Chocolate Avenue and Cocoa Street certainly is worth a snapshot. This spot is called the "Chocolate Crossroads of the World." Other Disneyesque touches include the streetlights shaped like candy kisses, some chocolate and some foilwrapped.

For a one-day outing, it might be best to head directly for the main parking lot at Hersheypark. There is no charge and free trams and shuttle buses will take you everywhere. If you start around 7:00 a.m., you should be able to arrive in Hershey about 9:00 or 9:30 a.m., just in time to enjoy a free ride through Chocolate World. You'll learn about chocolate from the growth of cocoa on tropical plantations to its processing at the Hershey plant.

Right in front of Chocolate World you catch a free bus up to Hershey Gardens. Laid out on 23 acres of grounds below Hotel Hershey, the gardens were begun in 1936 when Milton Hershey, founder of the company, was asked to contribute one million dollars to establish a National Rosarium in Washington. He decided instead to invest in a garden in his own community. His instructions were to establish "a very nice garden of roses."

The garden now includes 16 sections including the Italian, English Formal, Japanese, Colonial and Herb Gardens. Roses, however, are still the main attraction: the garden contains more than 30,000 bushes. In the spring there is a profusion of tulips, daffodils, azaleas and rhododendron. The gardens close in the fall with a 4,000-plant chrysanthemum display.

It is worth your time to stroll around the formal gardens of the Hotel Hershey. Its imposing and expensive restaurant overlooks the gardens but you can enjoy them even if you are not a guest at the hotel.

Another worthwhile attraction is the Hershey Museum of American Life with exhibits covering man's earliest explorations on this continent. A collection of antique weapons reveals the skillful dexterity of early inhabitants. Moving up through the Woodland Period of prehistory to the Indians of colonial time, displays highlight the dress and artifacts of Indians of the Eastern woodlands, Northwest coast, Great Plains, Southwest, Pacific Plateau, North Pacific coast and the Arctic.

Many household items, including dishes, furnishings, glassware and ornaments reflect the changing pattern of American life. Military displays cover early encounters, including the War of 1812, the war against Mexico in 1846 to 1848, the Spanish–American War and World War I.

The Hershey Museum of American Life is open 10:00 a.m. to 5:00 p.m.; hours are extended to 6:00 p.m. during the summer months. An admission is charged.

Then, of course, there is Hersheypark, the oldest of the theme parks, dating from 1906. It was totally redeveloped in 1971 and offers a wide selection of rides, comparable to any theme park in the northeast as well as a new feature called ZooAmerica.

Directions: Take Beltway Exit 27, I-95, to the Baltimore Beltway, I-695. Take Route 83 north to Harrisburg and then follow Route 322 east to Hershey.

KENILWORTH AQUATIC GARDENS
Lotus Land

A spot all too often missed in Washington is the Kenilworth Aquatic Gardens. Here the National Park Service maintains 11 acres of ponds planted with colorful waterlilies and lotuses. It is delightful to weave in and out on the narrow footpaths among the ponds containing more than 100,000 flowering water plants. The large lily pads, some more than six feet in diameter, look deceptively like giant stepping stones extending across the artificial ponds. If you walk quietly you can find frogs sunning themselves on the lily pads, turtles, and an occasional harmless water snake that will thrill the children. Aquatic plants include water hyacinth, water poppy, rose mallow, water primrose, wild iris, bamboo, elephant ears, cattails, umbrella ears, lilies and lotus.

The plants are most beautiful in the morning languorously opening in the early sun and their heady fragrance permeating the air. Approximately 70 varieties of day-blooming lilies begin their peak season in mid-June. The hundreds of lotuses are at their best in late July and early August and unbelievably impressive. Each plant grows as tall as a person and has blooms the size of basketballs.

The Kenilworth Aquatic Gardens are open at no charge from 7:30 a.m. to 6:00 p.m. but keep in mind that many of the lilies close during the heat of the day. If you visit in the late afternoon, you may catch some of the night blooming tropical lilies. Whenever you visit, but especially at dusk, be sure to apply an insect repellant as water does attract mosquitoes.

Directions: Kenilworth Aquatic Gardens is located inside the Beltway in northeast Washington. Take Kenilworth Avenue, southbound, to Quarles Street. Bear right and cross the Eastern Avenue Overpass, then turn left onto Douglas Street and turn right for the Gardens.

MASON NECK NATIONAL WILDLIFE REFUGE AND GUNSTON HALL
Home for the Eagle, Home for the Man

Eighteen miles from Washington, D.C., in Virginia is the first national wildlife refuge established specifically for the protection of our national bird, the bald eagle. This 1,920-acre refuge serves not only as a resting place for the bald eagle but as a home to a wide variety of wildlife. It is a blend of terrain including uplands forest, wooded swamps and riverfront marshland.

The upland forest area is radiant in the fall with its yellow, orange and red foliage. Since Mason Neck is located on the Atlantic Flyway, migratory birds such as black ducks, mallards, teal, Canadian geese and whistling swans come here in the fall by the thousands.

The Great Marsh, a 285-acre portion of the sanctuary, is an appealing place for the migrating birds to rest and serves in the summer as a home for snowy egrets, great blue herons and gulls, just a few of the more than 226 species of birds spotted in the refuge.

The refuge is a sanctuary in the best sense of the word; it is designed for the birds and other wildlife rather than for people. Although there are trails of various lengths through certain sections of the refuge, the major part consists of untamed dense forest and inaccessible swamp and marshland that offer peace and protection to nesting birds. The refuge is open free of charge during daylight hours from April 1 through November 30.

On one trip you can combine the natural beauty of the refuge with the architectural beauty of Gunston Hall. This house, located on a 5,000-acre plantation, was built for one of Virginia's Founding Fathers, George Mason. He is responsible for the outstanding boxwood gardens which, along with the twin summer houses, overlook the Potomac and Colonel Mason's Deer Park. The Chippendale dining room and the Palladian drawing room with its fine carved woodwork are just two of the rooms that give Gunston Hall the reputation of having had one of the most impressive interiors of any building in the Colonial period. Gunston Hall is open daily except Christmas from 9:30 a.m. to 5:00 p.m. Admission is charged.

Directions: From the Beltway take Virginia Exit 1, U.S. 1 south, to Gunston Hall and to State Road 242 which will take you directly into Mason Neck.

NORTHERN NECK
Explore George's Neck of the Woods

Virginia's Northern Neck abounds with natural charm. This narrow peninsula lies between the Potomac and Rappahannock Rivers. At almost every turn of the road, you come upon an inlet, creek or river.

At the upper end of the Neck you can visit the George Washington Birthplace National Monument, a place of bucolic tranquility. The view from the Visitor's Center of the quiet waters of Pope's Creek is worth the drive, and the meandering trail up to the plantation house offers numerous scenic vistas as does the second walking trail in this park.

The 14-minute film "A Childhood Place," which, like the colonial living farm itself, re-creates life at Pope's Creek, also emphasizes the natural beauty to be found on the Northern Neck. Changing seasons, the cycle of the crops and the transitory pleasure of migratory birds are all beautifully portrayed. Visitors sense that so much of what they see around them now was here when George Washington was a boy at Pope's Creek Plantation. Although he was born here, George

Washington's family moved to what later became known as Mount Vernon when he was 3½ years old. As an adolescent, George spent summers here with his half-brother, Augustine, after the death of their father.

The location of the original house is carefully marked and a Memorial House stands nearby. This eight-room house is furnished with period pieces and gives visitors a glimpse of the life-style enjoyed by the Washington family. So also do the artifacts recovered during the archeological excavations of the site and now on display at the Visitor's Center.

You will also see a decorated and fully operational kitchen house, weaving room and farm workshop. The natural features include a colonial herb and flower garden as well as the farm area. During the summer months there are special weekend demonstrations of crafts and farm related work. To obtain a schedule of summer activities call (804)224-0196 or write Superintendent, George Washington Birthplace National Monument, Washington's Birthplace, Virginia 22575.

There is a picnic area overlooking the water. This park is also completely accessible to disabled visitors. Transportation is available from the Visitor's Center to the historic area for those who can't walk. The George Washington Birthplace National Monument is open daily, except Christmas and New Year's Day, from 9:00 a.m. to 5:00 p.m.

You can also picnic at the nearby Westmoreland State Park where there is both an Olympic-size swimming pool and a beach on the Potomac River. Here too, you will be able to glimpse the river as you explore the scenic woodland hiking trails.

Just past this state park and still not more than 15 minutes from the Washington plantation is the Lee family home— Stratford Hall. It is amazing to find the ancestral homes of these two important American families practically side-by-side. The house on this 1,600-acre plantation incorporates the Italian style of placing the major living areas on the second floor, rather than the first-floor arrangement common to most plantation homes. There is also a garden, stable and working gristmill. Stratford Hall is open daily, except Christmas, from 9:00 a.m. to 4:30 p.m. For more details see Historic Plantations excursion. You can tour both of these historic plantations on a one-day foray and still have time for a swim.

Directions: Take Maryland Beltway Exit 7, Route 5, south to Route 301 and continue south to Route 3. All of these attractions are located off Route 3. George Washington's Birthplace National Monument is on Route 204 off Route 3; Stratford Hall is off Route 214. Westmoreland State Park is directly off Route 3.

OCEAN CITY LIFE SAVING STATION MUSEUM
Bathing Suits and Rescue Pursuits

Nostalgia buffs are really in for a treat when they visit the Ocean City Life Saving Station Museum, located at the very end of the Boardwalk on the inlet at Ocean City, Maryland. Whether you are a first time visitor to this popular resort or a regular you will enjoy this Ocean City retrospective.

The first Ocean City Life Saving Station opened on December 25, 1878. It was part of the network of stations positioned along America's 10,000-mile coastline. The station now serving as a museum was built in 1891 when a larger, more modern station was required.

The first room of the museum presents an encapsulated look at the Life Saving Service from its inception in 1848 until 1915 when it merged with the Revenue Cutter Service to form the U.S. Coast Guard. In the station's boat room, where equipment to effect rescues was kept while the station was operational, you can still see the apparatus used in early sea rescues. The largest piece is the surf rescue boat, a carefully restored 26-foot, double-ended, self-bailing vessel. This surfboat, one of the last models of its kind, was originally used at Caffey's Inlet in North Carolina.

A smaller metal boat is more unusual. This surfcar, or lifecar, measured 11 feet by 4 feet and weighed 225 pounds. It was developed to aid rescuers in getting more passengers off distressed vessels. The breeches buoy could handle only a single person, while the watertight surfcar held two to four. The surfcar was crucial to the saving of lives on the immigrant-laden ships that were frequently beached along the Atlantic Coast.

These are only some of the larger pieces in the collection, believed to be the largest of its kind in the country. In addition to seeing the memorabilia, you can watch a short movie showing the rescue of the *Olaf Bergh*. In 1946 this Norwegian freighter mistook the Fenwick Light for the entrance to the Delaware Bay and ran aground at 94th Street in Ocean City. She was hugging the shore in fear of German submarines. One photograph shows the Norwegian consul watching the removal of the crew by breeches buoy.

The adjoining room contains the museum's collection of articles reclaimed by divers from shipwrecks, as well as a shell collection and knot board. Those familiar with Ocean City will be interested in comparing the large aerial photograph of the beach resort taken in the mid-1940s with the 1981 picture. There is also an enlargement of a picture taken after the severe March storm of 1962.

It is when visitors go upstairs that the museum elicits their most heartfelt response because here they meet Laughing Sal. Remember the over-size lady who stood, bowing, waving her arms and laughing uproariously as you entered the Jester's Funhouse on the Boardwalk? That was Laughing Sal. She was memorialized by John Barth in his *Lost in the Funhouse* stories when he wrote, "You couldn't hear it without laughing yourself." You can hear her laugh bellow out by just pushing a button. In fact, your visit to the museum is apt to be punctuated by that loud mirth as visitor after visitor goes by and pushes the button.

You may well have a laugh of your own as you peruse the collection of old-fashioned bathing suits that go back to the turn-of-the-century. In those days visits to the beach were a rarity so people rented bathing suits. Examples of these dapper rentals can be seen in the exhibit, as can a daring number from the early 1900s made of 10 yards of heavy wool. You'll see the progression from bloomers to bikinis.

The other major exhibit on the second floor is the building model display of eight well-known Boardwalk hotels. These buildings were painstakingly re-created and are exact right down to corner door hinges and miniature tourists along the Boardwalk.

The Ocean City Life Saving Station Museum is open during June, July, August and September from 11:00 a.m. to 10:00 p.m. daily. During the months of May and October it is open Thursday through Saturday from 10:00 a.m. to 4:00 p.m. During the rest of the year it is open on weekends from noon to 4:00 p.m. A nominal admission is charged.

Directions: Take Beltway Exit 19, Route 50, to Ocean City. The museum is located at the south end of the Boardwalk.

OXON HILL FARM
Raising Cane

Both urban and suburban children can have a lark and a learning experience on a trip to Oxon Hill Farm. The National Park Service runs this large farm as it would have been in the late 19th century. Children can often pet the relatively tame cows, sheep, goats and donkeys that graze in a large fenced pasture. Other livestock includes horses, pigs, ducks, chickens, turkeys and rabbits.

Learning about farm life includes becoming familiar with the well-marked rows of vegetables—lettuce, tomatoes, squash, onions, green beans, corn, peas and beets. The equipment used for farming is also accessible. Youngsters may climb on the farm wagons and tractors and learn about such machinery as the hand-operated corn shredder, the cultivators and a windmill pump.

At various times during the day men wearing bib overalls and women in long cotton work dresses can be observed feeding the animals, milking the cows, and planting, tending and harvesting the produce. Events at the farm center around the season. During the winter farm tools are repaired and the fields are made ready for spring when the crops are sown. In May the sheep are relieved of their heavy winter coats. Summer means vegetables can be picked from the kitchen garden and by mid-summer grain can be harvested with the old-fashioned binder and threshing machine. By late summer the farmer is ready to cut winter fodder for the animals. In the fall the sorghum cane is cut. At the farm's sorghum mill the cane is stripped and mashed, and the run-off is boiled until it forms a sweet syrup.

On weekend afternoons there are usually special demonstrations, plus horse and wagon rides and square dancing. To find out about special events, call (301)839-1177 or 839-1176. The Oxon Hill Farm is open at no charge from 8:30 a.m. to 5:00 p.m. daily.

Directions: Take Maryland Beltway Exit 3, Indian Head Highway south, then turn right at the first light. Quickly take another right at the next light onto a road which will take you over the Beltway and into the parking lot for Oxon Hill Farm.

PISCATAWAY PARK AND THE NATIONAL COLONIAL FARM
The 18th Century is That-Away at Piscataway

If you want to get an excellent perspective on early America visit Piscataway Park in Accokeek, Maryland. This park encompasses the site of five known prehistoric groups, an important town of the Piscataway Indian empire, and shares a parking area today with a re-created colonial farm.

The Accokeek Creek prehistoric site is a registered National Historic Landmark. It is one of the oldest sites to be so recognized. The first group to camp here were the Marcey Creek People during the Archaic Period. Later artifacts indicate the Pope's Creek People were here between 100 B.C. and 300 A.D. The Middle Woodland Period of prehistory saw two groups inhabiting this site—the Accokeek Creek People and the Mockley People.

The last group were the Potomac Creek People, who evolved into the Piscataway Tribe. During the Indian epoch in 1608, Captain John Smith stopped at the Piscataway town he called Moyaone. This was one of the major towns of the Piscataway empire and had been standing on this location over 300 years prior to Smith's arrival.

Nearby, on the banks of the Potomac River, lies The National Colonial Farm, a re-created 18th-century middle class plantation. Its costumed staff members use old-fashioned implements and methods to tend the crops, livestock and orchard that would have been typical of a Maryland farm during the 1700s.

One popular feature of the farm is the Rosamonde Bierne Memorial Herb Garden. Under the careful supervision of the knowledgeable staff who have planted and used the more than 50 herbs growing here, you are invited to smell, touch and sometimes taste the various specimens. In colonial times herbs were used in cooking, medicine and cosmetics. The farm's Herb Shop sells a number of herbal products.

Farm buildings include an outkitchen, kept separate from the main house to reduce the fire hazard, and an authentic tobacco barn of the late 1700s brought here from the Annapolis area.

Piscataway Park also has a nature trail along the Potomac shore. Bring your camera to capture the marvelous sight of Mount Vernon on the opposite bank of the river and binoculars to catch the birds.

Another part of the park is Hard Bargain Farm, an environmental study area used primarily for schools and other groups. This farm of the early 1900s is open to the general public twice yearly, in the spring and fall. It makes an interesting comparison with The National Colonial Farm. Groups of ten or more can write or call anytime during the year to arrange a farm tour. The phone number is (301)292-5665 and the address is the Alice Ferguson Foundation, Hard Bargain Farm, 2001 Bryan Point Road, Accokeek, Maryland 20607.

The National Colonial Farm is open 10:00 a.m. to 5:00 p.m. every day except Mondays, Thanksgiving, Christmas and New Year's Day. Visitors older than 12 pay a nominal admission. There is a picnic area, the Saylor Memorial Grove and Pier, near the farm entrance.

Directions: Take Maryland Beltway Exit 3 to Route 210, Indian Head Highway south. Proceed 10 miles to the traffic light at Bryan Point Road, Accokeek, Maryland. Make a right turn onto Bryan Point Road and continue 4 miles to the farm and park; the parking lot is on the left.

ST. MARY'S CITY
The Past is Present

"St. Maries Citty" is an outdoor museum of living history where 17th-century oaths mingle with oratory. You can watch ongoing archaeological work, climb aboard a reconstructed, square-rigged pinnace, or hoe some sotweed.

Diverse dramatics are presented along the banks of the St. Mary's River on summer weekends. In the 1676 State House you can take part in a trial being pleaded before Lord Philip Calvert, governor of the colony. Various townspeople testify in colorful terms and visitors are included in the authentic re-enactments as both jurors and witnesses. Testimony from early court records has been carefully studied to make these presentations historically accurate.

While watching the trial, look around the assembly chamber. This is where the early colonial legislature met to advise their Royal Proprietor. It was to this colonial body in 1648, that Margaret Brent applied requesting the right to vote. She was a landowner, lawyer and sole executor of Governor Leonard Calvert's estate. Her request was denied. A dramatization of her efforts to win equal rights is presented as part of the St. Mary's Summer Festival.

A second play based on the life of a Maryland house builder, or housewright, called Daniel Clocker also is shown. In this play you'll meet a newcomer to the colony and Clocker will regale the "young fop" with advice on living in the new settlement. This play is presented at the Godiah Spray Tobacco Plantation, where throughout the summer living history vignettes are offered on Saturday and Sunday afternoons. The programs presented at the Plantation have an interesting continuity because they are based on an actual record kept by Robert Cole during the 1660s. Each year life at the farm changes as family members are born, die, leave the farm to be educated or marry and move away. You can watch as they go about their daily routine, preparing and serving meals for the family, indentured help and the neighborhood priest who frequently drops in for a visit at dinner time.

The Godiah Spray Plantation offers an interesting contrast between the rural English style of architecture and its subsequent adaption by colonial builders. The plantation house and the old barn have been built by the English method and the new barn and the freedman's cottage by the new world technique.

Costumed guides also will be on hand to acquaint you with the Maryland *Dove*, docked at the foot of the hill beneath the State House. It was in March, 1634, that the *Ark* and the *Dove* first landed in Maryland. The 140 settlers had a rough four months crossing the Atlantic. The *Dove* had become separated from the principal ship, the *Ark*, during a violent storm. It was with great thanksgiving that Father Andrew White offered a Mass to celebrate the safe arrival of the ships on the island of St. Clement's. A cross marks the spot of this first service just a short distance from St. Mary's on St. Clement's Island.

It is hard to imagine as you explore the *Dove* that a ship this small could carry supplies for 140 settlers. The *Dove* was considered large enough to cross the Atlantic but small enough to serve as a trading ship in the coastal rivers and bays of the New World.

Living history sketches are presented at the *Dove* on summer weekends. A character representing William Stone, early governor of Maryland, is one of the principals. Another personality is an enterprising if not entirely respectable go-getter. The third is a comely indentured servant who is sold into servitude.

In addition to these regularly scheduled activities there are special weekends planned throughout the summer months. St. Mary's summer season regularly begins in mid-June with Charter Day which commemorates the signing of the Maryland Charter. The province of Maryland was granted by Charles I in 1632 to the Calvert family as a feudal barony. According to the Charter the Calverts would deliver to the King or his heirs and successors "two Indian arrows of those parts, to be delivered at the said castle of Windsor, every year, on Tuesday in Easter week: and also the fifth part of all gold and silver ore which shall happen from time to time, to be found within the aforesaid limits." Historical exhibits, period music, living history and regional cuisine are all part of the Charter Day celebration. Other special weekends held annually are Militia Days and Children's Festival.

You can picnic at St. Mary's at tables overlooking the river on the State House grounds or near the Chancellor's Point Natural History Center, the last major exhibit area at St. Mary's City. Located on 66 acres, this natural history park attempts to illustrate how man has interacted with the surrounding land and water since prehistoric times. On Aboriginal Culture Day held in mid-October, you'll have a chance to try to flintknap an arrowhead or scoop out a dugout canoe. If you're really adventurous you can taste such authentic early dishes as raccoon stew and baked eel.

A pamphlet available at the nature center tells you where Indian camps once stood and about the fossils found here from 12 million years ago when a shallow sea extended all the way to Washington. The nature center is open year round, except Christmas Day, from dawn to dusk.

St. Mary's is reached by a pleasant drive through the Maryland countryside down Route 5. Exhibits are open daily during the summer months from 10:00 a.m. to 5:00 p.m.

but there is more going on during the weekends. Archaeological tours of excavation sites and work in progress are conducted Wednesday through Sunday from 10:00 a.m. to 3:00 p.m. June through September.

Directions: Take Maryland Beltway Exit 7, Route 5, south to St. Mary's City. It is approximately 1½ hours from Washington.

ST. PETERS VILLAGE
Victoriana Updated

A drive past Pennsylvania's rolling farmlands, rippling streams, open meadows and gentle hills offers all kinds of visual delights. With St. Peters as a destination you can have a mini-holiday and step back in time to the Victorian era.

The village of St. Peters was built in 1860 to house the workers of the French Creek Granite Company. In the mid-1880s it was developed as a summer resort. Now, more than a hundred years later, the calendar has been turned back and St. Peters has been restored to its former charm. Main Street is lined with craft and gift shops, many of which are closed on Mondays. Note that the General Store has an ice cream parlour.

Midday meals are available at the restored inn at St. Peters. Lunch is served Monday through Saturday from 11:30 a.m. until 2:00 p.m. in the Victorian dining room and also on the outdoor patio where you will have a view of the French Creek Falls. The stream drops 155 feet in less than one-half mile. For later dining the inn is open on Monday through Thursday from 5:30 to 9:00 p.m., Friday and Saturday from 5:30 to 10:00 p.m. and on Sunday from 1:00 to 7:00 p.m. For reservations call (215)469-6277.

If alfresco dining suits your style better, then a short one-mile drive will bring you to French Creek State Park, a 6,844-acre natural site with fishing, swimming, hiking, camping and picnicking facilities. There are three lakes within this park—Hopewell, Scotts Run and Six Penny. From Memorial Day weekend to Labor Day you can swim at a guarded beach at Six Penny Lake from 11:00 a.m. to 7:00 p.m. unless posted otherwise.

Scotts Run is a stocked trout fishing area. Brook and rainbow trout are caught here from pre-season to Memorial Day and during the winter trout season. Hopewell Lake has a wide variety of fish and can be tackled by fishermen under 16 without a license; all others need licenses.

Winter sports at French Creek State Park include cross country skiing as well as sledding and tobogganing. A small section of Hopewell Lake is maintained for ice skating, and ice fishing is also permitted.

Adjacent to the park is Hopewell Village National Historic Site. This restored iron-making village re-creates life here between 1820 and 1840. Ore was forged as early as 1771 and from that ore cannons and rifles were made for the patriots in the American Revolution. At the Visitor's Center an easy-to-follow explanation of how an iron furnace operated provides the background you'll need to appreciate the Walking Tour. Included among 17 stops are the ironmaster's house, tenant houses, the village store and the old iron furnace.

During July and August history really comes alive at Hopewell Village as costumed molders, blacksmiths, candlemakers, cooks and seamstresses demonstrate and tell about their life and work. Hopewell is open daily, without charge, from 9:00 a.m. until 5:00 p.m.

Handicapped visitors to Hopewell Village may tour the area with a park guide by car, by wheelchair or on foot. Guides also give special service to heart patients and the elderly.

Near the park is the quaint village of Birchrunville. It is called "little Switzerland" because the village sits high on a hill well above the tops of the church steeples in the valley. This hilltop setting plus nearby Hall-Sheeder covered bridge, built in 1850 over French Creek, were made to order for camera buffs.

Directions: Take Beltway Exit 27, I-95, north to the Wilmington exit on Route 202 north; bear left onto Route 100 which will take you through Birchrunville and onto Route 23 to St. Peters and Hopewell Village.

STAR ROSE GARDENS
A Rosy Perspective

A two-hour drive from Washington will bring you to the Conard-Pyle Star Rose Gardens, the largest growers of roses east of the Mississippi River. You can walk or drive through fields of fragrant roses that extend as far as your eyes can see. Although the gardens were once more extensive, there are still 30 acres of roses to beguile you. Visitors are welcome at no charge from dawn to dusk daily from June to October.

The 3,500 select roses planted in the Robert Pyle Memorial Garden by the Conard-Pyle Company are all clearly labeled. Many of them are All-American Award winners. If you are interested in the new varieties being developed you should arrange in advance to take a conducted tour of the research and development fields given Monday through Friday. Write the Star Rose Garden, The Conard-Pyle Company, West Grove, Pennsylvania 19390.

A novel event held annually is Red Rose Rent Day. It's on the Saturday following Labor Day. One red rose is presented to a direct descendant of William Penn in lieu of rent. This public ceremony is used to introduce garden fanciers to new roses and other plants.

Adjacent to the rose fields there is a delightful spot to enjoy a lunch break named (what else?) the Red Rose Inn. The inn is on part of the land once rented from William Penn.

Directions: Take Beltway Exit 27, I-95, to the Wilmington area; then take the Route 48 exit and continue to Route 41. Proceed on Route 41 until it intersects with U.S. 1 at West Grove, where you will find the Star Rose fields.

TANGIER ISLAND
Getting there is Half the Fun

Most of us know the story of how Manhattan Island was purchased from the Indians for a collection of beads but are unaware that Virginia has a similar story. In 1666, Captain John Smith sold Tangier Island in the Chesapeake Bay for two overcoats, which, by implication, made it a more valuable island than Manhattan. You can judge the worth of Tangier Island for yourself and have a delightful time doing so by taking an excursion there. The trip is long but exciting, especially the 1¾-hour ferry ride to Tangier.

The ferry, the *Captain Thomas*, can carry only 150 passengers, so you must make reservations beforehand: (804)333-4656. You can arrange to store your bike on the ferry at the same time. The Virginia State Travel Office provides a brochure on the ferry and Tangier Island. For information call (804)786-2061.

The ferry leaves at 10:00 a.m. from Reedville, Virginia, a three-hour drive from the Washington Beltway. The breeze off the water makes the trip comfortable even in August. You'll see crabbing boats and oyster fishermen in their tonging boats and get some idea of what Tangier must have looked like during the War of 1812 when the British based their fleet here and preyed on Baltimore and Washington shipping.

Tangier Island is only a mile wide and five miles long; three-quarters of its landmass is marshland. The small white houses of the 814 residents ring the treeless unpolluted island. Most of the residents walk or bicycle. There are but three cars on the island; you can rent a golf cart at a modest fee for a trip around the island, but a better way to see it is to bring your own bike. All the paths are paved and are only eight-feet wide.

Exploring the Island, you visit the old church and the graveyard where the graves rest above the marshy ground. Signs on many of the cottages you pass advertise handmade sun bonnets and aprons. Tangier is a wintering place for Canadian geese, so you will see plenty of waterfowl. If you decide to picnic, there is a country store where you can pick up something cold to drink.

Many visitors forego picnicking for the pleasure of sampling the excellent food at Mrs. Crockett's Chesapeake House. At this family-style restaurant you are seated at long tables and served heaping platters of crab cakes, clam fritters and Virginia ham. There are a multitude of tasty vegetables and homemade rolls and desserts. Many people like the food so much they come back to Tangier just for the cooking. Overnight accommodations are also available at Mrs. Crockett's. Call (804)891-2331.

Directions: From the Washington Beltway take Virginia Exit 4 onto I-95. Go south to just past Fredericksburg. Take the Route 17 Bypass, go left and continue on the Route 17 Bypass south to Tappahannock. Turn left and take Route 360 past Warsaw to Reedville and then follow ferry signs. Remember the ferry leaves at 10:00 a.m., and you will need three-hours' driving time from the Washington Beltway.

VINEYARDS
Don't Tread on Me

Connoisseurs may develop complicated rituals for choosing just the right wine, but the rankest amateur may have a lot of fun and learn a great deal about wine by visiting one of a number of local vineyards.

Of the Maryland vineyards the closest and one of the most hospitable is Provenza Vineyard in Montgomery County. After taking an enlightening tour conducted by the very people involved in the day-to-day wine making process, you will be able to taste and purchase wines made at Provenza. Visits must be planned in advance and reservations are necessary; call (301)277-2447. Tours are given on weekends at 1:00 p.m.

Another Maryland vineyard, the Berrywine Plantation Winery near Mt. Airy, hosts a number of wine-related festivals throughout the year in addition to offering tours. Berrywine-ers refer to themselves as the "Baskin Robbins of the wine industry" because they make 30 varieties of wine. After taking a tour you get a chance to sample elderberry, peach, damson plum, apple, blackberry, cherry, pear and strawberry as well as grape wines. Tours start at 10:00 a.m. daily, except Sunday when they begin at 1:00 p.m., and continue throughout the day. Closed Wednesdays and holidays.

Out past Frederick, Maryland, in Myersville is Byrd Vineyard which not only has vineyard tours but also a 15-minute slide presentation on how grape vines are grafted. Byrd Vineyard is open from June through November from 1:00 to 5:00 p.m. on weekdays. Weekend hours are 1:00 to 6:00 p.m. Closed on Tuesdays.

Virginia has over 40 vineyards. Those in the Middleburg area are closest to Washington and the best time to visit them is during the Virginia Wine Festival held annually in late August. You can, of course, explore at other times.

Meredyth Vineyards is the largest and can be visited without an appointment from 10:00 a.m. to 4:00 p.m. daily, except on major holidays. Just down the road is Highbury Vineyard, an experimental vineyard owned and operated by Robert de Treville Lawrence, the editor and publisher of *The Vinifera Wine Growers Journal.* There is not much to see at Highbury but Mr. Lawrence is an acknowledged expert. Also in the Middleburg area is Piedmont Vineyard which offers tours and tasting from 10:00 a.m. until 4:00 p.m. Tuesday through Saturday.

Directions: For Provenza Vineyard take Beltway Exit 28, New Hampshire Avenue, past Brighton Dam Road to Green Bridge Road, just ½-mile past Brighton Dam. At Green Bridge Road make a left and then another left at the Provenza sign, at 805 Green Bridge Road in Brookville, Maryland.

For Berrywine Plantation Winery take Beltway Exit 35, I-270, to the Damascus exit, Route 27. Follow Route 27 to the Mt. Airy Business District and then follow signs to the winery.

Use the same Beltway exit for Byrd Vineyard and continue on I-270 for ten miles past Frederick, to Exit 42 at Myersville. Follow Main Street through town to Church Hill Road. Turn right on Church Hill Road and continue to Byrd Vineyard on the left.

For the Middleburg vineyards take Beltway Exit 8, Route 50, to Middleburg. At the yellow blinker in Middleburg turn left. This becomes Route 776. Follow it for 2½ miles to Route 628. Make a right turn on Route 628 and drive 2½ miles to the Meredyth entrance. For Highbury, go back down Route 628 and go right on Route 679 for one mile. Make a left on another leg of Route 628, a one-way dirt road. After you visit at the winery continue up the dirt road and make a right on Route 601. Another right turn will put you on Route 626 heading towards Middleburg. Before you reach Middleburg you will see Piedmont Vineyards on your left. If you want to skip Highbury, simply take Route 679 until it intersects Route 626 and turn right. Again, Piedmont will be on your left before you reach Middleburg.

WHITE WATER RAFTING
Nature's Own Wild Water

For a very different and unforgettable adventure try a white water raft trip. Novices should consider the Youghiogheny River in Pennsylvania, though parts of the Upper Youghiogheny can be deadly. In West Virginia the New and Shenandoah Rivers are recommended for beginners, and the Cheat and Gauley Rivers for the more experienced.

Because most of us are cushioned from the elemental forces of nature it can be a genuine thrill to discover nature's ferocity. White water trips have tranquil periods too when you just relax and enjoy the unspoiled scenery and fresh, clean air.

Raft trips are not really dangerous when they are done under the supervision of trained outfitters. The commercial rafting companies have an outstanding safety record. In West Virginia alone more than 10,000 people raft each year and in the last ten years there has been only one serious accident.

The most exciting spot to sit in a raft is at the very front where you feel the full impact of the rapids and riffles. The more timid may want to forego that thrill and sit towards the back. Most rafts hold between four and eight people and companies do not usually allow any passengers under the age of ten. Some outfitters offer a "rubber ducky," which is a one-man inflatable kayak for advanced rafters.

Prices differ at the various rafting concerns so you might want to check not only the classification of the rapids but also the price before booking. Because rafting has become increasingly popular, reservations should be made as far in advance as possible. Trips go on regardless of the weather and you should be prepared to be thoroughly drenched. Many concerns rent paddling wet suits for cool weather rafting. If you bring your own covering, bring either a wet suit or wool clothing, as wool retains your body heat even when wet. You should also carry a complete set of dry clothes to change into after the trip.

You can reserve rafting trips with the following outfitters:

MARYLAND

River and Trail Outfitters
Box 246, Valley Road
Knoxville, MD 21758
(301)834-9950
Rafting on the Shenandoah River.

PENNSYLVANIA

Mountain Stream and Trail Outfitters
Box 106
Ohiopyle, PA 15470
(800)245-4090
Raft tours on the Youghiogheny, Cheat and Gauley Rivers.

Whitewater Adventures, Inc.
Box 31
Ohiopyle, PA 15470
(412)329-8850
Raft tours on the Youghiogheny and Cheat Rivers.

Wilderness Voyageurs, Inc.
Box 97
Ohiopyle, PA 15470
(412)329-4552
Rafting on the Youghiogheny River.

WEST VIRGINIA

Appalachian Wildwaters, Inc.
Box 126
Albright, WV 26519
(800)624-8060
Raft tours on Cheat, New and Gauley (ducky tours on Cheat) Rivers.

Blue Ridge Outfitters
Route 340
Harpers Ferry, WV 25425
(304)725-3444
Raft tours on the Shenandoah River.

Cheat River Outfitters
Box 196
Albright, WV 26519
(304)329-9816
Raft and ducky tours on Cheat River.

Mountain River Tours, Inc.
Box 88-E
Hico, WV 25854
(304)658-5817
Rafting on the New and Gauley Rivers.

Transmontaine Outfitters Ltd.
Box 325
Davis, WV 26260
(304)259-5117
Raft tours on the Cheat River.

Wildwater Expedition Unlimited, Inc.
Box 55
Thurmond, WV 25936
(304)469-2551
Rafting on the New and Gauley Rivers.

ZWAANENDAEL MUSEUM
Delaware Dutch Treat

Unicorn legends are well known, but you may not have heard about the unicorn that caused the massacre of the first Dutch settlers in Delaware. This story is told at the Zwaanendael Museum in Lewes which exhibits a large wooden unicorn resembling the heraldic unicorn the settlers brought over from Holland.

Henry Hudson had discovered the Delaware Bay in 1609. Twenty-eight settlers under the leadership of David Pietersen de Vries established the whaling colony of Zwaanendael in 1631. The curious Delaware Indians wanted the wooden unicorn, so the story goes, and when the Indians were thwarted, they burned the stockade and massacred the settlers.

The Zwaanendael Museum has a model of the first fort the Dutch built. Even the name they gave their settlement suggests legends because it means the Valley of the Swans.

The museum traces the land's history back to the beginning of man's presence here. There is a display showing the development of the arrowhead from the Paleo to the Woodland periods of prehistory.

Lewes, as the town is now called, next figured prominently in history when it was bombarded by the British on April 6 and 7, 1813. Flags, uniforms and weapons serve as reminders of that conflict.

The museum's collection includes a wide variety of domestic articles—handmade coverlets, quilts and samplers speak for the skills of yesteryear. China and silverware indicate changing tastes. There are also a few pieces of 17th-century pewter.

Another display area is devoted to antique toys. An 1860s stage coach is driven by a team of miniature horses. A later form of transportation is depicted with the 1922 Toonerville Trolley, complete with driver. There are dishes, dolls, puzzles, cradles and carriages.

The medicinal display has a number of interesting features. Do you know the derivation of "sugar coating"? You'll find out when you read about the pill roller recovered from a drug store in Milton, Delaware. The "paste," or main component of the pill, was laid on the iron cutter and sliced to size. Then the segments were put in a round box with sugar and shaken till they were properly shaped and coated.

There is also a surgical case, circa 1861, which might have given you pause had your doctor brought it with him on a house call, for one of the instruments is a formidable saw. A wide collection of apothecary bottles completes the exhibit.

The exterior of the museum is of equal interest. Built in 1931 to commemorate the 1631 settlement, it is a replica of the Town Hall in Hoorn, Holland, the home town of the first settlers. The brick building with its colorful blue trim and red and white shutters has a statue of de Vries atop its peaked facade.

While in Lewes you can take an escorted walking tour or set off on your own with the helpful map and tourist brochure put out by the Lewes Chamber of Commerce. The map lists 28 places of interest on the walking tour, chief among them some very old houses: the Joshua Fisher House begun in 1727 or 1728 and the Ryves Holt House, the oldest house in town, known to have been standing in 1685. The Joshua Fisher House is now a visitor's center; the Ryves Holt House is privately owned. The Maull House, a good example of early Dutch architecture that is currently being restored, was built in 1750. According to local lore it was here in 1803 that Jerome Bonaparte, the brother of Napoleon, brought his wife when stormy seas forced them ashore. The story is that Betsy Bonaparte refused to be seated at an elaborate dinner until the silver candlesticks from the ship were brought to the table.

Another old house which survived a barrage in the War of 1812 is known today as the Cannonball House and Marine Museum. Within the house are a series of nautical exhibits. Opposite the town post office is the 1812 Memorial Park where a defense battery stood. You'll see four large guns and a smaller one that is reputed to have been taken from a pirate ship. On the lower terrace of the park is a World War I naval gun.

After a morning's historical tour you can have an afternoon at the beach. Lewes offers a choice of the Delaware Bay at the public beach or the Atlantic Ocean at Cape Henlopen State Park. This 1,200-acre park is located at the edge of Lewes where the bay meets the ocean. If you have the energy, you should climb Hamburger Hill on the Seaside Nature Trail. You'll be rewarded with a splendid view of the two lighthouses on the Delaware capes.

During the summer months there are escorted morning walking tours. Call (302)645-9127 or stop at the Lewes Historical Society, Shipcarpenter and Third Street, for more information. The Zwaanendael Museum is open at no charge Tuesday through Saturday from 10:00 a.m. to 4:30 p.m. and Sunday from 1:30 to 4:30 p.m. The museum is closed Mondays and holidays.

Directions: Take Beltway Exit 19, Route 50, across the Bay Bridge to Route 404. Take Route 404 to Bridgeville where you will pick up Route 18 to Georgetown. At Georgetown continue on Route 9 to Lewes. The Zwaanendael Museum is located at the intersection of Kings Highway and Savannah Road.

SUMMER CALENDAR OF EVENTS

JUNE

EARLY

Great Maryland Strawberry Wine Festival— Berrywine Plantations, MD (301)662-8687

Local arts and crafts are demonstrated and sold, music is provided, and you can tour the winery and taste the new strawberry wine at this annual festival. Time: 10:00 a.m. to 6:00 p.m. on Saturday and 1:00 to 6:00 p.m. on Sunday.

Delmarva Chicken Festival—Alternating Sites (302)856-2971

Although it may be for the birds, it's fun to attend this annual tribute to a popular area taste treat, the chicken. Each year contestants take part in a chicken cooking contest and a booklet is prepared with the winners's recipes. Flea market, craft displays and a great chicken barbecue are all part of this festival. Kids like the assortment of rides. This is a weekend-long event.

Waterfront Festival—Alexandria, VA (703)549-8300 or (703)549-0205

This is a family-oriented festival featuring historic ship tours, boat races, nautical exhibits, water safety demonstrations, boat rides, an art show, music and numerous food booths all at the picturesque Alexandria waterfront. Events begin on Friday and continue through Sunday.

Torchlight Tattoos—Fort Washington, MD (301)292-2112

Once a month through the summer and into October Fort Washington brings alive the ghosts of the past as volunteers recreate camp life by torchlight. Visitors are briefed so that they can ask pertinent questions about the defenses of Washington. You can watch as the men walk post, polish their equipment, mend uniforms and tell tales around the campfire. Tattoos are held at 8:00, 9:00 and 10:00 p.m.

Antique Car Show—Oatlands, VA (703)777-3174

Along with a wide range of vintage vehicles there is also a craft fair and flea market at this annual event. Music, hay rides and a tour of this Greek Revival mansion make for a day with something for everyone. Time: 9:00 a.m. to 4:00 p.m.

Sundays at Fort Ward—Fort Ward Museum—Alexandria, VA (703)838-4848

Each Sunday a different Civil War living history vignette, musical performance, firing demonstration or drill is held at Fort Ward Museum. Time: 1:00 to 4:00 p.m.

Harborfest—Norfolk Waterfront, VA (804)441-5266

Weekend-long festivities featuring tall ships, boat races, nautical exhibits, ethnic foods, musical entertainment and fireworks make this an enjoyable event.

Turn-of-the-Century Sunday Afternoons—Clara Barton National Historic Site, MD (301)492-6245

Ice Cream socials, barbershop quartets, folk music, old-fashioned games, 19th-century home crafts, historical fashions and even old-time photography are just some of the Sunday afternoon programs at the Clara Barton House. Programs generally run from 1:00 or 2:00 until 4:00 p.m.

MID

Antique Car Show—Sully Plantation, VA (703)941-5000

Antique, classic and special interest cars are on display for this annual event. A frequently featured activity is the assembling of a complete Model T Ford in less than 15 minutes. Wagon rides, entertainment and food add to this show. You can also tour the historic house built in 1794. Time: 10:00 a.m. to 5:00 p.m.

Arts and Crafts Celebration—Gunston Hall Plantation, VA (703)550-9220

Along the shady lane approaching historic Gunston Hall costumed craftsmen demonstrate their 18th- and 19th-century skills. Music of this bygone era also is featured. You can enjoy a movie about Gunston Hall at the Visitor's Center and tour this lovely old home, noted for its beautiful woodwork. Time: Noon to 5:00 p.m.

Flag Day Celebration—Fort McHenry, MD (301)563-FLAG

At Fort McHenry, where the sight of the flag still flying after the Battle of Baltimore inspired Francis Scott Key to write the words for our national anthem, it is particularly appropriate to celebrate Flag Day with a "Pause for the Pledge," band concert and military drill team. Time: 3:00 to 5:00 p.m.

Carroll County Arts Day—Carroll County Farm Museum, MD (301)848-7775

At this County Arts Day you can observe such old-time crafts as blacksmithing, quilting, spinning, weaving and pottery making as well as an art show featuring all media. The entertainment, too, runs the gamut from jazz to ballet. Country food is available and you can tour the 19th-century farm house. Time: 10:00 a.m. to 5:00 p.m.

Steppingstone Museum's Annual Arts and Crafts Fair—Susquehanna State Park, MD (301)929-2299

Held the third weekend in June this old-time fair features local farm crafts and artists. Children enjoy the farm wagon rides. Time: 10:00 a.m. to 5:00 p.m. on Saturday and noon to 5:00 p.m. on Sunday.

Charter Day—St. Mary's City, MD (301)994-0779

Living History at St. Maries Citty kicks off the summer season with the annual commemoration of the signing of the original Maryland Charter. Historical vignettes bring to life the important events that occurred here at Maryland's first capital. Living History includes scenes at the Godiah Spray Plantation, the *Dove* and a trial in the Reconstructed State House of 1676. Charter Day events are from 11:00 a.m. to 5:00 p.m.; Living History continues on summer weekends 1:00 to 4:00 p.m.

Annapolis Arts Festival—City Dock, MD (301)267-7922

In addition to a wide range of arts and crafts there are performances of bluegrass, country, jazz, and big band music. This is a weekend-long event.

LATE

Maryland Forces in Garrison—Fort Frederick State Park, MD (301)842-2155
At Fort Frederick reactivated Maryland Forces garrison the fort and bring to life the days when this was a frontier outpost during the French and Indian War (1755–1763). You can see marching, drilling and training in the ranger tactics the Maryland Forces once used. Time: 1:00 to 4:00 p.m.

Victorian Wedding and Reception—Mary Surratt House, MD (301)894-6717
The historic landmark of the tragic aftermath of the Civil War, the assassination of Lincoln, is now the annual site of a happier event—a mock wedding of the Civil War period. The "wedding" takes place in the garden with the bride and her attendants in carefully styled Victorian dresses. The groom often wears a Confederate uniform. Guests can partake of wedding cake and punch in the drawing room. Upstairs the bedroom is strewn with the bride's Victorian era trousseau. There is an additional display of wedding related items and pictures in the library. Time: Noon to 4:00 p.m.

JULY

EARLY

Old Timey 4th of July—Maymont Park—Richmond, VA (804)358-7166
Croquet games, relay races and carriage rides provide family fun. You can also enjoy the beautiful gardens, tour the Dooley mansion and explore the Thalhimer Small Animal Habitat. Lots of music and plenty of food add to this old-fashioned 4th. This is an all day event.

Heritage Festival—Fredericksburg, VA (703)373-1776
This annual 4th of July celebration of Fredericksburg's colonial, Revolutionary and Civil War roots boasts a wide range of city-wide activities highlighted by the Great Rappahan-

nock River Raft Race and the Reenactment of the Battle of Fredericksburg. There are also hay rides, boat rides, puppet shows, children's games, music, dancing, crafts, historical walking tours and much more. Events are scheduled Friday, Saturday and Sunday.

Yorktown's Old-Fashioned Fourth—Yorktown Victory Center, VA (804)887-1776
Enjoy this patriotic day in an appropriate setting at Yorktown where there is a parade, town fair, sing-a-long and fireworks.

July 4th Celebration—George Washington's Birthplace, VA (804)224-0196
You can see the way our forebearers may have celebrated at this colonial party with 18th-century crafts and an ox-driving demonstration. Next door to Washington's Birthplace, Stratford Hall Plantation has a free open house in honor of the Lee brothers, Richard Henry and Francis Lightfoot, the only two brothers to sign the Declaration of Independence.

Old-Fashioned Fourth of July Celebration—Colvin Run Mill, VA (703)941-5000
Homespun fun includes greased pole climbing contests, watermelon seed spittin' contests, three legged races, sack races, and an ice cream social. There is also music, square dancing and country food. Time: 11:00 a.m. to 5:00 p.m.

19th-Century Folk Days at New Market—New Market Battlefield Park, VA (703)740-3101
All manner of 19th-century crafts are demonstrated and sold. One demonstration features bread-baking in outdoor ovens. You can also see Civil War artillery and infantry drills. Time: 10:00 a.m. to 4:00 p.m.

Ash Lawn Summer Festival—Charlottesville, VA (804)293-9539
A Colonial Crafts Weekend in early July opens the seven-week annual summer festival at Ash Lawn. Theatrical performances are part of this festival as are 18th- and 19th-century craft demonstrations. Time: 11:00 a.m. to 6:00 p.m.

Custis-Fitzhugh Marriage—Boyhood Home of Robert E. Lee, VA (703)548-8484
This traditional occasion celebrates the linking of the Washington and Lee families. It was at this house that George Washington Parke Custis married Mary Fitzhugh on July

4, 1804. Twenty-seven years after their marriage, their daughter married Robert E. Lee. A tour of this historic house, refreshments and music augment the celebration. Time: 10:00 a.m. to 4:00 p.m.

Reenactment of the Battle of Gettysburg—Gettysburg National Military Park, PA (717)334-6274

Each year this pivotal Civil War battle is reenacted by costumed units representing the Union and Confederate forces; displays of Civil War memorabilia include collections of antique arms, uniforms, documents and photographs. Free lectures are part of this historic weekend-long event.

MID

Lotus Blossom Festival—Lilypons Water Gardens, MD (301)874-5133

Where else could you mix lotus blossoms at their peak, wine tasting, ballet and rides on a horse-drawn surrey? Local products, both artistic and culinary, are available at this weekend-long event. Time: Saturday 10:00 a.m. to 5:00 p.m., Sunday 11:30 a.m. to 5:00 p.m.

Bastille Day—Maryland Inn—Annapolis, MD (301)263-2641

For a change of pace celebrate another country's holiday at this event which commemorates the storming of the French Bastille in 1789. Entertainment, dancing and food are part of this annual party. Time: 11:00 a.m. to midnight.

Piscataway Indian Festival—Cedarville State Park, MD (301)884-2144

This annual event is an opportunity to learn about the Eastern Woodland Indians who inhabited the western part of Tidewater Maryland when the European settlers arrived in the New World. There are tribal songs and dances as well as Indian arts and crafts both on display and for sale. Time: Noon to 5:00 p.m.

Farm Craft Days—Belle Grove Plantation, VA (703)869-2028

This is the major folk festival of the Shenandoah Valley area and it is planned so that there is something of interest for everyone in the famiy. There are mule rides, puppet shows, sheep shearing demonstrations, rural crafts, and booths selling country food and handcrafted items. Time: 10:00 a.m. to 6:00 p.m.

Civil War Reenactment—Mary Surratt House, MD (301)868-1121

Costumed volunteers recreate Civil War units. They set up camp and give rifle demonstrations. You can also tour the Mary Surratt House. Time: Noon to 4:00 p.m.

Pork, Peanuts and Pine Festival—Chippokes Plantation State Park, VA (804)294-3944

Combining country taste treats, entertainment and a wide selection of arts and crafts, this festival will give you a good chance to get to know Chippokes, an out-of-the-way historical attraction near Williamsburg that spans the centuries.

LATE

Virginia Scottish Games—Alexandria Episcopal High School grounds, VA (703)549-0205

This two-day Celtic festival features pipers, highland dancers, drummers, fencers and fiddlers from 26 clans across the U.S., Canada and Europe. You can purchase Scottish food and wares in the tents colorfully decorated with the clans's tartans. An unusual array of ancient games are part of the hepthalon tournament. You can see the caber toss, stone put, sheaf toss, weight toss and other events.

Military Field Days—Fort Frederick State Park, MD (301)842-2155

At most military encampments you're given a close-up look at one period from America's past. But at these Military Field Days the three major confrontations fought on American soil are represented. Hundreds of uniformed men set up camps, engage in tactical demonstrations and fight mock battles from the French and Indian War, the American Revolution and the Civil War. Time: 1:00 to 4:00 p.m.

Pony Round-Up and Penning—Chincoteague, VA (804)336-6161

Each year the wild ponies of Assateague Island are rounded up, and they swim to Chincoteague where they are auctioned off. Those that are unsold are returned to Assateague.

This popular and unusual event is augmented by a Firemen's Carnival on Chincoteague that features seafood, entertainment and carnival rides. This is a weekend-long event.

St. Mary's Summer Country Feast—St. Mary's City, MD (301)794-0779

Country cooking, vignettes and historic sites combine to make this annual event one of the special weekends at St. Mary's City.

AUGUST

EARLY

Old Fashioned Corn Roast—Union Mills Homestead, MD (301)848-2288

This old-time festival is part of a tradition that goes back to 1797 when the Shriver family started their convivial corn roast. You can watch the corn being roasted on iron stoves and then partake of a barbecued chicken lunch. A span of 185 years of American rural life can be observed at the Union Mills Homestead. Time: 2:00 to 6:00 p.m.

Jonathan Hager Frontier Crafts Day—City Park, Hagerstown, MD (301)791-3130

Picnic along Hagerstown's lake, enjoy a wide variety of frontier crafts, and tour the historic old Hager House and the Washington County Museum of Fine Arts at this day-long celebration. Time: 11:00 a.m. to 5:00 p.m.

Hoover Days—Shenandoah National Park, VA (703)999-2243 ext. 39

Once a year the National Park Service hosts Hoover Days to celebrate Herbert Hoover's birthday on August 10. This weekend is the only time the camp built by Herbert Hoover is open to the public. He was the first President to build a summer White House get-away. When he left the White House he also left his camp to be used by future Presidents and their official families. Tours and guided hikes are scheduled.

Children's Day—Oatlands, VA (703)777-3174

A special day for the youngsters features a wide variety of lawn games. A marionette show, clowns, a fortune teller and animals will entertain; food is available. Time: Noon to 5:00 p.m.

Cylburn All American Selections Display Day— Cylburn Arboretum, MD (301)542-3109

Get a jump on other garden enthusiasts by attending this advance display of the best new varieties of seed growing flowers and vegetables.

MID

Tavern Days—Gadsby's Tavern Museum, VA (703)838-4242

Life in an 18th-century tavern is recreated. There is food, drink, entertainment and music. Children may design tavern signs or play old-fashioned games. Time: 10:00 a.m. to 5:00 p.m. and 7:00 to 9:00 p.m.

Deer Creek Fiddlers' Convention—Carroll County Farm Museum, MD (301)848-7775

Hear some of the best of the old-time music players as they compete on fiddles, banjos, guitars and mandolins. There are bands and individual competitors. Food is available at this annual event. You can also tour the Main House and outbuildings which are filled with antique farm furniture and equipment. Time: Noon to 5:00 p.m.

Leitersburg Peach Festival—Leitersburg, MD (301)791-1621

This festival in the heart of Western Maryland's peach orchard country not only has fresh peaches, but a juried arts and crafts show, live bluegrass music, pony rides, covered wagon rides and a Civil War camp as well. General Lee's march through Leitersburg during the retreat from Gettysburg is recreated. Time: 10:00 a.m. to 6:00 p.m.

Child Games Day—Steppingstone Museum— Susquehanna State Park, MD (301)939-2299

Children enjoy playing games their grandparents once played. This museum preserves and demonstrates the rural arts and crafts of the 1880–1910 period. The event is held the third Sunday in August from 1:00 to 5:00 p.m.

Reenactment of the Battle of Fort Stevens—Fort Ward Museum Park, VA (703)838-4848
Authentic uniforms, weapons, equipment and field tents all recreate the tense moments of Civil War action during the summer of 1864. A living history enactment of camp life precedes the annual reenactment of the Battle of Fort Stevens, one of the 68 forts guarding Washington. Time: Saturday 1:00 to 4:00 p.m.; Sunday pre-battle activities are at noon with the battle reenactment at 3:00 p.m.

August Court Days—Leesburg, VA (703)777-0519
In colonial times the circuit court opening was an occasion for dancing, feasting and obtaining community news. You can relive an 18th-century court opening at this annual fair. There are craft demonstrations, live music, a children's fair, pony rides, dancing in the street and reenactments of actual court cases. Vignettes illustrate various forms of colonial punishment. Time: 9:00 a.m. to 5:00 p.m.

Balloon Festival—The Flying Circus Aerodrome, VA (703)439-8661
Watch while operators inflate a sizable number of hot air balloons which float in colorful profusion over the Flying Circus Aerodrome field. This is an additional feature to the weekend extravaganza of 14 aerial acts. Stunt flying, sky diving and wing walking are all part of this barnstorming show. Showtime 2:30 p.m.

Corn Harvest Festival—National Colonial Farm, MD (301)283-2113
You can help, or just watch, freshly picked corn being shucked before it is cooked in huge iron kettles over an open fire. In addition to enjoying the hot, buttered corn you can watch craftsmen demonstrating a variety of colonial skills. Time: 1:00 to 4:00 p.m.

C&O Canal Boat Festival—Cumberland, MD (301)724-7992
At the North Branch Canal Park you can enjoy an arts and craft festival in a restored canal park. The original stone lock from the C&O Canal still remains. Displays of the old mining days and the early railroad era are part of this boat

festival. Old time crafts, horse and buggy rides and blue-grass and country music are all part of the fun. Time: 10:00 a.m. to 6:00 p.m.

LATE

Sully Quilt Show—Sully Plantation, VA (703)437-1794
You can see the intricate patterns, colors and stitches of traditional and contemporary quilts at this annual quilt show. Quiltmakers will be exhibiting and selling their work which includes pillows, vests, purses, book covers, tote bags and other items. Quilting workshops will also be held. Time: 11:00 a.m. to 5:00 p.m.

Maryland Forces in Garrison—Fort Frederick State Park, MD (301)842-2155
For this event the historical time machine stops at 1755 to recreate military life on the western frontier during the French and Indian War. Activities include marching, drilling and training in range tactics as well as a chance for visitors to explore Fort Frederick. Time: 9:00 a.m. to 6:00 p.m.

Calvert County Jousting Tournament—Port Republic, MD (301)586-0565
This is one of Maryland's oldest tournaments where you can watch the state's official sport. You can also tour the restored one room school house and Christ Church, which were built in colonial times. A bazaar and country supper complete the fun. Time: 1:00 to 4:00 p.m.

Summer Candlelight Tour—London Town Publik House and Gardens, MD (301)956-4900
The glow of candlelight provides the appropriate atmosphere to explore this restored colonial ferry tavern. Costumed guides will escort visitors and there will be music and refreshments. Time: 7:00 to 9:30 p.m.

Virginia Wine Festival and Vineyard Tour—Middleburg, VA (703)754-8564
Wine seminars, wine-tasting tours of five Middleburg area vineyards, a grape-stomping contest, pony rides, jousting, balloon rides and plenty to eat and drink are all part of this yearly event. Time: 10:00 a.m. to 5:00 p.m.

AUTUMN

BLACKWATER NATIONAL WILDLIFE REFUGE
Duck, Duck, Drake

Blackwater is a wildlife refuge located on the Atlantic Flyway, the migratory path for millions of birds which extends from Canada to Florida. Blackwater, established in Maryland in 1932, encompasses 14,263 acres of tidal marshland, freshwater ponds and woodland areas and has become one of the chief wintering areas for the Canadian goose as well as a haven for the endangered southern bald eagle and the Delmarva Peninsula fox squirrel. During peak periods in the fall there are sometimes as many as 80,000 Canadian geese and 40,000 ducks in the refuge at the same time. More than 250 species have been sighted including snow geese, mallards, black ducks, pintail, widgeon, teal, whistling swans, shovelers and many more.

The best way to see Blackwater is to take the Wildlife Drive which winds along a canal and through the marshland. Often you come close enough to the ten-pound geese that you feel you could touch them. An observation tower enables you to get a panoramic view of the unspoiled landscape. It is exhilarating to see thousands of honking geese flying in V-formations. Blackwater National Wildlife Refuge and the Wildlife Drive are open at no charge seven days a week during daylight hours. The Visitor's Center is open September through May from 7:30 a.m. to 4:00 p.m. daily. It is closed Christmas Day. Additional information can be obtained at the Visitor's Center or by calling (301)228-2677.

Directions: From Beltway Exit 19, take U.S. 50 to Cambridge, Maryland, then go right on Route 16 to Church Creek. From there, take Route 335 four miles and turn left to the Visitor's Center.

CHINCOTEAGUE ISLAND
Watch the Waterfowl and Wild Ponies

As cold weather moves down the Atlantic coastline, so do the migratory birds. A major stop on their journey is Chincoteague Island in Virginia. In fact, a large number of geese, swans and waterfowl spend the winter at this refuge.

During Waterfowl Week in late November, a 13-mile service road that is usually closed to automobile traffic is opened to allow additional access to the interior of Chincoteague National Wildlife Refuge. The road takes you past man-made fresh water ponds. These ponds, or impoundments, are areas that were diked to trap rain water. The vegetation that grows in the impoundments helps feed the thousands of waterfowl that visit the refuge each fall. The refuge at Chincoteague was established primarily for the 15,000 snow geese that stop here from November to March, but more than 275 other species have been identified within the refuge as well.

An extra advantage of exploring the refuge when the service road is open is that you are more likely to get a close look at the wild ponies. These ponies, the ones featured in the book and the movie *Misty*, are believed to be survivors of a wrecked Spanish galleon. They eat so much dune and marsh grass some look as though they have on saddles instead of extra girth. It is certainly obvious that these wild ponies are strangers to curry combs. Their manes and coats are shabby and untrimmed. The forelocks on many cover their eyes. It is very important not to feed these ponies; a little bit of "junk" food multiplied by all the visitors to Chincoteague could lead to an unhealthy dependence. Also, it is not always safe to feed or pet them. Each year some visitors are bitten or kicked. If you miss the ponies at the refuge you can stop and see some for a nominal charge at the miniature pony farm in the town of Chincoteague.

Another resident of the island is the Sika deer. These deer, native to Japan, were transported to the island in 1923 because they were adaptable to the climate and would make a unique addition to the local wildlife population.

Chincoteague hardly needs these exotic residents to attract visitors; just walking along the deserted, natural beach on a pleasant fall day can provide a relaxing change of pace. If you tire of looking for your own shells, visit the Oyster Museum in town. The museum is open on weekends from 11:00 a.m. to 5:00 p.m. and charges a nominal admission.

If you can't make the trip to Chincoteague during Waterfowl Week there are shorter automobile routes open all year, as well as hiking and bike trails. One interesting path leads to the Assateague Lighthouse. Although visitors are not permitted to climb the 100-year-old tower, it offers a thrilling sight thrusting out of the flat marshland into the sky. Bicycles can be rented from the Refuge Motel in Chincoteague and interpretative tours are available on selected weekends.

While you are in the area you may want to stop at the NASA/Wallops Flight Center open for self-guided walking tours Thursday through Monday from 10:00 a.m. to 4:00 p.m. and on federal holidays except Thanksgiving, Christmas and New Year's Day.

Wallops is responsible for preparing, assembling and launching space vehicles to obtain scientific information. There have been 19 satellites launched from Wallops Flight Center. The Visitor's Center offers a video presentation on the work of NASA as well as exhibits on America's space flight program.

Directions: Take Beltway Exit 19, Route 50, to Salisbury, Maryland. From there follow Route 13 to Virginia; five miles past the state line, turn left on Route 175 to Chincoteague. Wallops Visitor's Center is on your right on Route 175. Take a left at the red light entering Chincoteague for the Oyster Museum. Then take a left on Maddox Boulevard for approximately 2 miles and the Oyster Museum will be on your left. To reach the Chincoteague National Wildlife Refuge, continue on Maddox Boulevard; the Visitor's Center will be on the left as you enter the refuge.

EASTERN NECK WILDLIFE REFUGE
Birds of a Feather Flock Together

Those who like their wildlife viewing really wild should try a visit to Eastern Neck, an island retreat in the Chesapeake Bay. It can be reached by a bridge but there is no Visitor's Center, only a long walkway over the marsh that leads to a raised platform. The observation platform gives the viewer an ideal vantage point from which to watch some of the thousands of Canadian geese that stop here on their way south in the fall. You should bring your binoculars because some of the wildlife is hard to spot at this distance. When there is a large flock of geese at the refuge the noise sounds like thousands of people cheering, something like the crowds at a football game.

Because the refuge is a mixture of marsh and woodlands, deer, squirrels, rabbits and other wildlife as well as numerous varieties of waterfowl can be seen living here. It is interesting to reflect while visiting Eastern Neck Wildlife Refuge that the first white man arrived here in 1650, and the wildlife those explorers encountered was much like what you can see today.

There is a well-marked nature trail through the woodlands across the road from the boardwalk at Tubby Cove. It is here that you will see the Delmarva Peninsula fox squirrel, an animal on the endangered species list. If you are observant you may spot the leafy nests of these squirrels in the trees along the trail.

The Eastern Neck Wildlife Refuge is open seven days a week at no charge. If you visit in the spring and can supply your own canoe, you can enjoy an activity popular with the locals: crabbing along the mud flats of the recreation area. Those without a canoe may want to wade out with a net and a bushel basket. Enthusiasts who have done this recommend setting your bushel basket in an inner tube while you net your catch. Blue crabs are in evidence as early as May but July is the high season for crabbing.

See the description of Remington Farms and Chestertown for other excursions in this area.

Directions: From Beltway Exit 19, take Route 50 across the Bay Bridge. When Route 301 splits from Route 50, take the Route 301 split until you pass Chestertown. Then turn left on Route 20 to Rock Hall and go south on Route 445 to

Eastern Neck. The refuge is about 2½ hours from the Beltway.

ELLICOTT CITY
A Change of Pace Place

Sometimes it is hard to appreciate the attractions of a new destination just by reading about it. One man's "charming" may be another's "so what?" A spot that to some may be picturesque may offer nothing of interest to others. A visit to Ellicott City, however, fosters a more uniform reaction—there's something for everyone.

The village of Ellicott's Mills was founded in 1772. Although it was nearly washed away in two floods, the first in 1868 and the second after tropical storm Agnes in 1972, the town continues to thrive.

In addition to exploring the historic reminders of this former colonial mill town, you can browse through numerous craft, antique and specialty shops displaying wares from all over the world. They are open on weekends and can be found all along Main Street.

Many of the granite stores and houses nestled in the hills above the Patapsco River were built in the late 1700s and early 1800s. Look for the early settler's log cabin that was built in 1780. More than a century ago Ellicott City was admired for its institutions of higher education. One of its four schools was the Patapsco Female Institute, founded in 1837, the ruins of which now overlook the town. This finishing school for well-bred and well-off young ladies, whose parents paid the then grand sum of $300 a year, was considered one of the finest schools in the country. Also in Ellicott City is the old Colonial Inn and Opera House where John Wilkes Booth is said to have made his debut.

Of greatest interest historically is the Ellicott City B&O Railroad Station Museum. The Ellicott City station is the oldest existing railroad building in America. Built in 1831 of native granite just 13 miles from Baltimore, this was the B&O Railroad's first terminus. As part of the museum's Sight and Sound Show you'll see a model railroad track covering these first important miles. The show begins with a 17-minute slide presentation on the development of the railroad in America and the significant role played by this first B&O line. While the room lights are still off, small lights begin to gleam in the buildings along the model train display. The room lights then come on so you can see the train as it moves along the tracks.

In the museum you'll see an old B&O caboose, which can be rented for children's birthday parties, and such railroad artifacts as a stationmaster's office and living quarters, circa 1885.

A nominal admission is charged at the museum which is open April through December, Wednesday through Saturday, from 11:00 a.m. to 4:00 p.m. and Sunday from 12:00 to 5:00 p.m. The museum is also open at the same hours on winter weekends. It is closed on major holidays.

You can spend a whole day exploring Ellicott City. For lunch, picnic treats can be purchased at the old-fashioned market and dessert is certainly easy to find at the bakery. Also there are pubs, taverns and restaurants offering old-time ambience.

Directions: Take Beltway Exit 30, Route 29, out past Columbia; then take Old Columbia Pike into Ellicott City. This will intersect with Main Street; go right for the railroad museum.

FALLINGWATER
Mr. Wright Can't Be Wrong

The most famous of all the residences designed by one of America's greatest architects, Fallingwater lies a long day's journey from Washington. More than 50,000 visitors travel to Mill Run, Pennsylvania, every year to see the supreme example of Frank Lloyd Wright's "organic architecture." Wright believed that form should follow function and should maintain a oneness with nature. Fallingwater is regarded by architects all over the world as one of the finest examples of 20th-century architecture.

The house is a triumph; rising up above the two small waterfalls, it seems to have grown from the earth just as naturally as the trees around it. In every possible way Wright preserved the natural surroundings and made them part of the house. Rooms are angled around the trees and huge, jutting boulders are incorporated into the flooring. There is a moss garden growing within the house, and everywhere the bubbling of the waterfall can be heard.

Frank Lloyd Wright built Fallingwater in 1936 as a summer weekend retreat for Edgar J. Kaufman, a Pittsburgh department store owner. Mr. Kaufman's son had studied architecture with Wright at his workshop in Taliesin, Arizona, and his father, too, had become interested in Wright's innovative work. The house took a year to construct and the contractor who built it was aghast at the design. He was very reluctant to remove the supports used to build the cantilevered structure and would do so only under the personal supervision of Wright. In 1963, the house was given to the Western Pennsylvania Conservancy by Edgar Kaufman, Jr.

From April to mid-November it is open from 10:00 a.m. to 4:00 p.m. for guided tours. It is closed Mondays. Reservations are a good idea but not always necessary; write Fallingwater, R.D. 1, Mill Run, Pennsylvania 15464, or call (412)329-8501. It is a good idea to call before setting out as Fallingwater is about a five-hour drive from the Beltway. There is a light lunch restaurant at Fallingwater. Admission is charged.

Directions: Take Beltway Exit 35, I-270, to Hagerstown. Then follow Route 40 west past Cumberland into Pennsylvania to Farmington. Take Route 381 north to Mill Run and follow the signs to Fallingwater.

FREDERICK AND CATOCTIN MOUNTAIN PARK
A Pleasant Combo

A trip that combines historical with scenic interest is a journey through Frederick, Maryland, and the nearby Catoctin Mountain Park.

In 1776, the Maryland legislature established a military post in Fredericktown. Hessian soldiers captured by the Continental Army were used to construct the barracks and supply depot. The barracks were later used during the Civil War and, in one instance, served as a hospital for the wounded from the nearby Battle of the Monocacy. Visitors may view the barracks as well as other famous buildings from our nation's past at no charge.

Frederick is immortalized in John Greenleaf Whittier's poem written in 1864 and entitled "Barbara Fritchie":

*"The clustered spires of Frederick stand
Green-walled by the hills of Maryland."*

Barbara Fritchie is buried in Mount Olivet Cemetery, six blocks from her home at 154 West Patrick Street, where she, an ardent Unionist, is supposed to have waved her famous flag at the Confederate General "Stonewall" Jackson. The episode is recorded in Whittier's poem:

*"'Shoot if you must, this old grey head,
But spare your country's flag,' she said."*

Other important figures from American history are buried in the same cemetery including Francis Scott Key, who wrote *The Star Spangled Banner.*

On South Bentz Street you will see the home of Roger Brooke Taney, the fifth Chief Justice of the Supreme Court. Chief Justice Taney wrote the famous Dred Scott decision which established that slaves were the property of their masters and not citizens and that Congress had no power to exclude slavery from the territories. The Taney House is tastefully furnished in the style of the period, 1801–1823, when Judge Taney lived there. It is open by appointment only.

As you head away from Frederick toward Catoctin Mountain Park you may want to make a short detour to see one of the several photogenic covered bridges in this area. You'll find it eight miles out of Frederick, a short distance from Lewistown. If you continue on this road you come to the Albert Powell Trout Hatchery. To reach Catoctin Mountain Park continue on Route 15 for about a mile past Thurmont.

One of the biggest attractions in Catoctin Mountain Park is the Blue Blazes Whiskey Still operated on weekends by the National Park Service. This is a real still brought to western Maryland from the Smokey Mountains in Tennessee. (Not that there weren't stills in Maryland—moonshiners did operate in this area during Prohibition in the 1920s.) Just like the old-time stills the Blue Blazes works are hidden in a grove of beech trees. The still is operated on Saturdays and Sundays from Memorial Day weekend through October from 11:00 a.m. to 5:00 p.m.

Cunningham Falls State Park is another popular part of the Catoctin Mountain Park which has become well-known as the site of the Presidential retreat, Camp David. Although Camp David is off-limits to visitors, the rest of this 4,446-acre forest provides ample rewards. Cunningham Falls is spectacular because the waters of Big Hunting Creek cascade down a 40-foot rocky gorge. A trail leads from the West Picnic Area to Cunningham Falls and numerous wooded trails interweaving throughout the park offer, depending on how long a hike you want to take, panoramic vistas from lookouts such as Cat Rock, Bobs Hill and Isobel Rock. Within the park a 40-acre stocked lake provides trout fishing for adults with a license; children under 16 may fish without a license. The lake is also suitable for swimming and boating.

Cunningham Falls State Park is open daily from sunup to sunset. There is no admission charge for the park but entrance to the lake area, open only during the summer months, costs $3.00 per carload.

Directions: Catoctin Mountain Park is 60 miles from Washington. Take Beltway Exit 35 and follow Route 270 to Frederick. Take Route 15 out of Frederick to Thurmont and the eastern edge of the Park. The West Picnic Area with its trail to the Falls is located off Maryland Route 77.

GETTYSBURG MINIATURE HORSE FARM
Picture You upon a Mini-Horse

A trip to Gettysburg suggests historical monuments and battlefields but I'd like to recommend a quite different attraction—the Gettysburg Miniature Horse Farm. Children delight in horses no bigger than a German shepherd. The Lilliputians come in all breeds and colors: Appaloosa, Clydesdale, Arabian, English trotter, pinto, palomino, black and many others. They are extremely gentle and children love to pet their long, silky manes. You can put your child on one of these small horses for a quick picture at no charge. Young people also like the goats and sheep (in the new small animal area adjacent to the nature trail). Children can ride saddled miniature horses as they are led around the compound or take a ride on a wagon for a nominal fee. During daily training sessions, the horses entertain you with a free show of dancing, counting and responding to commands.

At present there are only 350 of these miniature horses in the world and the 50 horses at Gettysburg form the largest single group in the United States. The farm is open daily April to November, 9:00 a.m. to 5:00 p.m. Admission is charged. Special group rates are available upon request.

The Gettysburg area offers other attractions in the fall because it lies in orchard country. Markets abound with apples. You can see them being picked and buy them at a discount if you go to the orchards. Nearby Carroll Valley is known as a skiing area.

Directions: From the Beltway take Exit 35, I-270, to 15-N. Continue to 30-W, then make a left onto Knoxlyn. You will find that after you reach 30-W there will be signs to follow. To return by an alternate route through the apple fields, take a right out of Gettysburg onto Route 116. When you reach the Ski Liberty ski trails, turn left. This road will take you through the orchard area and back onto Route 116 at Fairfield. Continue west on Route 116 to the intersection of Route 97 and go into Emmitsburg. Take a right on Route 15 and follow this to I-270 at Frederick. I-270 takes you back to the Washington Beltway.

GUNPOWDER FALLS STATE PARK
Sure-Fire Fun

For their final eight-mile stretch, Big and Little Gunpowder Rivers join together in Maryland to flow into the Chesapeake Bay. There is a legend that the rivers got their names when early settlers gave gunpowder to the Indians who planted it along the riverbanks in hopes that it would grow. The Old Post Road passes the point where the Gunpowder River enters the Long Calm Ford, one of the most famous fording places of colonial days.

Within Gunpowder Falls State Park, whose 15,000 acres comprise Maryland's largest park, you will find many glimpses of America's past, including Jerusalem Mill, the only double-dormed mill in the United States. It was constructed in 1772 by David Lee. Behind the mill is a two-story building where Lee manufactured guns during the Revolutionary War.

There is a covered bridge on Jericho Road over the Little Gunpowder River near the Jerusalem Mill.

Near the Hereford area of the park is the 140-foot Pretty Boy Dam. Close to the dam stand the remains of the Clipper Paper Company built in 1775 by William Hoffman. The paper used by the Continental Congress was manufactured here.

Fishermen enjoy visiting Gunpowder Falls State Park. The renowned Chesapeake Bay delicacy, the blue crab, can be found in abundance from late summer through early fall in the Hammerman area. This area also has a 600-foot beach with a lifeguard and seven separate places to picnic. In the Hereford area of the park licensed fishermen can try their luck for bass, carp and catfish. At the mouth of the Gunpowder River you can catch striped bass, perch and pickerel.

Other activities that you can enjoy include hiking and bird watching. There is much in the park to interest amateur geologists. The park is open year-round during daylight hours. The only charge is an entrance fee for the Hammerman Area.

Directions: From the Beltway take Exit 22, the Baltimore-Washington Parkway, to the Baltimore Beltway (695). To reach the Hereford Area take Route 83 off Route 695. For the Hammerman Area take Route 40 off Route 695. From Route 40 take Ebenezer Road to the town of Chase. Hammerman Area is located on Graces Quarter's Road outside Chase.

HARPERS FERRY NATIONAL HISTORICAL PARK
Raid Harpers Ferry and Relive American History

An excursion to West Virginia offers a rare chance for historical sightseeing in an area of breathtaking natural beauty. Nestled in a rocky gorge in the Appalachian Mountains where the Shenandoah River enters the Potomac River is Harpers Ferry, the scene of John Brown's Raid and several Civil War skirmishes. The town was established in 1747; many pre-Civil War buildings still remain in spite of the fact that in 1862 General "Stonewall" Jackson captured the city. You may take an extensive walking tour which begins at the Visitor's Center and leads to the old fort and to Jefferson Rock. The Visitor's Center is located in the Old Stagecoach Inn and will provide you with a pamphlet to guide you on the walking tour. The tour includes historic old houses such as Harper House and the Master Armorer's House, which is now a gun-making museum. The houses are open to visitors in the summer. In addition, the tour includes natural sites such as Jefferson Rock where Thomas Jefferson looked out over the rugged countryside and proclaimed the panoramic view "stupendous" and "worth a voyage across the Atlantic."

For hiking enthusiasts, a three-mile hike follows the Appalachian Trail or an alternate hike leads to the ruins of a stone fort on Maryland Heights. The trail ascends to an almost bare ridge with a spectacular view of the Shenandoah and Potomac valleys. Additional information is available at the Visitor's Center; you can write Superintendent, P.O. Box 65, Harpers Ferry, West Virginia 25425, for a free brochure entitled *A Visitor's Guide to Harpers Ferry.*

Directions: Take Beltway Exit 35, I-270. Proceed to the outskirts of Frederick, then west on Route 340 to the park. It is 53 miles from the Beltway.

HAWK MOUNTAIN AND WK&S STEAM RAILROAD
Your Own Eyrie

Seeing birds of prey in the wild takes us back to the time before increased urbanization separated us from all but caged wildlife. Residents of the Washington–Baltimore urban sprawl are fortunate to have places such as Hawk Mountain, Pennsylvania, to escape to.

Hawk Mountain is the first sanctuary in the United States created for the protection of migratory birds of prey such as the hawk, vulture, falcon and eagle and ten other species. An invigorating one-mile hike takes you to a rocky overlook where you can peer far down the valley and far up to the wild birds in flight. This cloud-like perch is particularly attractive in the fall when the foliage is at its peak. The birds migrate from August through December.

Hawks and eagles are daytime fliers and use the mountains to capitalize on the air currents created by the mountain ridges. These currents permit the birds to glide for long stretches and thus enable them to conserve their energy for the remainder of their migration. Hawk Mountain is at the southern edge of the convection currents so the birds often rest here; the rest of the journey southward entails much wing beating.

The Hawk Mountain Sanctuary encompasses 2,000 acres of the Allegheny Mountain range. There is a Visitor's Center with exhibits of mounted birds of prey to aid you in identifying the birds you might see. Admission to the sanctuary is charged. It is about a four-hour drive from the Washington Beltway to Hawk Mountain.

This outing with its extended bird watching may seem a bit slow for younger children so as a special treat you can include a stop at the WK&S Steam Railroad, the Hawk Mountain line. You can take a 40-minute ride in an authentic heavy-weight passenger car from the Reading and Lackawanna railroads. Another option is the 35-minute trolley trip. From September through November when most bird watchers visit Hawk Mountain, the trains run on weekends from 1:00 to 4:30 p.m. From March through June, hours are 1:00 to 5:00 p.m. The WK&S is closed December through February. For fare information call (215)756-6469 or (215)437-1239.

Directions: Take Beltway Exit 27, I-95, north for Hawk Mountain. At the Baltimore Beltway head west toward Towson. Take I-83 north past Harrisburg. From there you will merge with I-78/US-22. Follow this to the Pennsylvania Route 61 Exit which will read Pottsville, Port Clinton. Take this for 4.5 miles to Pennsylvania Route 895, then go east for 2.5 miles to Drehersville. From there follow the signs for two miles to the Hawk Mountain Sanctuary.

For the WK&S return to Route 61, and head south until it crosses Route 22 (I-78). Turn left on Route 22 and continue to Krumsville. Go left on Pennsylvania Route 739 to Kempton and the Railroad Station.

INDIAN RESERVATIONS
No Need to Wire Ahead

There are certain holidays that remind us of our historical past—Thanksgiving is certainly one. From grade school on, Americans associate November with reflections on our colonial past, the joining of settlers and Indians to give thanks. In the Washington area when your thoughts turn to the role played by the Indians in our past, you can bring those long-ago years to life by visiting Virginia's two Indian reservations.

When the English arrived in Virginia in 1607 the area they settled was part of the Powhatan Confederation. Of the 30 Algonquin-speaking tribes in this network two remain, the Pamunkey and the Mattaponi.

Located side-by-side near West Point, Virginia, these two tribes have endured. Though they both have museums, they use very different approaches to presenting the past. At the Pamunkey Indian Reservation an interpretive museum will give you a very complete picture of the tribe's roots anchored in prehistoric times. One excellent display traces specific tools as they changed from crude implements in the Archaic Period to more detailed and accurate pieces in the Historic Period. The changes in pottery design are also traced through the decades. Pottery and other Indian handicrafts can be purchased at the Trading Post and Gift Shop.

There is another point of interest, the ongoing 16th-century Pamunkey Village project. Both the completed wigwams and those that are still being constructed show very clearly how the Indians utilized the materials at hand to build their homes.

You can visit the Pamunkey Indian Reservation daily from 9:00 a.m. to 5:00 p.m. Admission is charged.

Across the highway at the Mattaponi's Stone Age Indian Museum there is a one-room collection that presents artifacts from the tribe's long history in an overlapping array that bewilders many visitors. Children, though, often enjoy this display more than the well ordered educational approach.

There are individual pieces rich with history—a headdress worn by Powhatan and a necklace which belonged to Pocahontas. Tomahawks, medicine bags and fossils are particular favorites of young adventurers.

The Mattaponi Stone Age Indian Museum is open on weekends from 10:00 a.m. to 6:00 p.m. A small admission is charged.

Directions: Take Virginia Beltway Exit 4, I-95, south to the outskirts of Richmond. From there take Route 360 north for about 15 miles to Route 30 south. There will be signs off Route 30 for both reservations. From Route 30 take Route 633 eight miles to the Pamunkey Indian reservation. The Mattaponi is almost directly across the highway and signs will indicate the turn for this second reservation. From Route 30 you will make a left onto Route 640 and another left onto Route 624 for the Mattaponi Reservation.

LADEW TOPIARY GARDENS
Yew-All Will Love It

If you have trouble keeping your evergreens green and your hedges clipped you will appreciate the amount of time, work and skill involved in maintaining the more than one-third mile of stately yew and hemlock hedges at Ladew Topiary Gardens in Maryland. Topiary is the art of trimming and training shrubs and trees into ornamental shapes. It was much in vogue in the English country gardens during the Tudor and Elizabethan periods. The Garden Club of America has called this "the most outstanding topiary garden in America."

The Ladew Gardens, started more than 50 years ago, have 15 seasonal flower gardens surrounding the topiary. These gardens are interspersed with fountains, streams, statuary and fanciful buildings. Visitors will see topiary poodles, sea horses, birds of paradise, lyrebirds and rows of pyramid-topped hedges. One particularly entrancing area is the great bowl surrounded by terraces and hedges, one section of which is sculpted into shapes of swans swimming in rippling water. But the major attraction of this 250-acre estate is an unbelievable life-size hunt scene depicting a hunter, his horse, a fox and the hounds in full cry. The unique manor house (open Wednesday and Sunday at additional charge) contains fine collections of china, furniture, paintings and fox hunting memorabilia.

Ladew Topiary Gardens are open from mid-April through October Tuesdays through Saturdays from 10:00 a.m. to 4:00 p.m. and Sundays from noon to 5:00 p.m. Admission is charged. For information on special events call (301)557-9466. It is a one-hour drive from the Washington Beltway.

Directions: Take Exit 27, I-95, north from the Washington Beltway. At the Baltimore Beltway, 695, go west toward Towson. From the Baltimore Beltway take Exit 27 north to Route 146. Follow Route 146 past Jacksonville for about five miles. The Gardens are on the right. Be careful to stay on Route 146 where it divides just past Loch Raven Reservoir.

LEXINGTON MARKET AND INNER HARBOR
The Sub: Eat It at the Market, Tour It at the Harbor

The sign over the door invites you to visit "World Famous Lexington Market." Though it hardly rivals the Los Angeles Farmers Market, this Baltimore market is certainly a thriving example of an old-fashioned farmers market. Located in three large buildings in the heart of downtown Baltimore, it has parking garages under each building!

A cornucopia of fruits and vegetables and other fresh produce awaits you in the market's 100 stalls. A wide range of meat, poultry and fish is offered by butchers who cut the fresh meat and clean the fish to order. Some stands offer prepared foods, so you might want to visit around lunchtime and try some Sicilian pizza, Polish sausage, hot soft pretzels, barbecued chicken or steamed crabs. Although you will not find the prices any lower than those in the supermarket, shopping at the market is an intriguing experience for anyone brought up on prepackaged foods. Lexington Market is open 8:00 a.m. to 6:00 p.m. daily except Sundays and holidays.

From Lexington Market take S. Paca to Pratt Street, go left on Pratt Street and head down to the Inner Harbor area. On the southern rim of the harbor is the Maryland Science Center. This is not a collection of static displays but rather an assortment of experiments and programs that actively involve both children and adults. The Davis Planetarium, a part of the Science Center, has shows about the United States space program, UFOs and futuristic space forays. In its Boyd Theatre all kinds of props, projectors, demonstrations and experiments encourage one to explore nature's laws. For younger visitors the K.I.D.S. (Key Into the Discovery of Science) room lets 4- to 7-year-olds investigate the scientific world at a level they can enjoy and appreciate.

The Maryland Science Center has a rather steep admission price. To get the most for your dollar, allow adequate time to explore all the experiments, exhibits and special programs. Hours during the summer months are daily 10:00 a.m. to 8:00 p.m. After Labor Day and until the last week of June it is open Monday through Thursday from 10:00 a.m. to 5:00 p.m., Fridays and Saturdays from 10:00 a.m. until 10:00 p.m. and on Sundays from noon to 6:00 p.m.

Docked at the Inner Harbor you will see the *USS Constellation*, described in the spring selection with Cylburn Arboretum and Sherwood Gardens, and the *USS Torsk*, one of the high speed attack subs launched during World War II. The *USS Torsk* saw action off Japan and was the command sub of a Wolf Pack called "Lou's Tiger Sharks." She holds the world record for submersion with 11,884 dives to her credit.

If you have never been inside a submarine this will be some experience. The crew's quarters where 36 men slept are about 14 feet by 30 feet. The narrow bunks are only 18 inches apart. Visitors can tour the *USS Torsk* from Memorial Day to the end of September on Monday through Thursday from noon to 8:00 p.m. From October through Memorial Day hours are 10:30 a.m. to 4:30 p.m. Admission is charged.

There is also the outstanding National Aquarium. In 1982 more people visited the Inner Harbor than Disneyland, according to Baltimore's Tourist Office, and the big attraction was this fascinating aquatic world. The aquarium hardly qualifies as an offbeat excursion but it is too captivating to be passed by. Seeing the Atlantic Coral Reef is the next best thing to snorkeling in the Caribbean.

If you want to explore the harbor on your own, rowboats, pedal boats and sailboats can be rented from early spring until late October. The rental area is adjacent to the *Constellation* dock. There are also excursion boats that depart from the dock and cruise down the Patapsco River to Fort McHenry. The *Port Welcome* and *Port Baltimore* sail out into the Chesapeake Bay for trips to Annapolis and Maryland's Eastern Shore. For cruise information call (301)383-5705.

Directions: Take Beltway Exit 22, the Baltimore-Washington Parkway, which leads into Russell Street and then becomes S. Paca. Proceed up S. Paca Street to the Lexington Market. For the Inner Harbor take S. Paca to Pratt Street and go left on Pratt and down to the Inner Harbor. To return from the harbor, turn right on Lombard Street and go down to Greene Street and make a left. This will lead back to Russell Street and the Baltimore-Washington Parkway.

MARY SURRATT HOUSE
Conspirator in Crinolines

The Mary Surratt House in Clinton, Maryland, calls up the tragic past of its owner. The house was one of the stops on the blood-stained trail of John Wilkes Booth after he had assassinated Abraham Lincoln. For her role in that criminal conspiracy Mary Surratt was the first woman executed by the Federal Government. Who was she and how did she become involved in one of the blackest crimes in the annals of American history?

The restored house you can explore today was built in 1852 by John Surratt. It served as home for his family, as a tavern and gathering place for the community as well as the post office and polling place. It was perhaps inevitable that southern Maryland dissidents who were unhappy with their state's northern status would gather here. By 1862 John Surratt had died and Mary had sole responsibility for her three children. Her youngest son, John Jr., left college to help her run the tavern and fell under the sway of the Confederate sympathizers; in fact, the tavern became a safe house for agents of the Confederacy.

It was this involvement that led to the day when Mary Surratt left field glasses and guns at the tavern for John Wilkes Booth. This action cost her her life. She was executed on July 7, 1865. It is worth noting that when her son, John, was tried for virtually the same crime in 1867 the court decided it did not have sufficient evidence to convict him.

Both floors of the Mary Surratt House are furnished with antiques from the early to mid-Victorian era. In late June this bygone period is evoked in a Victorian Wedding that has become one of the Surratt Society's most popular annual events. Another program the Society sponsors is the twice-yearly John Wilkes Booth Escape Trail Tour that guides you over the route he took from Ford's Theatre to the site of the farm, now the Fort A. P. Hill military base, where Booth was finally cornered and shot.

The Mary Surratt House is open March through December on Thursday and Friday from 11:00 a.m. to 3:00 p.m. and on weekends from noon to 4:00 p.m. Admission is charged.

Directions: Take Maryland Beltway Exit 7, Route 5, Branch Avenue to Woodyard Road, Route 223 in Clinton. Take a right on Woodyard Road, then turn left at the second traffic light onto Brandywine Road. The Mary Surratt House is on the left at 9110 Brandywine Road.

MERCER TRIO
Tools, Tiles and Trails

Most collectors have to winnow acquisitions when they outgrow storage space. Not Dr. Henry Chapman Mercer. He built a castle in Doylestown, Pennsylvania, to contain his collection of 40,000 artifacts. Built in 1916, the Mercer Museum is operated today by the Bucks County Historical Society. Hobbyists, history buffs and art enthusiasts are amazed by the magnitude of Mercer's collection. The necessary implements for more than 40 crafts are represented here.

Mercer's home, Fonthill, is also in Doylestown and is open to the public. The mansion contains Dr. Mercer's engaging private tile and print collection. On the grounds surrounding the estate are wooded paths maintained by the Department of Parks and Recreations.

The Mercer Museum is open 10:00 a.m. to 4:30 p.m. Monday through Saturday. On Sunday it is open 1:00 p.m. until 4:30 p.m. Fonthill has 50-minute tours every 15 minutes from 10:00 a.m. to 3:30 p.m. Admission is charged for both places and they are closed during January and February.

While in the Doylestown area you might try to fit in a visit to the Moravian Pottery and Tile Works, also built by Dr. Mercer. Mercer Tiles, unique patented picture tiles, have been used worldwide. One of the best collections of the tiles is in Harrisburg's State Capitol Building where 400 tiles depict Pennsylvania history from colonial times to the 20th century.

The Moravian Pottery and Tile Works is open Wednesday through Sunday, 10:00 a.m. to 4:00 p.m. Admission is charged for this attraction.

Directions: From the Beltway take Exit 27, I-95, north into Wilmington, Delaware. From I-95 go north on Route 202 to the Pennsylvania Turnpike. Go east on the Pennsylvania Turnpike to Willow Grove, Exit 27. From Willow Grove travel north on Route 611 to Doylestown. Do not take the Doylestown Bypass. Route 611 becomes South Main Street.

To reach the Mercer Museum, drive to the first traffic light and turn right on Ashland Street. Turn right again onto Green Street; the museum and parking lot will be on your left.

To reach Fonthill, go back up Main Street four blocks to Court Street. Turn right on Court Street and drive six blocks to Fonthill, which is set back from the road on the left.

There is parking on the Fonthill estate serving both Fonthill and the Moravian Pottery and Tile Works.

NATIONAL RADIO ASTRONOMY OBSERVATORY
Studying the Universe with Radio Waves

A full day's trip on which half of the fun is getting there is an excursion to the National Radio Astronomy Observatory at Green Bank, West Virginia. Your route will take you through some of the most spectacular fall foliage on the East Coast.

Green Bank was chosen as the site for the National Radio Astronomy Observatory because it is sparsely populated and its mountains serve as a shield against man-made radio and electrical noise. In fact, the Federal Communications Commission imposes a National Radio Quiet Zone to minimize potential sources of radio interference with the delicate task of collecting and measuring extremely faint radio waves from celestial objects.

There are conducted tours on the hour from 9:00 a.m. to 4:00 p.m. during the summer from mid-June through Labor Day. A fall visit will have to be planned for a weekend because from Labor Day through October tours are held only on Saturday and Sunday at the same hours. The free tours begin with an introductory film on radio astronomy and the Observatory. After the film there is a narrated bus tour of the area that takes you to the giant radio telescopes. You will learn how radio waves from outer space are detected and how they are used to study the universe. The giant antennas, one 300 feet in diameter, are an unusual sight in such a pastoral setting.

Just a short ten-minute drive from Green Bank is another attraction which offers a nostalgic return to the past via a ride on an authentically restored early-1900s steam powered logger. Cass Scenic Railroad is in an 855-acre state park.

From Memorial Day to Labor Day you can take a two-and-a-half hour round trip through the Monongahela National Forest to Whittaker. A longer four-and-a-half hour round trip to Bald Knob would not be feasible for a one-day excursion from Washington. No reservations are needed for these rides. For up-to-date information on fares call the toll-free number, (800)624-8632.

You should plan to leave Washington early in the morning as this trip takes about 5½ hours from the Beltway. Your first stop should be the Cass Scenic Railroad for their trip to Whittaker. If you arrive in Cass with some time to spare before the train leaves you can catch the displays of railroad memorabilia and old photos at the History Museum or sample the wares at the old country store. You may even want to purchase picnic supplies and enjoy lunch in the park. After your train ride you will have time for a visit to the National Radio Astronomy Observatory before heading home.

Directions: From the Beltway take Virginia Exit 9, I-66 west, to Route 81 south. Continue to Harrisonburg and take Route 33 west for 55 miles to Route 28. Turn left and take Route 28 south for 33 miles to Green Bank. The National Radio Astronomy Observatory is on the right. The Cass Scenic Railroad is 4 miles farther on Route 28.

NEW HOPE
Arts and Crafts, Barges and Trains

A trip to Bucks County, Pennsylvania, offers something for all members of the family: quaint shops, historical landmarks, barge rides on the Delaware canal, a wild flower preserve and a steam train ride through the Pennsylvania countryside. There is so much to do that you will have to choose judiciously in planning a one-day excursion.

Because New Hope is about a four-hour drive from the Washington area, you might want to head there first and then branch out. New Hope is an artists' colony with many galleries and the well-known Bucks County Playhouse which operates April through November with matinees on Wednesday, Thursday and Sunday at 2:00 p.m. For up-to-date ticket and performance information call (215)862-2041.

A welcome fortifying first stop might be the ice cream parlor on Main Street. Don't think Main Street completes your window shopping in New Hope. Some of the most unusual shops are on the side streets such as Ney Alley. For those who are not content to see the exterior of old towns such as this without exploring at least one house, there is the Parry Mansion on Cannon Square. It is open courtesy of the Historical Society from 2:00 to 5:00 p.m. Friday through Monday. Each of the mansion's ten rooms reflect the decor and life-style of a different period from the late 18th to the early 20th century.

Young children bored with in-town browsing will relish the mule-drawn barge trips on the historic Delaware canal. From May through mid-September the barge trips run daily about every hour. During April and from mid-September to mid-November the barge rides are on Wednesday, Saturday and Sunday. Reservations may be made for this popular ride by calling (215)862-2842. If you can't arrange a ride along the canal, don't miss the chance to take a short walk along the towpath. From 1828 to 1931 mule-drawn barges carried goods through New Hope until outcompeted by the railroad.

You can experience for yourself the difference between canal and rail transportation by taking an 8½-mile train ride on the New Hope Steam Railway. This rail line was constructed between 1889 and 1890 and opened its first passenger car service in 1891. The old New Hope Station with its unusual architectural witches' peak, the railroad museum in the freight station and the ticket office and gift shop in the baggage car will bring back the days of early locomotive travel. Movie buffs may recognize the curved trestle bridge used for last minute rescue scenes in the *Perils of Pauline* matinee serials. The train chugs through some of the most beautiful rolling farmland in the east to Lahaska and then back to New Hope.

From May through October the train leaves on Saturday at 1:30 and 3:30 p.m., on Sunday at 1:15, 2:45 and 4:15 p.m. The train runs only on Sunday during November and rides then are at 1:30 and 3:15 p.m. For more information call (215)750-0872.

If you have a weekend to spend in Bucks County, consider stopping at either Washington Crossing Historic Park or Peddler's Village in Lahaska. Washington Crossing Historic Park, just a few miles from New Hope, marks the spot where George Washington and his 2,400 men crossed the Delaware on Christmas night, 1776. They attacked the Hessian troops and went on to capture Trenton. Various historic buildings bring to life those momentous times. In the spring and early summer nature lovers won't want to miss Bowman's Hill Wildflower Preserve. This northern portion of the park just three miles from New Hope has 100 acres filled with roughly 800 species of wild flowers, bog flowers, unusual orchids and other plants.

Further diversion is offered by some 40 craft and gift shops in Peddler's Village just up Route 202 from New Hope. There are stores in a reproduced grist mill, an early Pennsylvania log barn, brick paths, sidewalk benches, flowers and a number of eateries. Shops are open year-round 10:00 a.m. to 5:00 p.m. Monday through Saturday and 12:00 to 5:00 p.m. on Sunday.

Directions: Take Beltway Exit 27, I-95, north past Philadelphia. Use the New Hope exit and take Route 32, River Road, to New Hope. You will reach the turn-off on Route 532 for Washington Crossing Historic Park before you come to New Hope. For Lahaska take Route 202 from New Hope to Peddler's Village at the intersection of Route 202 and Route 263.

POPE-LEIGHEY HOUSE AND WOODLAWN PLANTATION
Dual Dream House

An interesting architectural contrast between the old and the new can be seen at Woodlawn Plantation. On the grounds of this colonial estate you see a Federal-style plantation house built in the early 19th century and a Frank Lloyd Wright suburban house from the mid-20th century.

The Pope-Leighey House is the unexpected surprise. It was moved to this plantation site in 1964 from its original location in Falls Church, Virginia. Built there in 1940, it was the second of Wright's Usonian houses, built by him to provide a well-designed house for people of modest income. Five Usonian houses were built along the east coast. As Wright himself explained it, "To give the little family the benefit of industrial advantages of the era in which they live, something else must be done for them than to plan another little imitation of a mansion. Simplifications must take place. They must themselves see life in somewhat simplified terms."

Although this Usonian house is made of cypress rather than concrete like Wright's later ones, it does readily demonstrate his contributions to modern architecture. The house has unplastered cypress paneling both inside and out. It is built on a concrete slab and blends cypress, brick and glass. The flat roof and carport have since become standard features on suburban homes. Wright's ability to achieve organic unity and use space and light are very much in evidence in the design of the Pope-Leighey House.

It is fortunate that the landscape at Woodlawn Plantation resembles the house's original surroundings 15 miles away in Falls Church because the integration of a building with its natural setting was an important consideration for Wright. The Pope-Leighey House was moved here in 1964 when Interstate Highway 66 was being built. The house was dismantled, moved and then reassembled, fortunately by the same master craftsman who had originally built the house and furniture. It is well to remember when visiting this house that it was indeed a prototype.

The plantation house that shares the grounds was, on the other hand, a deliberate copy. The house was designed to resemble Kenmore, the family home of Lawrence Lewis, son of George Washington's sister, Betty. It was furnished with family pieces collected by his bride, Nellie Parke Custis, from her home, Mount Vernon. Nellie was the stepdaughter of George Washington and he gave her the land for this home as part of her dowry.

Woodlawn, in addition to being attractively furnished with period pieces, has one special room for youngsters, The Touch and Try Room. Old-fashioned games and toys are here to be enjoyed, not displayed as museum pieces. On pleasant days the hoops and stilts can be used on the lawn.

The Pope-Leighey House is normally open from 9:30 a.m. to 4:30 p.m. on weekends from March through October, but the illness of Mrs. Leighey, who has life tenancy, has forced a temporary closing of the interior. Call (703)557-7880 before visiting to see if the house is open. Woodlawn Plantation is open at the same hours year-round except Christmas Day.

Directions: From the Beltway take Exit 1, U.S. 1, south for 14 miles to the Woodlawn Plantation and the Pope-Leighey House on the right.

PUMPKIN PATCHES
Maybe You'll Find the Great Pumpkin

Halloween can become more than a time for children to dress up in costumes; it can also mean pumpkin picking time. A pumpkin they have found themselves can be a real treat and a nice way to spend a crisp October day.

During the month of October, Robin Hill Farm Nursery sponsors a Pumpkin Harvest Farm Tour. The tour of this southern Maryland farm includes a stop at the tobacco operations; a chance to see pigs, horses, cows, goats, chickens and waterfowl, to enjoy a straw ride on the big hay wagon, to wander around the pumpkin field and find just the right jack-o'-lantern. The pumpkins are reasonably priced. You can arrange to visit any day in October by calling (301)579-6844.

If you want a slightly longer hike to the pumpkin patch visit Potomac Vegetable Farm in Vienna, Virginia. You may have to walk about a half mile to the pumpkin field but on a nice day that can be part of the fun. Both here and at Robin Hill you can bring a picnic lunch to make your outing more festive. Potomac Vegetable Farm is open daily from 8:30 a.m. to dusk; for more information call (703)759-2119.

Directions: From the Beltway take Maryland Exit 11, Route 4 to Route 301. Go south on Route 301 for about four miles to Croom Road (Maryland Route 382). Take a left on Croom Road and go about eight miles to Robin Hill Farm Nursery. While in this area you might want to stop at Patuxent Park where there are numerous migratory waterfowl in the fall.

For Potomac Vegetable Farm take Virginia Exit 11S from the Beltway. Take Route 123 to the intersection of Route 7. Follow Route 7 west for about four miles to the farm.

The following is a list of additional local pumpkin patches.

MARYLAND

Anne Arundel County

Belvoir Berry Farm
Linda Brown
1489 Generals Highway
Crownsville, MD 21032
(301)923-2107

Open: May through November
Pick-Your-Own (PYO) Selections: Pumpkins, Thornless
Blackberries and Strawberries
Special Comments: You can arrange hayrides for birthday
parties; you can also cut your own firewood.

Baltimore County

Rutkowski & Taylor Farm
J. Taylor and A. Rutkowski
11211 Raphel Road
Upper Falls, MD 21156
(301)592-8785
Open: May through November
PYO Selections: Pumpkins, Strawberries and a complete
selection of vegetables
Special Comments: There are hayrides and farm tours.

Frederick County

Glade-Link Farms
Shirley A. Wisner
9332 Links Road
Walkersville, MD 21793
(301)898-7181
Open: Spring, summer and fall
PYO Selections: Pumpkins, Blueberries, Strawberries,
Broccoli and Cauliflower

Howard County

Larriland Farm
G. Lawrence Moore
2525 Florence Road
Woodbine, MD 21797
(301)854-6110
Open: Late May through October and again in December
PYO Selections: Pumpkins, Apples, Blackberries, Red
Raspberries, Peaches, Strawberries and a complete
selection of vegetables
Special Comments: There is a farm festival the first
weekend in October; you can arrange farm tours and
hayrides; also available are Christmas trees, country hams
and firewood.

Charles County

Cedar Hill Farm
Route 5
Waldorf, MD 20601
(301)843-6801
Open: Summer and fall
PYO Selections: Pumpkins, fall greens and a complete
selection of vegetables
Special Comments: Cider is sold at the farm.

Montgomery County

Butler's Orchard
George H. Butler, Jr.
22200 Davis Mill Road
Germantown, MD 20874
(301)972-3299
Open: Spring, summer and fall
PYO Selections: Pumpkins, Thornless Blackberries, Red
Raspberries, Strawberries and a complete selection of
vegetables
Special Comments: There are free hayrides on October
weekends.

Rock Hill Orchard
Richard A. Biggs
28600 Ridge Road
Mt. Airy, MD 21771
(301)831-7427
Open: June through November
PYO Selections: Pumpkins, Red Raspberries, Strawberries
and a complete selection of vegetables
Special Comments: There are fall pumpkin tours;
grapevine wreaths and herbal products are available.

Prince George's County

Cherry Hill Farm
William A. Gallahan & Sons
12300 Gallahan Road
Clinton, MD 20735
(301)292-4642 or 292-1928
Open: April through November

PYO Selections: Pumpkins, Apples, Blueberries, Strawberries and a complete selection of vegetables
Special Comments: There are wagon rides to and from the fields and children's wagon rides during October.

E. A. Parker & Sons
Rod and Chris Parker
12720 Parker Lane
Clinton, MD 20735
(301)292-3940
Open: Spring, summer and fall
PYO Selections: Pumpkins, Thornless Blackberries, Table Grapes, Strawberries and a complete selection of vegetables
Special Comments: You can arrange hayrides in the fall; organic grains flour and canning supplies are available.

Miller Farms
Henry P. Miller and Charles P. Miller
10200 Piscataway Road
Clinton, MD 20735
(301)207-5878, 297-4562
Open: May to December
PYO Selections: Pumpkins, Strawberries and a complete selection of vegetables

VIRGINIA

Fairfax County

Cox Farms
Gina Richard
2599 Chain Bridge Road
Vienna, VA 22180
(703)281-0165
Open: June through October
PYO Selections: Pumpkins and Strawberries
Special Comments: Children can enjoy cider, hayrides and picking pumpkins from mid to late October.

Fauquier County

Manor Lane Berry Farm
Jack and Louise Vinis
Rt. 2, Box 103
Warrenton, VA 22186
(703)347-4883
Open: May through October
PYO Selections: Pumpkins and Strawberries

Frederick County

Raspberry Ridge Farms
Jack K. Jenkins
Rt. 1, Box 273
Winchester, VA 22601
(703)662-4552
Open: June through October
PYO Selections: Pumpkins and a complete selection of
vegetables

Loudoun County

Chantilly Farm Market
Tim Hutchinson or Claire Crockett
Rt. 2, Box 238-B
Leesburg, VA 22075
(703)777-4041
Open: June through October
PYO Selections: Pumpkins, Strawberries, Sugar Snap
Peas, Eggplant, Corn and Tomatoes

Cochran's Vegetable Farm
George B. and Emily B. Cochran
P.O. Box 3
Lincoln, VA 22078
(703)338-7248 or 338-7002
Open: May through October
PYO Selections: Pumpkins, Strawberries and a complete
selection of vegetables

Spotsylvania County

Belvedere Plantation
M. R. Fulks
Star Rt. TWT, Box 125
Fredericksburg, VA 22401
(703)371-8494 or 690-1255 (toll free/dial direct number
from northern Virginia and Washington, D.C.)
Open: May through October
PYO Selections: Pumpkins, Strawberries, Thornless
Blackberries and a complete selection of vegetables
Special Comments: There is a picnic area available.

Strasburg Rail Road
*If Your Trip to Hollywood's Been Derailed, Try the
Strasburg R. R.*

A dults and children alike will delight in a ride into the
past on an old-fashioned turn-of-the-century steam train
at the Strasburg Rail Road. Located in the heart of the
Pennsylvania Dutch country, just a little over a two-hour
drive from the Washington Beltway, Strasburg Rail Road
has been in operation for more than 150 years. It is the
second oldest railroad still in use in the United States.

For a very reasonable rate you can take a nine-mile round-
trip ride on the trains which depart hourly during the week
and every 30 minutes on weekend afternoons. The coaches
are faithfully restored with kerosene lamps, potbelly stoves,
inlaid wood paneling and plush seats. The trains blend perfectly with the rustic countryside. During the nine-mile ride,
the conductor talks about the old trains as well as the area
through which you are passing.

Many of the train coaches have interesting histories such
as Number 3556, the oldest standard-gauge coach in the
world, and Willow Brook, which is 60 years old and was
featured in the MGM movie *Raintree County.* Four other
coaches, including an open observation coach, were built
at Strasburg and featured in the movie *Hello, Dolly!* At the
old time railroad station, for an additional 25¢ per person,
you can climb aboard a railroad president's car. The Strasburg Rail Road operates year-round except from mid-
December to mid-January. There are many restaurants in

the area that feature Pennsylvania Dutch food, which is a must if you have never tasted it. The names of the foods, such as shoofly pie, are enchantment in themselves.

If you visit this area on Saturday, stop at the Southern Market in Lancaster just off Penn Square on Queen Street. Farm families bring their produce here to sell in the old-fashioned stalls. Three miles east of Lancaster on Route 462 is a working Amish farm you can tour year-round. Guided tours through the house and around the farm show you how the Amish live. For more information call (717)392-0832.

Directions: From the Beltway take Exit 27, I-95, to the Baltimore Beltway (695) and go northwest toward Towson. Then take Exit 24, I-83, north around York. From there take Route 30 east through Lancaster to Route 896. Turn right and proceed south on Route 896 to Strasburg. At the town square in Strasburg turn left and follow Route 741 to the Rail Road. For additional information about the Strasburg Rail Road, call (717)687-7522.

SUGAR LOAF MOUNTAIN
Sweetens Nature

The goal of many day-trips is to find a good vantage point from which to enjoy and appreciate nature's bounty. One of the best views, particularly during the autumn foliage display, is from the top of Sugar Loaf Mountain near Dickerson, Maryland.

First charted as early as 1707, Sugar Loaf rises 1,283 feet above sea level. This little mountain rises up in dramatic contrast to the farmland at its foot. It was named Sugar Loaf by early pioneers and hunters because its shape recalled to them the sugar loaves their wives and mothers prepared.

On a clear day you may not be able to see forever, but you will see spread below you a land rich in our country's history. To the south you can see Bull Run; to the west, Catoctin and the Blue Ridge Mountains; and to the north, the Frederick Valley.

In 1775 during the French and Indian War, Braddock passed Sugar Loaf as he led his men to defeat at the Battle of Fort Duquesne. The mountain served as a lookout post during the Civil War. In 1862 from this spot Lee was sighted by a Union soldier as he crossed the Potomac prior to the bloody Battle of Antietam. In fact, soldiers wounded in that battle were treated in the log cabin still standing at the foot of Sugar Loaf.

The mountain was acquired by Gordon Strong after he discovered it while on a vacation in 1902. He bought the property gradually over the years, naming his Georgian-Colonial estate built in 1912 and the land on which it stood—Stronghold. The Strongs entertained many distinguished guests. When President Franklin Roosevelt visited the mountain in the early 1940s he wanted to obtain it. He was persuaded instead to turn his attention to the 10,000 acres in Thurmont which the government already owned. There he built his presidential retreat and named it, at Gordon Strong's suggestion, Shangri-La. President Eisenhower renamed it Camp David.

When you visit you'll understand why President Roosevelt was so taken with Sugar Loaf Mountain, now preserved as a Registered National Natural Landmark. There are three walking trails and one horse trail. The 5½-mile trail across the mountain peak was devised and is maintained by the local chapter of the Appalachian Trail.

For those who want a shorter hike there is a winding road that extends up the mountain for about a mile with a number of overlooks to give you several perspectives from which to enjoy the surrounding countryside. At the end of the paved road there is a ¼-mile trail to the mountain top.

At the fourth level you'll find picnic tables and rustic facilities. A snack bar is open on weekends and holidays. You can visit Sugar Loaf Mountain from 7:00 a.m. to sunset daily without charge. It is now owned and operated by Stronghold, Inc., established by Gordon Strong in 1946 so that the public could enjoy and appreciate Sugar Loaf's natural beauty.

Directions: Take Beltway Exit 35, I-270, for about 28 miles to the Hyattstown Exit. Circle under I-270 and go west on Route 109 for 3.3 miles to Comus. Make a right on Route 95 for 2½ miles to Sugar Loaf Mountain.

THEODORE ROOSEVELT ISLAND
Rough, Ready and Rustic

An 88-acre wilderness preserve nestles between two booming metropolitan areas—Arlington, Virginia and Washington, D.C. The natural terrain of Theodore Roosevelt Island has been left undisturbed, the underbrush tangled, the trees untrimmed; if you ignore the jets landing at nearby National Airport, you will discover a peaceful retreat. On any visit you are likely to see people hiking and bicycling on the trails. It's also a popular place with pet owners because dogs may be taken along the trails if they are leashed.

The island park was presented to the American people in 1932 as a memorial to one of the country's most conservation-minded presidents, Theodore Roosevelt. Roosevelt deplored the despoliation of our natural resources. During his administration he created the U.S. Forest Service, five national parks, 51 bird sanctuaries and four game reserves. He focused the attention of the people on the wanton destruction that had been prevalent. The island serves as a living tribute to his foresightedness.

A large standing sculpture of Theodore Roosevelt dominates the northern section of the island. The 17-foot bronze statue in front of a 30-foot granite shaft presents an imposing sight. Surrounding the statue are terraced areas with enclosed boxwood plantings and urn-shaped fountains. A water-filled moat circles all and is spanned by marble footbridges.

On Saturdays at 2:00 p.m. there are history talks on Theodore Roosevelt and on Sundays at 2:00 p.m. guided nature walks. On weekend mornings at 8:30 a.m. Bird Walks are conducted on a prior reservation basis. The well-marked trails, however, enable anyone to be his own guide. Signs deal with various environmental aspects—the weathering process, the swamp, the fall line and many others. Any remaining questions you might have will be answered by the park guides.

There are three trails to take: the Swamp Trail, the Upland Trail and the Woods Trail. These are all short walks because the total trail length on the island is 2½ miles. The Swamp Trail provides a number of scenic vistas. You can watch people sculling on the Potomac from large boulders at the water's edge, or sit on a bench and enjoy a delightful view of the Kennedy Center or the Lincoln Memorial framed by the Theodore Roosevelt Bridge.

The marsh area with its cattails, pickerelweed and arrow arum provides the perfect terrain for marsh wrens, red-winged blackbirds and kingfishers. Muskrats, turtles and frogs are also common. The mudflats are rooting grounds for willows, red maples and ash trees and are home to the raccoons. Theodore Roosevelt Island is right off the Atlantic Flyway and in spring and fall black ducks, mallards, great blue herons, grosbeaks and many other birds rest here.

The Upland and Woods Trails wander through elms, tulip trees, maples and oaks. Here you can see downy woodpeckers, chickadees and wood thrushes with their neighbors the grey squirrels, chipmunks, red and grey foxes and cottontails. The island is a wildlife sanctuary and the plants, animals and birds are protected by law.

Theodore Roosevelt Island is open daily at no charge from 9:30 a.m. to dusk. For more information call (703)285-2601.

Directions: Theodore Roosevelt Island is inside the Beltway. From Washington take either George Mason Memorial Bridge or the Theodore Roosevelt Bridge onto the George Washington Memorial Parkway. The park entrance and parking lot is well marked and is on the east side of the Parkway near the Theodore Roosevelt Bridge in Virginia.

THUNDERBIRD MUSEUM AND ARCHEOLOGICAL PARK
Can You Dig It?

If you are tired of commercial attractions and find prehistory interesting, Thunderbird Museum and Archeological Park in Virginia is the place for you. You can learn much about what America was like thousands of years before Columbus landed.

The museum shows man's 11,000 years of prehistory in the Shenandoah Valley. A narrated color slide program introduces you to the basic techniques of archeology and to the history of the area. The Thunderbird complex of sites is one of the oldest and most important archeological discoveries in the eastern United States and is one of the first prehistoric sites in Virginia to be designated a National Historic Landmark. These excavations are at the site of the only known undisturbed and unmixed North American Paleo-Indian base camp. A base camp was a focal place, whether permanent or not, for the tribe's activities. This is an extremely important archeological find not only as a base camp with the remains of the earliest dwellings in North America but also because it contains remains of a hunting and butchering camp. Another distinction is that it is the only known stratified site spanning the period from 10,000 to 6,000 B.C.

When Paleo-Indians occupied Thunderbird much of the American continent was under a glacier and giant mastodons prowled the countryside. The ancient Indians hunted for meat with stone weapons made from the native yellow jasper and returned to this base camp in the Flint Run area. After 6,000 B.C., the Indian way of life altered with environmental change. Camps became smaller, plant food gathering and fishing increased in importance, and stone other than jasper was used for tools.

America's prehistory is presented through a walking tour of the excavations. It is instructive to watch the painstaking work of archeological discovery. Workers don't just dig out the artifacts; they carefully and methodically uncover them, removing the layers of soil. It is vitally important to record the exact arrangements of the finds. The sites are open year-round, and archeologists work and give talks throughout the summer season; the Corral Site (2,000 to 1,000 B.C.) and the historic Aenon Mill Site (destroyed in the flood of 1870) are the focus of the walking tour. These are reached either on foot from the nature trail, or you may drive down to the excavation area.

In addition to the archeological exhibits of the museum and excavations, there are picnic tables if you want to bring lunch and a museum shop where you may purchase local crafts, Pamunkey Indian pottery, books, or small souvenirs. Admission to the museum and park is charged. The Thunderbird Museum and Archeological Park is open daily from mid-March through mid-November from 10:00 a.m. to 5:00 p.m. It is located about an hour and 30 minutes from the Beltway.

Directions: Take Virginia Exit 9, Route I-66, from the Beltway to the first exit for Front Royal, at Linden, Virginia. Continue on Route 55 to Front Royal. When you reach Front Royal turn south on Route 340 and follow it for seven miles.

Thunderbird Museum and Archeological Park is on your right, off state Route 737.

WASHINGTON MONUMENT STATE PARK
It's Monumental, by George!

As America becomes more history conscious, new attention will focus on the Washington Monument State Park in Maryland. On July 4, 1827, the state park became the first monument to be dedicated to George Washington. The park's land was part of the territory surveyed by George Washington for Lord Fairfax. Climb to the top of the 35-foot tower and you'll get a view of many historical sites: the 1862 Antietam battlefield; Harpers Ferry, the scene of John Brown's raid; the part of Virginia traversed by General Sheridan on his famous ride. Your view will take in a majestic panorama of three states: Maryland, Virginia and West Virginia. The monument that stands today is not the original 1827 structure but a reconstruction made by the Civilian Conservation Corps in 1934.

The state park surrounding the monument encompasses 108 acres and has 36 miles of trails for hiking and bird watching. This part of the Cumberland Valley is on the flyway for migratory birds, and eagles and hawks may be seen from the tower as they make their seasonal north-south trip. The Appalachian Trail passes through the park at the base of the monument and there are numerous smaller trails for hiking enthusiasts.

When you visit Washington Monument State Park stop at the Visitor's Center to see the collection of Civil War mementos, Indian relics and an arsenal of artillery and firearms. There are many picnic sites, and 13 acres are set aside for tenting. The park is open year-round.

Directions: From the Washington Beltway take Exit 35, I-270, past Frederick to Route 40. Washington Monument State Park is located 1½ miles north of Alternate Route 40 at Zittlestown.

WHEATON REGIONAL PARK AND BROOKSIDE GARDENS
Fragrance, Flora and Fauna

Parks today have so much to offer that you can easily spend an entire day exploring one park's attractions; this is particularly true of Wheaton Regional Park in Maryland where there is so much to choose from you'd be lucky to be able to cover it all on one trip. You can enjoy Brookside Gardens, Old MacDonald's Farm, Wheaton Lines Railroad, Pine Lake, Brookside Nature Center, the riding stables, ice rink, playground area, pony rides and hiking trails.

Brookside Gardens is worth a visit all by itself in any season. There are several types of gardens within its 35 acres ranging from formal arrangements of flowering bulbs to the casual Azalea Garden. Two special areas are the Rose Garden and the Fragrance Garden. In September and October the chrysanthemums bloom outside and in November they are trained into lavish flowering cascades, upright columns and miniature tree shapes in the conservatories. At Easter time lilies, azaleas, hydrangeas and fuchsias reign supreme. The Christmas display is a blaze of poinsettias, cyclamen, Jerusalem cherry and kalanchoe.

Brookside Gardens is open free to the public daily from 9:00 a.m. to 5:00 p.m. except Christmas Day. For more information call (301)949-8230.

A very popular feature of Wheaton Regional Park is Old MacDonald's Farm, a miniature Maryland farm with barn, smokehouse, brick oven, windmill, a silo and a wide variety of farm animals. There is no admission charge. Behind the farm is a five-acre lake, Pine Lake, where from 10:00 a.m. to sunset you can fish from the shore for bass, bluegill, crappie and catfish. Fishermen of all ages are welcome to try their luck and no license is required for those 16 and under.

Children will be excited by the Wheaton Lines Railroad, which wanders on its two-mile track through meadow, woodland and around Pine Lake. The train is a reproduction of an 1865 steam engine with vintage cars, switch and signals. The ride over bridges and through tunnels is a real bargain at 75¢ per person.

There are miles of hiking and bicycle trails through the unspoiled interior of the park. Maps of the park trails are available throughout the park, and bicycles can be rented during the summer. For the loner, there is a ¾-mile well-marked nature trail. The Brookside Nature Center offers interpretative exhibits of the local ecology.

Wheaton also offers the latest in innovative play equipment as well as a stagecoach. The park can accommodate more than 2,000 picnickers. Athletes will find the year-round ice rink, athletic fields and tennis courts well-suited to their needs. There is also a riding stable with horses for rent and woodland bridle paths.

Directions: From the Beltway take Exit 31 north on Georgia Avenue. Take a right on Arcola Avenue and a left on Kemp Mill Road to the park entrance.

AUTUMN CALENDAR OF EVENTS

SEPTEMBER

EARLY

International Children's Festival—Wolf Trap Farm Park, VA (703)941-1527
Over 100 performances by talented young artists from around the world make up this yearly festival. You can enjoy story-telling, puppeteering, magic, music and mime. There are many activities that encourage the young audience to join the fun. Time: 11:00 a.m. to 4:00 p.m.

Gunston Hall Car Show—Gunston Hall Plantation, VA (703)550-9220
This popular car show awards trophies for the Oldest Car, the Best Car in Class, which includes Antique, Classic, Sports and Special Interest, and both Foreign and Domestic cars. The drivers are encouraged to wear costumes, making quite a spectacle. Music, refreshments and the opportunity to tour the gracious colonial mansion all add to the fun. Time: 11:30 a.m. to 3:30 p.m.

Maryland Renaissance Festival—Columbia, MD (301)685-1445 or (301)596-4673

Entertainment, crafts, games and food recreate the 16th century at this Medieval fair. Hundreds of costumed participants bring alive the pageantry of this long-ago time. Time: 10:30 a.m. to 6:00 p.m.

Steam Show Days—Carroll County Farm Museum, MD (301)374-2607

You can see displays of steam and gasoline engines, antique cars, sawmilling, old time machinery, and also browse through a flea market and sample the food at this country showcase. Time: 10:00 a.m. to dusk.

John Wilkes Booth Escape Route Tour—Mary Surratt House, MD (301)326-6945 or (301)868-1121

The second tour of the year sponsored by the Mary Surratt Society retraces Booth's route after his assassination of Lincoln. The bus begins at the Surratt House, proceeds to Ford's Theatre, and then retraces Booth's stops to Port Royal, Virginia. Time: 7:30 a.m. to 7:30 p.m.

Boonesborough Days—Boonesboro, MD (301)432-6115

This weekend-long event features more than 125 old-fashioned crafts in a juried show. The work will be demonstrated, judged and sold. Folk music, square dancing, barbershop singing and lots of homemade food are part of the festivities. Time: 11:00 a.m. to 6:00 p.m.

Civil War Days—Gathland State Park & Burkittsville, MD (301)293-2420 or (301)834-6109

Two days of historical pageantry will include Civil War encampments and a reenactment of the Battle of South Mountain. There will also be square dancing, folk music, crafts and food booths. Time: 10:00 a.m. to 5:00 p.m.

Draft Horse Day—Belle Grove Plantation, VA (703)869-2028

This day celebrates "The Horse at Work" and includes riding exhibitions, a work-horse show and a draft-horse pulling contest. For the children there are wagon and mule rides plus log-pulling and obstacle course contests for those a little older. This is a good chance to tour the mansion that Thomas Jefferson helped design and where James Madison spent his honeymoon. Time: 10:00 a.m. to 6:00 p.m.

Oatlands Needlework Exhibition—Oatlands Plantation, VA (703)777-3174

This show focuses on adult and junior needlework competitions with changing special exhibits each year. Throughout the exhibit professionals are on hand to demonstrate various needle art techniques. Time: 10:00 a.m. to 5:00 p.m.

Red Rose Rent Day—Star Rose Gardens, PA (215)869-2426

Each year on the Saturday following Labor Day a ceremony is held in which one red rose is paid to a direct descendant of William Penn. This occasion is used to present new varieties of roses and other plants to interested gardeners. Saturday afternoon event.

MID

Spanish Heritage Week—Clara Barton National Historic Site, MD (301)492-6245

A special program dealing with the Red Cross in Cuba during the Spanish–American War is held annually during Spanish Heritage Week. Clara Barton and the American Red Cross helped both Cuban civilians and American servicemen. Time: 2:00 to 4:00 p.m.

Forklift Rodeo—Baltimore Museum of Industry, MD (301)727-4808

Unsung industrial heroes maneuver their forklifts through a specially designed obstacle course. Prizes are awarded in this very different competition. Time: 10:00 a.m. to 5:00 p.m.

Defenders Day—Fort McHenry, MD (301)962-4290

Military pageantry marks the celebration of the 1814 Battle of Baltimore. There is patriotic music and drills, a mock bombardment of Fort McHenry and the raising of a replica of the Star-Spangled Banner. A fireworks display will bring the event to a close. Time: 6:30 to 9:30 p.m. Earlier on the same day in Baltimore there is the nation's largest patriotic parade celebrating "I Am An American Day." The parade is from 2:00 to 6:00 p.m. around Patterson Park in Baltimore. Call (301)342-2404).

Candlelight Walking Tour of Chestertown—Chestertown, MD (301)778-0330 or (301)778-1141

One evening each year private homes from the 18th, 19th and 20th centuries are open to the public. Historic Chestertown has numerous antique, gift and craft shops that can be visited in the afternoon before the evening candlelight tour from 6:00 to 10:00 p.m.

Quilt Show—Fredericksburg, VA (703)373-1776

Several of Fredericksburg's historic buildings play host to this Quilt Show which customarily displays more than 40 treasured quilts. There are also lectures by quilt experts, quilting demonstrations and the display and sale of both old and new quilts. Time: 9:00 a.m. to 5:00 p.m.

Trolley Car Extravaganza—National Capital Trolley Museum, Washington, D.C. (301)384-9797

All 14 of the museum's operable cars are in action or on display. In addition to several European cars you can see two Washington Snow Sweepers and a work car, all built before 1906. You can also take a trolley ride. Time: 1:30 to 3:30 p.m.

Pre-Revolutionary War Days—Claude Moore Colonial Farm at Turkey Run, VA (703)442-7557

Muskets and merriment are predominant on this 18th-century farm. In addition to the soldiers on hand to fire their muskets there will be a flea market with 18th-century reproduction items. Your attention will be divided between old-fashioned music and old-time chores. Time: 1:00 to 4:00 p.m.

Fall Festival at Furnacetown—Snow Hill, MD (301)957-1870 or (301)957-1919

Each year a diverse group of Eastern Shore artists and artisans join this festival to demonstrate and sell their wares. You can enjoy buggy rides, watch a forging demonstration or see an exhibit of antique engines. A bluegrass concert and barbecued chicken dinner complete the festival. Time: 10:00 a.m. to 6:00 p.m. on Saturday and 11:00 a.m. to 6:00 p.m. on Sunday.

Ways of Wood—Colvin Run Mill Park, VA (703)759-2771

You can watch or take part in Lumberjack Day contests like speedchopping, logrolling and sawing with a crosscut saw.

There is also storytelling and folk music as well as wood-carving lessons and demonstrations of traditional hand-made crafts. Time: 11:00 a.m. to 5:00 p.m.

Shenandoah Vineyards Harvest Festival—Edinburg, VA (703)984-8699

In addition to touring Shenandoah Vineyards you can help stomp the grapes, enjoy free wine tastings and browse through an arts and crafts sale. There will be bluegrass music and mountain cloggers plus a barrel-rolling contest. Time: 10:00 a.m. to 6:00 p.m.

Country Fair and Auction—Ellicott City, MD (301)992-2483

An auction of country crafts and antiques as well as demonstrations of handmade collectibles are enhanced by tours of Ellicott City. Country and bluegrass music add to this one-day event. Time: 11:00 a.m. to 5:00 p.m.

LATE

New Market Days—New Market Main Street, MD (301)831-6010

The "Antique Capital of Maryland" holds its fall festival with country food, buggy rides, historical displays, entertainment and lots to discover in the town's 40 antique shops. Time: 10:00 a.m. to 5:00 p.m.

Governor's Invitational Firelock Match—Fort Frederick State Park, MD (301)842-2155

Reactivated 18th-century units from several states take part in both individual and team competitions. The individual events include working with pistols, rifles, muskets and tomahawks. Team events include drill, musket, rifle and cannon competition. Time: 1:00 to 4:00 p.m.

Old Alexandria Tour of Homes—Alexandria, VA (703)751-9335

Historic and renovated private homes in Old Town Alexandria are featured in this walking tour. Tea is customarily served in the afternoon from 2:30 to 4:30 p.m.; the event runs from 11:00 a.m. until 5:00 p.m.

Historic Tours of Fairmount Park—Philadelphia, PA (215)686-1776

Each fall a number of special tours are planned to the mansions and botanical areas in Fairmount Park. You are escorted via the Fairmount Park trolley to the Horticulture Center and the Japanese House, or the Far Country Arboretum and Bird Sanctuary. Other tours encompass the Laurel Hill Cemetery, the John Bartram House and Gardens, Germantown or Cedar Grove and Solitude Mansions. Tours may vary from year to year.

Blessing of the Fleet—St. Clement's Island, MD (301)884-4369

An historical pageant celebrating Lord Baltimore's Proclamation of Freedom of Conscience For All and a religious ceremony and blessing of the fleet are just part of the day's events. There is also a boat parade, a draft horse pulling contest, entertainment and food concessions. Time: 10:00 a.m. to 5:00 p.m.

OCTOBER

EARLY

State House Quilt Show—Reconstructed State House—St. Mary's City, MD (301)994-0779

Old and new quilts are on display at this historical site in St. Mary's City, Maryland. You can watch demonstrations of quilt making, browse among the many quilts on exhibit and even purchase a quilt at this annual event. Time: 10:30 a.m. to 4:30 p.m.

Fall Festival—Rose Hill Manor—Frederick, MD (301)694-1650

There are three museums to see at Rose Hill Manor Park while you enjoy this country festival. A carriage museum, farm museum and children's touch and see museum are part of the ongoing fun at this Frederick, Maryland, attraction. During the Fall Festival you can also see a variety of crafts demonstrated and exhibited, watch country butchering, apple butter making, and enjoy entertainment and homemade food. Time: 10:00 a.m. to 5:00 p.m. on Saturday and noon to 5:00 p.m. on Sunday.

Fall Harvest Days—Carroll County Farm Museum, MD (301)848-7775

This is the biggest annual event at Carroll Country Farm Museum. A wide variety of 19th-century farming skills are demonstrated: quilting, broom making, tinsmithing, butchering, apple butter making and others. You can enjoy country food and entertainment from 10:00 a.m. to 5:00 p.m.

Victorian Craft Fair—Mary Surratt House, MD (301)868-1121

Rediscover domestic life in the 19th-century at this two-day fair featuring such crafts as weaving, spinning, rug looming, braiding, English smocking, quilting, lacemaking, needlework, bookbinding, chair caning, woodworking and basketry. Costumed docents conduct guided tours of the house. Time: Noon to 4:00 p.m.

Patuxent River Appreciation Days—Calvert Marine Museum, MD (301)326-3719

This festival focuses on the economic, cultural, scenic, historic and recreational importance of the Patuxent River. There are nautical demonstrations, boat rides, seafood and a parade. Time: 10:00 a.m. to 6:00 p.m.

Harvest Festival—Byrd Vineyards, MD (301)293-1110

Special winery tours, wine tasting and a slide presentation are part of this annual autumn festival held from 10:00 a.m. to 6:00 p.m. on Saturday and noon to 6:00 p.m. on Sunday.

Waterford Homes Tour and Crafts Exhibit— Waterford, VA (703)882-3018

This festival, which runs Friday through Sunday, is held in the 18th-century National Historic Landmark Village of Waterford, Virginia. Historic buildings are open and there are craft demonstrations, entertainment and art exhibits. Time: 10:00 a.m. to 5:00 p.m.

Carriage Drive and Competition—Morven Park, VA (703)777-2414

This annual driving meet includes a Driving Test, a Timed Marathon and a Concours D'Elegance. This is a marvelous time to tour the historical home at Morven Park as well as enjoy a wide variety of carriages in action. Time: Noon to 4:00 p.m.

The First Virginia Regiment of the Continental Line Encampment—Gunston Hall, VA (703)550-9220

Costumed 18th-century citizen soldiers and their families will participate in a living history encampment. You can watch vignettes of camp life, as the regiment members cook, sew, repair gear, drill, play games and engage in other typical activities of the Revolutionary period. Time: 9:30 a.m. to 5:00 p.m.

Festival of Leaves—Front Royal, VA (703)635-3185

The highlight of this festival is the Reenactment of the Battle of Front Royal fought by Mosby Rangers. The festival also features a parade, historical displays, a colonial bazaar, arts and crafts show, quilt show, carriage and pony rides plus archeological exhibits from Thunderbird Museum. Time: 10:00 a.m. to 5:00 p.m. on Saturday and noon to 5:00 p.m. on Sunday.

MID

Autumn Glory Festival—Oakland, Deep Creek Lake, MD (301)334-3888

Up around Deep Creek Lake where the autumn leaves provide their own glory this annual festival is a popular weekend event. There is a parade, an arts and craft bazaar, antique show, a Five-String Banjo Contest and a Fiddlers Championship. This is a weekend-long event.

Oktober Wine Festival—Berrywine Plantation, MD (301)662-8687

One of the yearly events at Berrywine Plantations is this fall festival featuring arts and crafts, wine making demonstrations and tasting, plenty of Italian food and even helicopter rides. Time: 10:00 a.m. to 6:00 p.m.

Needlework Show—London Town Publik House, MD (301)956-4900

A judged competition and a display of needlework provide an added incentive to visit this 18th-century ferry stop. The time is 10:00 a.m. to 4:00 p.m. on Saturday and noon to 4:00 p.m. on Sunday.

Aboriginal Culture Day—Chancellor's Point Natural History Center—St. Mary's City, MD (301)994-4900

One of the most unusual local annual events takes place each fall in St. Mary's City with this festival that lets you discover what it was really like to live on this continent before the coming of the Europeans. At Aboriginal Life Day you can take part in stone tool making, friction fire starting, clay and stone pottery making, bow and arrow construction, as well as digging out an Indian canoe. There are games for children plus such unusual fare as raccoon stew. Time: Noon to 4:00 p.m.

Celebration of Lafayette's Visit to Alexandria— Boyhood Home of Robert E. Lee, VA (703)548-8454

This is the annual commemoration of the historic 1824 visit by the Marquis de Lafayette to "Light Horse Harry" Lee's widow. The event is celebrated with music and refreshments and tours of the house by costumed docents. Time: 10:00 a.m. to 4:00 p.m.

Fall Festival of Needlework—Woodlawn Plantation, VA (703)557-7881

A week-long series of needlework workshops is held each autumn at Woodlawn Plantation. Each workshop is an all day event.

Harvest Days, "Our Musical Heritage"—Sully Plantation, VA (703)437-1794

This special program enables you to enjoy the wide variety of music and dance of the South, from the 18th century to the late 19th century. You can watch traditional craft demonstrations and listen as musical instrument makers explain the sounds created by the different instruments. Horse drawn wagons take you to the back fields of the historic plantation. A variety of country food rounds out this festival. Time: 11:00 a.m. to 5:00 p.m.

Election Day 1860—Harpers Ferry, WV (304)535-6610

At this annual event over 100 people dressed in period costumes dramatize the tension between North and South one year after the John Brown Raid on the eve of the 1860 Presidential election. This is an all day event.

Fall Festival—Oxon Hill Farm, MD (301)839-1177

This annual event is a day of craft demonstrations, music, dancing, antique farm machinery demonstrations and homemade food. You can see demonstrations of dyeing, weaving, woodworking, blacksmithing, quilting, basketry and more. Cloggers and an old-time string band will perform. Time: 10:00 a.m. to 4:00 p.m.

American Craft Days—Decatur House Museum, Washington, D.C. (202)673-4030

This annual event features craftsmen and artisans demonstrating and selling wares which are pertinent to the Decatur House urban setting of the 1820s. You can see the art of paper making, stenciling, tole painting, floorcloths, band boxes, tinware, silhouettes, scrimshaw, marbled papers and many more. This three-day event is from 10:00 a.m. to 4:00 p.m. A period luncheon will be served.

Historic Hike—Heritage Weekend—Annapolis, MD (301)267-8149

This is your chance to walk with knowledgeable guides in architecture, urban planning and historical restoration through examples of 300 years of architectural development in the historic district of Annapolis. Time: 10:30 a.m. to 3:30 p.m.

Chesapeake Appreciation Days—Sandy Point State Park, MD (301)757-4100

Activities on land, water and in the air make this a very special event. Air shows with antique aircraft, skipjack races and plenty of craft exhibits provide something for everyone. You can also get your fill of Maryland seafood. Time: 10:00 a.m. to 5:00 p.m.

All Hallows Eve—Colvin Run Mill Park, VA (703)759-2771

This historic grist mill is filled each year with ghosts, goblins, a swamp monster and other assorted ghoulish characters. Such traditional favorites as apple bobbing and pumpkin carving are part of the fun. Time: 7:00 to 9:00 p.m.

NOVEMBER

EARLY

Chrysanthemum Display Conservatory— Brookside Gardens, MD (301)949-8230

This is the most spectacular display of the year at Brookside Gardens Conservatory. The display features Japanese cascade mums, upright columns, hanging baskets, miniature tree mums and bedding mums in addition to the regular conservatory collection. Time: 9:00 a.m. to 5:00 p.m.

Athenian Agora—Greek Orthodox Cathedral— Baltimore, MD (301)727-1831

Bousouki music, Greek folk dancing and such popular national culinary specialties as baklava, souvlakia, moussaka and retsina create the illusion that you have journeyed to Greece itself. You can tour the Greek Orthodox Cathedral, browse through rooms featuring Greek jewelry, religious icons, handicrafts and boutique items. Join in the fun from 10:00 a.m. to 9:00 p.m. on Friday and Saturday and from noon to 6:00 p.m. on Sunday and enjoy the food and music.

Washington Review of the Troops—Gadsby's Tavern, VA (703)549-0205

Washington's last military act, his 1798 review of the troops, took place in front of Gadsby's Tavern. Each year in November this historic occasion is reenacted at 11:00 a.m. A yearly bake sale is also held from 9:00 to 11:30 a.m.

Historic Carriage Drive—Rose Hill Manor, MD (301)694-1650

A parade of antique carriages leaves Rose Hill Manor and is guided by costumed drivers through Frederick's historic district. Departure time is customarily at 1:30 p.m.

Christmas at Oatlands—Oatlands Plantation, VA (703)777-3174

For over a decade visitors have found inspiration for their own holiday decorations while enjoying the arrangements at Oatlands which recreate celebrations of the 1880s. Throughout the 13 exhibit rooms at Oatlands the Christmas finery is recreated based on records kept by the family. The house is lit by candles for special open houses. Christmas refreshments are served. Time: 10:00 a.m. to 5:00 p.m.

Virginia Thanksgiving Festival—Berkeley Plantation, VA (703)293-5350

Two years before the Pilgrims landed at Plymouth Rock the colonists in Virginia celebrated a Thanksgiving ceremony. On the first Sunday in November at Berkeley Plantation this historic first Thanksgiving is reenacted, with Captain Woodlief and his companions again coming ashore from their replica of the *Margaret*. Indians too are on hand to take part in this ceremony. You can partake of Virginia hams, yams and apple cider. Time: 11:00 a.m. to 5:00 p.m., with the reenactment at 2:00 p.m.

MID

Waterfowl Festival—Easton, MD (301)822-4567

You can see waterfowl art, decorative and working decoys, nautical artifacts, antique guns, and an old-fashioned auction at this yearly festival. A popular event is the Duck and Goose Calling Contest. Time: 10:00 a.m. to 8:00 p.m. on Friday and Saturday and 10:00 a.m. to 5:00 p.m. on Sunday.

Victorian Collection Show—Mary Surratt House, MD (301)868-1121

In addition to touring the Mary Surratt House you can see a display of unusual Victorian memorabilia. Time: Noon to 4:00 p.m.

Christmas Shopping Faire—Reconstructed State House—St. Mary's City, MD (301)994-0779

This unique holiday event takes its cue from the setting of the Reconstructed State House and features reproduction items from the 17th and 18th centuries for some unusual gift giving ideas. Work by southern Maryland craftspeople is also available. You can enjoy a cup of wassail as you warm yourself in front of the huge fireplace. Time: 11:00 a.m. to 4:00 p.m.

LATE

Gift Shop Christmas Bazaar—Carroll County Farm Museum, MD (301)848-7775

You can purchase work by local craftspeople as well as hand-crafted items and tree decorations from around the world at this annual event. Time: Noon to 5:00 p.m.

Waterfowl Week—Chincoteague National Wildlife Refuge, VA (804)336-6122

This a once-a-year opportunity to use normally closed park roads at Chincoteague National Wildlife Refuge. It gives you a great chance to get close to the wild ponies of Chincoteague as well as the opportunity to spot a wide range of waterfowl. This special week coincides with the migration of Canadian and Snow Geese. Observation of Waterfowl Week is a week-long event.

Thanksgiving Conservatory Display—Longwood Gardens, PA (215)380-6741

If you have the time you can't beat this annual display of chrysanthemums. Longwood has more and bigger flowers than you will see at local conservatories. Time: 10:00 a.m. to 5:00 p.m.

SUGGESTED READINGS

Discovering Historic America Mid-Atlantic States, ed. S. Allen Chambers, E. P. Dutton, Inc., New York, 1983.

Free Stuff for Travelers, ed. Tom Grady, Meadowbrook Press, Deephaven, Minnesota, 1981.

Going Places with Children in Washington, Green Acres School, ed. Katherine Tippett and E. Susan Parsons, Maryland, 1982.

Excursions: Daytripping In and Around Pennsylvania's Dutch Country, the Delaware Valley and Poconos, Sally M. and David C. Keehn, Hastings House, New York, 1982.

Natural Washington, Bill and Phyllis Thomas, Holt, Rinehart and Winston, New York, 1980.

Old Alexandria, Nettie Allen Voges, EPM Publications, Inc., McLean, Virginia, 1975.

One-Day Trips to Beauty and Bounty, Jane Ockershausen Smith, EPM Publications, Inc., McLean, Virginia, 1983.

One-Day Trips through History, Jane Ockershausen Smith, EPM Publications, Inc., McLean, Virginia, 1982.

The Best Free Attractions in the Eastern States, John Whitman, Meadowbrook Press, Deephaven, Minnesota, 1981.

The Great Public Gardens of the Eastern United States, Doris M. Stone, Pantheon Books, New York, 1982.

The Great Weekend Escape Book, Michael Spring, E. P. Dutton, Inc., New York, 1982.

Weekender's Guide to the Four Seasons, Robert Shosteck, Potomac Books, Inc., Washington, D.C., 1982.

TOPICAL CROSS REFERENCE

ARTS AND CRAFTS

FOR THE HANDICAPPED

GARDENS

HISTORICAL

MUSEUMS

PLACES ACCESSIBLE BY BOAT

SCENIC

WILDLIFE/ANIMALS

GENERAL INTEREST

INDEX